STUDIES IN AFRICAN LITERATURE
▼▼▼▼▼▼▼▼▼▼▼▼▼▼▼▼▼▼▼▼▼▼

*Aeroplane Mirrors*

Recent Titles in STUDIES IN AFRICAN LITERATURE
▼▼▼▼▼▼▼▼▼▼▼▼▼▼▼▼▼▼▼▼▼▼▼▼▼▼▼▼▼▼▼

The Marabout and the Muse: New Approaches to Islam in African Literature
*Kenneth W. Harrow, editor*

Bessie Head: Thunder Behind Her Ears
*Gillian Stead Eilersen*

New Writing from Southern Africa: Authors Who Have Become
Prominent Since 1980
*Emmanuel Ngara, editor*

Ngugi wa Thiong'o: An Exploration of His Writings, Second Edition
*David Cook and Michael Okenimkpe*

Writers in Politics: A Re-Engagement with Issues of Literature and Society
*Ngugi wa Thiong'o*

The African Novel in English: An Introduction
*M. Keith Booker*

A Teacher's Guide to African Narratives
*Sara Talis O'Brien*

Women's Voices in a Man's World: Women and the Pastoral Tradition in
Northern Somali Orature, c. 1899–1980
*Lidwien Kapteijns with Maryan Omar Ali*

Running towards Us: New Writing from South Africa
*Isabel Balseiro, editor*

Alex La Guma: Politics and Resistance
*Nahem Yousaf*

Recasting Postcolonialism: Women Writing Between Worlds
*Anne Donadey*

Colonial Histories, Post-Colonial Memories
*Abdelmajid Hannoum*

# *Aeroplane Mirrors*

## Personal and Political Reflexivity in Post-Colonial Women's Novels

### Elizabeth Morgan

HEINEMANN
Portsmouth, NH

Heinemann
A division of Reed Elsevier Inc.
361 Hanover Street
Portsmouth, NH 03801–3912
www.heinemann.com

Offices and agents throughout the world.

© 2002 by Elizabeth Morgan

All rights reserved. No part of this book may be reproduced
in any form or by any electronic or mechanical means,
including information storage and retrieval systems, without
permission in writing from the publisher, except by a
reviewer, who may quote brief passages in a review.

ISBN 0–325–07058–X

**Library of Congress Cataloging-in-Publication Data**

Morgan, Elizabeth, 1943–
    Aeroplane mirrors : personal and political reflexivity in post-colonial women's novels / Elizabeth Morgan.
       p. cm.—(Studies in African literature, ISSN 1351–5713)
    Includes bibliographical references (p.  ) and index.
    ISBN 0–325–07058–X (alk. paper)
    1. African fiction—20th century—History and criticism.  2. African fiction—Women authors—History and criticism.  I. Title.  II. Series.
PN849.A35M67 2002
809.3'0082'0960904—dc21       2001016955

British Library Cataloguing in Publication Data is available.

Printed in the United States of America on acid-free paper.

06 05 04 03 02 SB 1 2 3 4 5 6 7 8 9

**Copyright Acknowledgments**

The author and publisher gratefully acknowledge permission to reproduce the following material:

Scattered excerpts from *Africa Wo/man Palava: The Nigerian Novel by Women* by Chikwenye Okonjo Ogunyemi are reprinted by permission of University of Chicago Press.

"I Give You Back" from the book *She Had Some Horses* by Joy Harjo, copyright © 1983 by Thunder's Mouth Press, appears by permission of the publisher, Thunder's Mouth Press.

Scattered excerpts from *When Rainclouds Gather* by Bessie Head are reprinted by permission of The Orion Publishing Group and John Johnson Limited.

Scattered excerpts from *Nervous Conditions* by Tsitsi Dangarembga, copyright 1989 by Tsitsi Dangarembga, appear by permission of Seal Press.

Scattered excerpts from *Our Sister Killjoy: or Reflections from a Blackeyed Squint* by Ama Ata Aidoo appear by permission of Ama Ata Aidoo.

Scattered excerpts from *A Sister to Scheherezade* by Assia Djebar OMBRE SULTANE, copyright © 1987 by Assia Djebar, are reprinted by permission of Quartet Books and Liepman AG.

Excerpts from *The Autobiography of My Mother* by Jamaica Kincaid, copyright © 1996 by Jamaica Kincaid, are reprinted by permission of Farrar, Straus, and Giroux, LLC. Extract from *The Autobiography of My Mother* by Jamaica Kincaid published by Jonathan Cape. Used by permission of The Random House Group Limited.

Excerpts from *God Dies by the Nile* by Nawal el Saadawi are reprinted by permission of St. Martin's Press and Zed Books.

For Peter, gifted son,
who loves women in all the right ways.

And for Cait, "other daughter,"
who, loving justice, was taken from us by
violence.

"My face always looks more beautiful in aeroplane mirrors. . . . [D]o my features change simply by crossing borders, or are aeroplane mirrors of better quality?"
—Nawal el Saadawi, *My Travels Around the World*

# Contents

Introduction: Feminist Debate and Subversive Fictions     xiii

## PART ONE: THEORETICAL FRAMEWORKS

1   The Fourth World Conference on Women:
Celebration of Unity or Diversity?     3

2   The Novel: European Monolith or
International Literary Marketplace?     21

3   Choosing a Language: *Neo*-Colonialism or *Post*-Colonialism?     39

## PART TWO: WOMEN'S NOVELS AND WOMEN'S ISSUES

4   Naming the Mother:
Reproduction and Domestic Labor     61

5   Resisting Arrest: Violence Against Women
and the Fight for *Human* Rights     89

6   Pen and Paper: Son Preference, Colonial
Models, and Education of the Girl Child     119

7   Feminization of Poverty:
Economic Justice and Issues of Power     151

8   Imaging Women:
Fighting Stereotypes and Building Agency     181

9  Conclusion: Unexpected Gifts                                211

Appendix A: *Beijing Declaration,
            Fourth World Conference on Women*              217

Appendix B: *Non-Governmental Organisation (NGO)
            Beijing Declaration, September 15, 1995*       223

Bibliography                                                  229

Index                                                         245

# Introduction: Feminist Debate and Subversive Fictions

> "This daughter of yours," Grandma announced, "is a trickster, all right. Can work her way through the crookedest situation. Straight into solid glass she walks and it melts for her."
> —Meena Alexander, *Manhattan Music*

Across the globe, women are writing their way out of obscurity. Their novels are being published, translated, and taught cross-culturally in ever increasing numbers. A group of women activists in El Salvador claim that Alice Walker is their inspiration, and Tsitsi Dangarembga's *Nervous Conditions* is read by adolescent women in North America desperate to understand their own relationship to parental and cultural authorities. The novel, more than any other genre, has become an international literary marketplace for the exchange of ideas and experiences, of despair and desire among the world's women, those who in many countries are tenders of the material marketplace as well.

But what are these women writing their way into? Is it into global awareness of "women's" issues and a unified agenda for addressing historic wrongs (as many of the United Nations documents on women and children's rights would suggest)? Or is it into a problematized, multivoiced, cultural debate where even the word *woman* has seemingly infinite meanings? And what might be the role of the storyteller in either of these worlds? Is it to unify the audience around common human experience or is it to validate the unique complications of any lived experience?

Very few people would argue that the contemporary novel represents a simple reflection of life, culture, or ideology. Thanks to modernist, postmodernist, and post-colonial theory, works of fiction are much more often approached as elaborate halls of mirrors, reflecting multiple, interactive social and psychic images that deny single or final interpretation. If women writers around the globe are engaged in such a decentered effort, a fairly easy argument to make, what then is their relationship to the work of policymakers and human rights advocates trying to improve the lot of women through consensual analysis and action? Are such approaches necessarily at odds?

Nawal el Saadawi, novelist, psychiatrist, and long-time advocate for women's health issues and political freedom in Egypt and beyond, seems to effect an intersection of the two when she asks, "Can I be a dissident without being creative?" Saadawi defines *creativity* as a demystification of the many names of power (father, god, husband, nation, human rights, even modernism and postmodernism) through paradox and double meaning. Thus, she seems intent on making literary language part of the public discourse itself. Where might such a linkage take us?

This study explores such questions. It is about women crossing borders. It is about women activists, philosophers, anthropologists, economists, poets, and novelists engaging and critiquing one another across geographical, religious, ethnic, class, and personal borders. It is blatantly cross-disciplinary, attempting to bring literary and development thinkers into a space where they can see and appreciate their reciprocity, where they can value normative demographics and resonate with particular cases. But more than that, where they can explore together a retelling of women's experience that both preserves the integrity of complex causality and moves toward new ways of relating (to) truth.

The questions this study explores about the difficult relationship of universalistic thinking to vastly diverse cultural and intracultural experience are widely interpreted. Julia Kristeva, psychoanalyst and social critic, asks if we as human beings can have any kind of a life together without giving up the desire to retreat into subjectivism and defensive nationhood, as well as avoiding the leveling effect of universal analysis (Smith 23). Martha Nussbaum, philosopher and development ethicist, focuses on the moral risk involved in seeking social change. If we judge a practice endorsed by specific cultural tradition as wrong, as a violation of "universal" human rights, she argues, we risk superimposing our own moral ideals on a "foreign" context. If we validate the practice based on cultural sovereignty, we risk suspending "critical judgment where real evil and real oppression" are present. But to "avoid the whole issue because the matter of proper judgment is so fiendishly difficult is . . . perhaps the worst option of all" ("Introduction," *Women, Culture, and Development* 1).

Seyla Benhabib, professor of government at Harvard University, argues for recognition of a global political reality by reminding us that "immigration, travel, communication, the world economy and ecological disasters" continually redefine and enlarge the context in which we can do (must do) significant moral reasoning ("Cultural Complexity" 244). Chandra Mohanty, a consistent advocate for decentralized analysis of women's issues, nonetheless reminds her readers that complex local struggles exist in a world "traversed with intersecting lines of power and resistance" ("Cartographies of Struggle" 2).

As if to illustrate these complications, novelist and poet Meena Alexander, born in India and having lived in Sudan and New York, asks how one can truly live in a multicultural world without acknowledging the hard overlapping realities that meet there: "The Muslim women raped in Surat, the Hindu women stoned in Jersey City co-exist in time; cleft by space they forge part of the fluid diasporic world, a world in which I must live and move and have my being" ("Translated Lives"). Bringing such unspeakable acts into open literary discourse is, for Alexander, both acknowledgment of and resistance to the violence that perpetuates them.

Important to this study is a realization that the relationship between a particular "I" and a generalized "we," between a particular "we" and generalized "they," is as much an issue for social analysts and activists as it has ever been for novelists, even as the two groups differ in points of origin, extension of language, and constituency. In this, it would seem that practitioners of either or both have the capacity to keep a vital critical spirit alive in the world, in themselves, and in each other.

## Public Debate: The Beijing Conference and Beyond

Recognizing that hegemonic feminism is no answer for the problems of the world's women, yet conceding that pockets of terrible oppression may be allowed to take place in the name of "sacred difference," more than 30,000 women, from 190 countries gathered in Beijing, China, in September 1995 for the UN's Fourth World Conference on Women and for the accompanying Non Governmental Organization (NGO) Forum on Women (moved to Huairou in the last days of planning). In assessing its ultimate impact, Deniz Kandiyoti, attending from the Middle East and representing the United Nations University, explains that this conference highlighted the complex processes of globalization in a post–cold war era, and took stock of the gender ramifications of such political and economic changes. Specifically, she notes that women of the southern nations took careful stock of the effects that structural adjustment programs[1] can have on women's lives; eastern European women explored the implications of market economies; women of the northern nations assessed the effects of growing unemployment and dismembered welfare systems on the lives of women and children. As Kandiyoti concludes, "This complexity made the expression of similar concerns over welfare provision and social services possible across very different contexts and regions" (3). She is here making a point that is emphasized many times in this study—only the recognition of difficult particular cases (which the novel is especially good at representing) makes collective conversation significant.

The 135-page *Beijing Declaration* and *Platform for Action* that resulted from deliberations of the Fourth World Conference on Women declares up front that it was about "acknowledging the voice of all women everywhere and taking note of the diversity of women and their roles and circumstances" (*Declaration #3*). There may well be debate about the operational validity of that statement (such a claim clearly cannot cover all deliberations at Beijing), but accounts of the proceedings of this global gathering indicate that it had a sophistication its precursors lacked.

Intersections of gender, race, and class seem to have been more carefully considered than before, as reflected in wording of the *Platform for Action* and, even more so, the *NGO Beijing Declaration*. In addition, both the UN Conference and the NGO Forum recognized that sexual politics—the right of a woman to control her own sexuality and reproductive functions—is integral with discussions of empowerment and economic opportunities for women, even if delegations had very different views of how this recognition might play itself out.[2] Language throughout the 1995 *Platform for Action* indicates that sexual rights and reproductive health are human rights impinging on a woman's status in "public and private life, including opportunities for education and economic and political empowerment" (paragraph 97).

Reservations to the *Platform*, as expressed by the Vatican and delegates from Muslim countries, attest to the explosive power of this reexamination of the sources of social vulnerability for women. It is particularly interesting to note that the Holy See, while finding the *Platform* too focused on sexual politics, nonetheless directed most of its reservations to those very issues, thus, validating the need for even more attention to their unraveling.[3]

A number of Muslim countries went on record saying that their endorsement of the *Platform* was contingent on compliance with religious and civil laws *already in place* at home. These qualifications reflect an ongoing and painful conflict among Muslim (and other) women attending the conference. In their home countries, women arguing for economic and personal rights are often accused of giving in to a new form of Western imperialism—first-world feminism. They are assured that what they think is articulation of universal women's rights is merely oppressive and hegemonic "foreign" ideology.

But as Iranian activist Mahnaz Afkhami and Erika Friedl point out, the arguments of anti-feminist Islamic fundamentalists (as well as secular nationalists) are themselves quite convoluted in that they take both a universalist and relativist tack simultaneously. If Islamic law is the true, god-declared behavioral code (as many Islamists claim), it supersedes any man-made law or treaty. But, in that there are different "schools" of Islam, human difference must be admitted into couplings of divine law and culture, forcing Islamists back on the relativist defense that every society has the right to practice its own customs, however they may be judged by international deliberative bodies (xii–xiii). Middle Eastern feminists often want to challenge these totalizing assumptions, but, with good reason, they are equally disturbed by "outside" definitions of a singular Muslim culture and by reductionist views of religious law.

This kind of disturbance prevails in many areas of global women's studies, and no desire to create a global agenda for women can afford to be cavalier about its reality. Thus, what becomes clear in all of this debate is the very necessity of entering it with as much agility as possible—both acknowledging the cultural construction of "women" and boldly claiming their agency as reconstructors. In an article tellingly entitled "Imagination as Subversion," Iranian activist Azar Nafisi asks, "What can one do when reality seems like a trap, when society offers no private or public spaces within which individuals can control and shape their lives" (70)? The answer she posits is a creation of space within one's imagination to shape and reshape that reality.

## Literary Discourse and Subversive Fictions

### The Power of Story

Azar Nafisi shapes her ideas about the power of imagination by revisiting Shahrzad (Scheherazade), spinning out tale after tale to save her very life. As the ancient plot goes, a Middle Eastern king, betrayed by his queen, marries a different virgin each night and kills her in the morning, until the shrewd and imaginative Shahrzad, daughter of the Vizier, deflects his vengeance by telling him a story every night for 1,001 nights. Unable to forego the pleasure of her artistry, the king lets her live from one telling to the other until he gets over his "lethal obsession." Nafisi argues that Shahrzad is a true subversive: instead of abdicating responsibility for life, she loiters at "unexpected corners of reality, redirecting life, subverting power, renaming relations, becoming immortal" (71). What might this myth mean to us?

In a modest little book entitled *Poetic Justice: The Literary Imagination and Public Life* (1995) Martha Nussbaum relates our need for moral imagination to the reading of novels. While working on "quality-of-life" assessment at the World Institute for Development Economics Research in Helsinki, Nussbaum and global economist Amartya Sen used Charles Dickens's *Hard Times* to ground their critique of standard paradigms of assessment—exposing the reductionism of such paradigms and their failure to address human complexity. Thus, she is willing to argue that one of the best ways to keep economics from becoming a "dismal science" is for students of economics to seek a "more complicated and philosophically adequate set of foundations" through reading novels (8)!

She argues that it is an essential component of any ethical stance that theoreticians enter imaginatively into the lives of the "subjects" they are considering and that they do so in such a way that they experience emotions about this participation (xvi). Novel reading provides a significant "rehearsal" for such engagement. Moreover, the novel allows readers to engage in a form of ethical reasoning that is context-specific without being solipsistic. As symbolic representation (or reflection) of reality, the novel contains both concrete action and abstract idea, multiple motives and unitary arrangement of detail, ultimately bringing experience, emotion, and analysis or interpretation into a single, complex rendering. What one encounters here is full of play and multifaceted significance, and, because it is vicarious, the reader can stand back far enough to take in the richness, without being overwhelmed by detail (43).

Nussbaum is not suggesting that novels replace political documents or economic analyses, but she is saying that political and economic treatises would be perfectly consistent with their goals if the view of human beings underlying them was that supplied by novels. "Government cannot investigate the life story of every citizen in the way a novel does with its characters; it can, however, know that each citizen has a complex history of this sort" (44).

**Reflexive Readings**

This study makes the claim that reading the *Platform for Action* coming out of the Fourth UN Conference on Women alongside global women's novels makes absolute sense. It is a way of keeping the concrete alive in the abstract, the particular essential to the universal, the playful in touch with the analytical, and the complex inherent in the unified. Furthermore, it exercises the "what if" factor in human thought, reminding us that if cultural systems and categories are created, they can be recreated, and that myths of renewal and empowerment have always preceded significant social change.

The title comes from Nawal el Saadawi's remark that she looks beautiful to herself in airplane mirrors; she also ponders whether this is a matter of the quality of the glass or the experience of crossing from one world to another. One suspects it has to do with animated features (a wide-eyed openness to the foreign). Mirrors feature widely in literature and literary criticism where writers are continually trying to unpack ideas of mimesis and identity. In the nineteenth century, Stendhal defined the *novel* as a "mirror walking along the road." And Gustave Flaubert created that remarkable scene where Madame Bovary stares at herself wide-eyed and amazed after her first love affair, reciting "I have a lover." She has, indeed, composed a face to meet her face in the mirror, writing her new identity into the very features she projects. Emma has crossed an essential line (for good or ill) and she will never be the same again.

Psychoanalysts certainly share this interest in mirror images, important crossings, and identity. As Julia Kristeva interprets Jacques Lacan's idea of the mirror stage, it is the moment when the child first sees him or herself and arrives at an illusion of a fixed identity. Before this, the child has babbled; now he or she enters the possibility of speech. Yet the "crossing" is itself a fiction, an anticipation of personal wholeness that so many experiences in life will belie. The fiction remains, nonetheless, a belief in (nostalgia for) singularity ("A Question of Subjectivity").

Complex stories, of the sort novels reproduce, often follow the same dialectic. Taking convoluted lives and circuitous events, the writer creates a single artifact, but part of the pleasure of reading the work is knowing that that singularity is artificial and made up, and that events could, in fact, often will take a very different shape than anticipated. The work is both fixed and quite surprising, articulated yet inviting interpretive play.

As the title of this study suggests, fictional reflexivity is both personal and political.[4] It addresses the complex selfhood of the reader—a foreignness of self to self—and draws the reader into foreignness of other sorts—of race, gender, age, class, geography, education, lifestyle, religion, and so on. In story, as in life, situations of alienation, oppression, and reconciliation vary interminably, even as systems of power draw on the same fears and vulnerabilities. Politics enters, not necessarily through fictional content, but through the writer's and reader's mutual acts of navigating patterns of meaning.

### Documents of Embattled Practice

This is a study of women's novels in political context. More specifically, *Aeroplane Mirrors* states in its subtitle that it is concerned with *post-colonial* women's novels. The term came into popular usage with the 1989 publication of *The Empire Writes Back: Theory and Practice in Post-Colonial Literatures*, by Bill Ashcroft, Gareth Griffiths, and Helen Triffen. Post-colonial is initially defined there as "all the culture affected by the imperial process from the moment of colonization to the present day" (2), but that definition is immediately amended to include recent cross-cultural criticism and its discourse. In terms of literature, post-colonial includes not only the psychological impetus to write that comes out of the historical experience of colonialism, but also the subversive strategies used by post-colonial writers to expose and resist systems of power (24, 33). This is the idea of writing back. As writers from former colonies dismantle the assumptions of colonial power, they are writing back to the centers of power, both in terms of revealing hidden information and of resisting the misuse of power that information unmasks. Part of what is revealed through these writings is that the "natives" are far more complex and unbanal than assumed.

For this study, *post-colonial* refers to the theoretical and literary discourse that reflects the experience of having been colonized and of resisting colonial powers. Especially, this study focuses on the experience of women whose lives have been controlled by both imperial and patriarchal systems of power and who are attempting in their writings to give new definitions to both marginality and to empowered and resistant selfhood.

*Aeroplane Mirrors* comes from a first-world perspective (the writer is what she is). It makes no claim to define and defend "third-world women's" fiction or to critique or evaluate it in the normal sense. There are plenty of regional critics and scholars to do that. What this book does explore is how Western readers can be impacted by the novels of women writers from the Eastern and Southern nations, writers who have only been readily available to them in recent times. How are these writers disorienting us, changing how we see the world, ourselves, and issues of women's rights? How are they changing our response to and participation in political discourse? How are they reorienting our ideas of feminism and making respectful, risky solidarities possible? How are they problematizing our concepts of culture in general and of specific cultures that have been all but hidden (often by our own volition) from us in the past? As Susie Tharu and K. Lalita describe this enterprise in the introduction to *Women Writing in India* (1993), Western women need to read these works "not as new *monuments* to existing institutions or cultures, . . . but as *documents* that display what is at stake in the embattled practices of self and agency, and in the making of a habitable world" (39).

To accomplish this, *Aeroplane Mirrors* has had to stay with writers who have composed in English or been widely translated to date. (The dates given in the pages of this study indicate the original dates of publication of works, while the bibliography lists current editions and translations used.) It stays with writers readily available in major book stores and through Internet book suppliers. That means concentrating less on new writers than on those who have established a critical following and have had the possibility of changing perceptions in the post-colonial period. It includes writers who were born outside of the so-called industrialized world but who have come to reside and work there.

Chapter 1 considers the historical, anthropological, and political contexts for the Fourth UN Conference on Women and how its deliberations and outcomes illustrate the ongoing tension between an articulation of universal human rights for women and recognition of significant differences in the needs of concrete, acculturated women.

Chapter 2 looks at the novel as an international literary marketplace, concentrating on the struggles and styles of post-colonial women writers. Most important, it explores the ethics of reading post-colonial women's novels in a first-world setting so that foreignness is neither minimized nor stigmatized.

Chapter 3 focuses on language. What does it mean for a Nigerian woman to choose to write in English? What does this say about her education, her relationship to a changing culture, her desire to be published, and her attempt to choose an audience? The chapter assesses how all language preserves estrangement, but especially how the language of women both reveals and strategically obscures the desires of their hearts and the intentions of their politics.

Chapters 4 through 8 explore how specific novels illuminate and complicate the critical areas of concern outlined by participants in the Fourth World Conference on Women. The underlying assumption throughout is that what happened at Beijing, with all of its complex antecedents and proceedings, provides a viable political context for understanding both the challenge and the influence of post-colonial women's fiction.

## Notes

1. Structural adjustment programs are the set of policy prescriptions for economic stability imposed by international lending organizations (the World Bank, the International Monetary Fund) as a condition for development or short-term emergency loans to governments. Debtor countries are forced to reduce social spending, increase exports, and often devalue currency as a means toward cutting inflation rates, establishing balance of payments, and guaranteeing debt repayment. These policies, geared toward economic stability, often shortchange initiatives for the alleviation of poverty and overburden women who are forced to compensate for the loss of social services (health, education, food subsidies) with their unpaid labor.

2. Anti-poverty measures outlined in previous conference documents concentrated on equality of opportunity and income generation, while tending to ignore the domestic and intimate lives of women (Mosse 156). This may have resulted from an assumption on the part of development professionals that the household is the proper unit of analysis, rather than what happens *in* the household in terms of forced labor and forced sex (Okin 279).

3. In the 1998 UN conference to establish an international tribunal to try war crimes, the Vatican continued to undermine concerns of the Beijing conference by insisting that "enforced pregnancy" not be described as a form of torture for fear that countries enforcing anti-abortion laws could become liable. Islamic countries and U.S. anti-abortion lobbyists joined the Vatican, and references to sexual crimes against women came close to being eliminated from the treaty (Stanley).

4. In the largest sense, that intended in this study, *politics* means the total complex of relationships that determine life in society. That can be complex indeed, as illustrated by the comments of Bharati Mukherjee at a conference on politics and imaginative writing: "I was born into a religion that placed me, a Brahmin, at the top of its hierarchy while condemning me, as a woman, to a role of subservience. The larger political entity to which I gave my first allegiance—India—was not even a sovereign nation when I was born" (24).

# PART ONE

# THEORETICAL FRAMEWORKS

# Chapter 1

## *The Fourth World Conference on Women: Celebration of Unity or Diversity?*

> Acknowledging the voices of all women everywhere and taking note of the diversity of women and their roles and circumstances, honouring the women who paved the way and inspired by the hope present in the world's youth . . . we reaffirm our commitment to the equal rights and inherent human dignity of women and men.
> —*Beijing Declaration,* Fourth World Conference on Women

## The Historical Context for Beijing

### Development History

The *Platform for Action,* emerging from the Fourth World Conference on Women in September 1995, was a long document with a long history. In the 1950s, economists and international policymakers began to talk about "development" as a way of conceptualizing and shaping changes taking place in newly independent nations of the Southern hemisphere. But from the very beginning, the term implied a "notion of historical change derived from Western European secular and scientific thought" (Charlton 7) and tended to project a linear course of economic growth commensurate with this paradigm.

The 1970s brought radical changes, both in the application of ethical theory to development models and in the recognition that women's issues were a vitally necessary part of the discussion. Ester Boserup's seminal study *Women's Role in Economic Development* (1970) is often cited as the beginning of this new consideration. Here Boserup looks at the gender complications of colonialism: the effects of urbanization on family dynamics, shifts in female labor patterns, the effects of Western diseases on patterns of care-taking, education for women biased toward domestication—complications wrought on diverse traditional patterns of gender socialization and carrying well into the post-colonial period.

In the early 1970s, the Women's Committee of the Society for International Development began to use the phrase "Women in Development" as a way of speaking to U.S. policymakers about the findings of Boserup and others who shared her interests (Mosse 158). Advocates of "Women in Development" argued that women needed first and foremost to be given equal opportunities in the workplace. Assuming that technical and vocational training for women would lead to their integration into the economic market, few stopped to ask if the system they would be entering was a good one or if more fundamental problems needed to be addressed (154). Third-world thinkers, in particular, found the emphasis on equality of opportunity to be a limiting preoccupation of first-world feminists.

In the latter half of the 1970s, "Women *and* Development" began to be used as a substitute phrase, one suggesting alliance of feminist concerns with class concerns under the rubric of Marxist analysis. This approach recognized that women have always done significant work—work that is fundamental to the functioning of societies everywhere—but that women's work has been controlled by men both inside and outside of the household such that women often do not fully participate in the means of exchange. Marxist feminists argued that improving class inequalities within nations and economic disparities between nations would lead to more political participation on the part of all persons, including women, and therefore the development of more income-generating options for women (Charlton 6, Ollenburger and Moore 20).

But this approach led to a denial that women are almost everywhere overburdened with work and to an overemphasis on the development of income-generating labor at the expense of addressing patriarchal ideology—"women's specific gender oppression" (Mosse 160). Such critique has led to an approach called "Gender and Development," suggesting that both men and women's roles need to be restructured in order for true equity to be possible. If the current oppression of women can be traced to "race, class, colonial history, and the position of Southern countries within the international economic order," as well as to family politics, job laws, and educational preparation, then all aspects need to be considered. Advocates of "Gender and Development" argue that women need to be empowered with knowledge and resources to change the very structures that have abused them (161).

### History of UN Involvement

The 1995 Conference in Beijing reflected all of these years of study and debate, and evidenced in its *Platform for Action* a complex understanding of the causality of women's problems, a sophisticated analysis of the solutions necessary, and a growing reliance on collective conversation as the way to arrive at either. It reflected the history of UN involvement with women's issues and with articulation of universal human rights as well.

In the late 1940s, the UN created a Commission on the Status of Women to promote nondiscrimination against women. In addition, the original *Charter* of the UN and the early *Universal Declaration of Human Rights* spoke of the dignity of all humankind. *Dignity* was here defined as an ability to speak and participate in the public world, to control one's own body and life in the private world, and to seek shelter, food, education, health, a secure environment, and employment in order to sustain life (Bunch, "Women's Human Rights" 160). Some years later, the UN's declaration of the Decade for Women (1975–85) gave rise to three global conferences on women's issues, the first in Mexico City (1975), the second in Copenhagen (1980), and the third in Nairobi (1985).

The conference in Mexico City was the context out of which UNIFEM, a United Nations Voluntary Fund (very much like UNICEF), was born. The conference in Copenhagen introduced to the world an all-important *Convention on the Elimination of All Forms of Discrimination Against Women*. And the conference in Nairobi produced a precursor to the 1995 *Platform for Action* entitled *Forward-looking Strategies for the Advancement of Women*.

Charlotte Bunch, director of the Center for Women's Global Leadership, and Valentine Moghadam, senior research fellow at the World Institute for Development Economics Research, view the growth of women-centered conferences and of women's political participation as tied to the concern for human and environmental rights at the very center of the UN mission. Bunch argues that, historically, way too much of human rights practice and jurisprudence has been shaped by male experience. But by asserting the universal dignity of all humankind, early UN documents left space for the equal participation of women in basic human freedoms. This has empowered the activism of women around other UN deliberations. As Bunch observes:

> Women are not waiting for permission to have our human rights recognized but rather are stating that issues like female infanticide and illiteracy, violence against women and female sexual slavery, reproductive health and women's poverty are fundamental to our humanity and must become cornerstones of human rights practice and global development agendas. ("Women's Human Rights and Development" 161).

Women were active in planning the World Summit for Children in 1991 and were instrumental in composing the *Convention on the Rights of the Child* that came up for ratification at that Summit. They were an important lobby at the World Conference on Human Rights at Vienna in 1993 and made sure that the *Vienna Declaration and Programme of Action* recognized that women's rights are "universal, inalienable, and indivisible and should not be subordinated to culture or religion" (Bunch 161). This was the first time that the UN specifically called for the "elimination of 'violence against women in public and private life' as a human rights obligation" (161) and instituted gender training for all UN personnel responsible for the promotion and protection of human rights. As an outcome of this conference, a Special Rapporteur on Violence Against Women was appointed.

These deliberations opened up space for the reaffirmation of women's rights to life, liberty, and security of person (including the right to safe motherhood and full, timely knowledge about reproductive health and sexuality) at the International Conference on Population and Development at Cairo in 1994. They also made possible the recognition of gender equality as a condition for a fair labor market, social integration, and the eradication of poverty at the Summit on Social Development in Copenhagen in 1995 (Heyzer 3).

Valentine Moghadam looks back on these accomplishments with both caution and hope. Although she argues that the causes of social and political strife for women are almost intractable and that movements to identify rights are always complex, she agrees that the UN "universal declarations" are a powerful starting point for significant discussion and action at both the country and international levels. In fact, she views the effort to move beyond "particularist rhetorics" and "exclusivist concepts of identity" in these documents as a possible way out of culturally ordained misogyny: "One answer to identity politics which seeks to control women is to disarticulate 'women' from 'culture,' deconstruct women as symbol, reconstruct women as human beings, and problematize women's rights as human rights" (22).

As a result of both governmental and nongovernmental attention to global conferences, and as a result of globalization itself and of its enforced needs for participatory interdependence among nations and ethnicities, UN conferences are assuming ever greater importance for both planning and policy for women. Furthermore, they call for social justice and ethical reasoning to be placed at the center of development discussion.

**Looking Toward Capabilities and Dialogic Community**

One publication that anticipated the Fourth World Conference on Women was a collection of essays by development philosophers arguing for responsible universalism through the human capabilities approach to economic development. Edited by Martha Nussbaum and Jonathan Glover, *Women, Culture, and Development: A Study of Human Capabilities* (1995) offers a way to avoid both "do-gooder colonialism" and "uncritical validation of the *status quo*" through assessing and promoting the fulfillment of shared human capabilities. This approach does not start with human resources but with human desires, such as the desire (right?) to live a life of normal length; to be adequately nourished; to seek sexual satisfaction and choice in matters of reproduction; to be able to reason and imagine; to be able to relate to other human beings, animals and plants; to laugh and play (83–85).

The degree to which a nation's citizens are capable of achieving these desires becomes a measure of the quality of life offered by that nation. Thus, whether individuals start from an orientation toward productive wage earning or reproductive (domestic) labor, their goals are valued. This places women in the quality-of-life equation in ways that gross national product and gross domestic product, focused on productive exchange alone, could never do.

People in a variety of cultures may aim for the same capability, but satisfy it in vastly different ways and with vastly different resources. Freedom to choose a particular venue for satisfaction is, in fact, an inherent part of the approach. But lest disparity of resources seem irrelevant, Nussbaum hastens to stress the "universal" side of this scheme by arguing that when resources are limited, it is more just to bring everyone over a reasonable line of capability to achieve than to allow an elite to achieve ever higher desires. In a world where the "feminization of poverty" is becoming a given, this has radical gender implications.

But where this approach is, perhaps, most radically important for the participation of women in the process of their own development is in its insistence on the value of inclusive conversation. Discovering what persons really care about and can afford to choose for their lives requires open negotiation of difference. As Linda Alcoff points out, because systems of power and restraint affect the choices of all members of a group, no area of investigation and struggle in society can be considered apolitical or beyond negotiation ("Democracy and Rationality" 225), and no voice can be labeled irrelevant. Those who have traditionally been silenced (often the female half of the human race) need to be allowed and encouraged to speak, for no "portion of the elite can accurately determine the needs of the oppressed in a process that is not characterized by democratic inclusiveness and symmetrical relations of co-operation" (233). This requires confrontation with racial, sexual, and economic forces and with the contradictions that drive any culture.

Seyla Benhabib reinforces this point by claiming that many romanticized views of cultural sovereignty (that each culture's way of organizing its members must be respected) are based on bad sociology—they imagine singularity of cultural identity when, in fact, all state and cultural identities are made of contradictions and debate that play themselves out in social institutions and in common discourse ("Cultural Complexity" 240). Thus, the call to "dialogical community" is a call to make public what is already present in a culture (albeit in a number of masked, ritualized, and privatized ways) and ultimately a call to reproduce dialogic community on a global level. She turns the universalist–relativist argument back on itself here, arguing for the universality of intracultural difference, and presupposing contradiction and the need for debate on all levels of negotiation. Such inclusiveness, attempted, although not always achieved, at the UN–NGO conferencing in Beijing, can only be a positive stage toward the full political participation of women.[1]

## The Anthropological Context for Beijing

### Assessing Difference

To consider the anthropological context for the Beijing Conference, one has to ask why a women's conference? If all culture is a matter of contradictions, debates, and shifting vantage points, what themes "for women" can emerge? Couldn't the UN just as easily have had a conference for tall persons, or persons with brown eyes?

In a now classic collection of essays by female anthropologists entitled *Women, Culture and Society* (1974), editor Michelle Zimbalist Rosaldo warns against necessitarian essentialism by paraphrasing sociologist Talcott Parsons and early feminist Simone de Beauvoir:

> I would suggest that anything so general as the universal asymmetry of sex roles is likely to be the result of a constellation of different factors, factors that are deeply involved in the foundation of human societies. Biology may be one of these, but biology becomes significant only as it is interpreted by human actors and associated with characteristic modes of action. (23)

Yet even in cautioning against overgeneralization in a matter so complex, Rosaldo holds to a foundational asymmetry between the constructed roles of males and females in culture, related to the fact that "men have no single commitment as enduring, time-consuming, and emotionally compelling—as close to seeming necessary and natural—as the relation of a woman to her infant child" (24) and so are freer to move into the broader arena of social construction. For Rosaldo, and other anthropologists, biology is an undeniable reality, but if biology is destiny it is because men (and women) have acquiesced to systems of authority and behavior that claim it to be so.

In this same volume of essays, Sherry Ortner presents a view of gender asymmetry connected to the split between nature and culture, such that public structures of male activity tend to take precedence over reproductive female functions. She argues that even when women are active participants in cultural processes, they are perceived as being more rooted in natural processes ("Is Female to Male" 73). So, although biological facts only take on significance within the framework of culture, they are hardly irrelevant to a culture's arguments for upholding structures of difference (and privilege). We certainly do not have to go far for evidence of this in the industrialized world, where professional women are often described as working mothers, whereas professional men are assumed to have no domestic life worth remarking on, unless, of course, that life promises scandalous details.

In the 1980s, historian Gerda Lerner initiated an inquiry into the origins of patriarchy,[2] observing that the female half of the world's population has been, to varying degrees, invisible in written accounts of culture (this, of course, overlaps with periodic and geographic silencing of other groups of persons because of race, class, political affiliation, etc.). Her attempts to reconstruct this history led her to the conclusion that gender asymmetry is related to patterns of exchange of material goods that occurred (at different times and in different places in the world) during the development of stable civilizations. In *The Creation of Patriarchy* (1986) Lerner interacts with the work of economic theorist Friedrich Engels and anthropologist Claude Levi-Strauss, among others, to assert that the early "exchange of women" was related to their valued ability to nurture, as well as give birth to human infants and thus ensure the future of the tribe. Exchange of women tended to create peaceful relationships between tribes (an exchanged woman, while respecting her origins, would remain loyal to the kinship relations of her children).

Most interestingly, Lerner speculates that this commodification of women's reproductive and nurturing capabilities took place with the full agreement of women, appearing to be a cogent strategy for peace and development. Its eventual emergence into exploitative systems of slavery and economic disenfranchisement would, at the time of its origin, have been completely unknown (52). So, although Lerner agrees with other theorists that the link between childbearing and childrearing is a cultural construction, she speculates that there may have been a period in history when, for the survival of the tribe, women were complicit in their own reification. Are the consequences of such a choice "essential" if the causes turn out to be nearly universal?

Martha Chen does a fine job of contextualizing the problematic nature of patriarchy in her study of women's right to employment in India. She notes that, according to the basic patriarchal kinship system in India, labor is divided by gender but further hierarchicalized according to caste, whereby the most telling symbol of a family's position in the caste system is what kind of work its women are allowed to do. The higher the caste, the more secluded women tend to be. The lower the caste, the more acceptable work outside the home becomes. But where this kind of hierarchy is vaguely based on economics, caste is sufficiently different from class to cause painful confusion. Poor women from higher castes, needing to work for the survival of themselves and their children, are often banned by family members from seeking employment.

To illustrate her point, Chen cites the case of Metha Bai, an upper caste widow who will probably "have to risk censure, abuse and even disinheritance by her in-laws if she seeks work in order to feed her sons" ("A Matter of Survival" 49). Where a woman like Bai may have been maintained by family in the past, economic straits may legislate against such support in the present, although the stigma attached to breaking seclusion remains in place and is validated by tradition. So, although male protection is far from guaranteed, women's seclusion is still a marker of caste through control of female labor.

Global deliberations on ways to resist the pervasive economic, domestic, and social disadvantaging of women indicate that questioning such assumed differences is foundational. What value does the division of human beings into male and female perform within any given culture? If binary oppositions (Black–White, East–West, fat–thin) often result in one member of the pair being privileged over the other, and if we concede that male persons have been more active in the formation of culture and its institutions than female persons, then how do women escape being defined negatively—as the other; the elusive entity; the one that is not male, not as readily theorized; the one subject to being named? And if this binary holds, what does it do to differences between and within groups of men, between and within groups of women? What does it say about male feminists and female rulers? Are we better off arguing for difference in a different key—for the multiplicity and heterogeneity that invade all categories under discussion?

## "Making" Gender

Chandra Mohanty has certainly contributed to this questioning in her demand that words like *patriarchy* and *women* be opened up for interpretation. As an activist for women's issues, Mohanty recognizes the necessity of naming categories of analysis. So for her, "women" names a discursively constructed group. Yet this name is not synonymous with "woman" as a material subject, as a person with a proper name, subject to a localized context, who suffers and resists suffering ("Under Western Eyes" 56). Resistant behavior is important for Mohanty, for, as she argues, if "women" are perceived as a fixed, transcultural category, understood as powerless (as other to male power), significant differences among women and their many ways of asserting power (overt as well as subversive) become invisible.[3] Likewise, if men are defined categorically as those who violate women, such behavior seems inevitable. "Defining women as archetypal victims freezes them into 'objects who defend themselves,' men into 'subjects who perpetuate violence' and society into powerless and powerful groups of people" (58).[4]

Mohanty argues that male and female behavior must be described (rather than predicted) as the activities of particular men and particular women who, although culturally conditioned, still have volition. By using that volition to act against oppressive customs and endemic systems of power, groups of women (and men) can establish complicated identities. In this sense, third-world "women" may come to constitute themselves as a strategic group who at particular historical junctures, and in contextualized ways, engage in political struggle against "class, race, gender and imperial hierarchies" (58).[5]

In this, Mohanty is rebelling against the cultural notion of (universal) "women" in the same way that feminist anthropologists of an earlier time rebelled against biological necessity—as a deterministic trap. In "The Use and Abuse of Anthropology," published in *Signs* (1980) and quoted by Mohanty in "Under Western Eyes," Michelle Rosaldo admits that in some ways anthropology is, like fiction, a hall of mirrors where anecdotal experience challenges every generalization but where "lurking in the oddest shapes and forms, we find a still familiar picture of ourselves" (39). The world we find ourselves in (whoever we are) is a world where social and cultural forms tend to be male dominated, but where these forms assume an infinite variety of shapes (394). She concludes, then, that gender must be understood in terms of social relationships and that gender inequality can only be understood in relationship to all other social inequalities.

Sherry Ortner's recent work likewise reflects the need to take differences among women's experiences seriously. Going back to the nature–culture dialectic in a 1996 piece entitled "So Is Female to Male as Nature is to Culture?" she admits that research subsequent to the original article reveals isolated societies where male dominance does not seem to be the order of the day. Yet egalitarianism in these cultures is, at best, complex, inconsistent, and fragile (175), indicating that a more interesting topic than empirical universality may be how gender has come to be a metaphor for talking about the relationship between nature and culture and vice versa.

Metaphoric discourse is important to Ortner in assessing how people deal with gender relations and, in fact, seize or deny the power of "rewriting" them. In "Making Gender," Ortner looks at Grimm's fairytales and notices that, in these stories, female agency is constantly being unmade by structures of power. Yet, it had to exist in the first place in order to be dismantled. From these tales she moves to a definition of the "serious games" played in any culture where human agents, equipped with "skill, intention, wit, knowledge, intelligence" are engaged in weaving "webs of relationships" that ultimately define who they are (1). What she notices is that agents of all sorts constantly stretch the limits of the game, even as they play it, being invented and inventing as they go. Like Mohanty, Ortner appears to be interested in defining women as agents rather than victims, foregrounding their ability to challenge patriarchal forces, and defining them collectively as holders of that power.[6] One wonders if she had Beijing in mind!

### Gender and Identity Politics

Two volumes of essays surrounding and supporting the Beijing Conference—*Identity Politics and Women: Cultural Reassertions and Feminisms in International Perspective*, published the year before, and *Muslim Women and the Politics of Participation: Implementing the Beijing Platform*, published two years after—make clear that all sides of the essentialism versus cultural relativism debate must remain in play, if solutions to women's problems are not to be ideologically hegemonic or myopically contextual. (Once again, it may be worth stating that women's stories and novels, by the very nature of stories, continually keep voices of difference in play and thereby perform a valuable function in such an effort.)

In her introduction to *Identity Politics*, Valentine Moghadam, like others, admits that the real issue for feminist analysis may not be distinguishing between "common culture" and "multiplicity of cultures," but recognizing that what is common in culture may be its internal multiplicity. She notes that social institutions in place among human beings mask more than they reveal and make as many claims *on* as *for* people (especially women), hardly articulating a unified identity for groups within the society or for the society itself. Among Muslim countries, a denial of such multiplicity often plays itself out politically in terms of women's issues being ascribed to "westoxication," "a plague from the west," and thereby dismissed as outside of coherent cultural boundaries. Muslim women, considered (by their essential nature!) to be most vulnerable to the Western virus that deprives them of their "chastity, modesty, and honor through notions of autonomy, sex appeal, and so on," must therefore be veiled as a cultural marker that they are distinctly other from all of that (13–14).

The fact that many Muslim women, even professional women and self-named feminists, choose the veil as a symbol of autonomy is a whole other complicating factor, as is a historical reminder that in 1979, middle-class women in Iran chose the veil in order to stand in solidarity with their working-class sisters during the Islamic revolution (Mohanty, "Under Western Eyes" 67). Some women have chosen the veil as a form of national dress, others have chosen it because it is economical and convenient. Reasons offered by male leaders for enforced veiling include the argument that women's sexuality is too powerful and disruptive to be openly displayed and the fact that an unveiled woman offends Islamic law. Veiling has had a long history in Judaic and Christian tradition (orthodox Jewish women cover their hair after marriage and Catholic nuns have done so up to the present day) and is differently related to class, region, occupation, and urban/rural status, as well as motive.[7] Recognition of anything less complicated in the advocacy for Muslim women's rights may invalidate the effort, no matter how sincere.

Essays in *Muslim Women and the Politics of Participation*, written in response to the Beijing Conference, continue the theme of respecting complexity. Editor Mahnaz Afkhami argues in her introduction that women and sympathetic men must not only challenge religious and political authorities but the very common sensical and easily habitualized behavior that takes place in "the family, the village, the workplace, the city, male–female relations" (xiii). Boutheina Cheriet turns this complicating gesture back on the very idea of human rights. She notes that the initial UN *Declaration of Human Rights* came out of a Europeanized enlightenment notion of inalienable rights, and, in the 1940s, its composers had little awareness of the history and colonial context of southern nations, including a notion of how abhorrent secular law was to Islamic nations. How could articulation of these rights be expected to communicate to de-colonized countries without "translation"? Seeing a continuation of this problem at Beijing and beyond, her solution for implementation of the *Platform for Action* is to encourage open debates within Muslim countries (and other non-European countries) over the *Critical Areas of Concern*, allowing women (and men) to explore them within their own particularized contexts and languages.

## The Fourth World Conference for Women and Its Debates

### Calling the Conference

All of this raises the question of what kinds of policy debates preceded the Fourth World Conference on Women and surrounded the composition of its *Platform for Action*. In 1990, the UN General Assembly endorsed a resolution from the Economic and Social Council to call a world conference on women in 1995 and requested that the Commission on the Status of Women serve as the planning committee for this conference. The Commission then appointed Gertrude Mongella from Tanzania as secretary general of the Fourth World Conference on Women and requested that she oversee preparation of a *Platform for Action*, based on and updating the Nairobi *Forward-Looking Strategies for the Advancement of Women*.

One of the most hotly contested issues was whether the word *gender* needed to be bracketed as a specialized term indicating cultural construction rather than the material facts of sexuality, or whether the term could stand alone for all forms of social differentiation based on but not limited to biology. Other issues involved the effect of structural adjustment programs, sustainable development, international human rights instruments, and economic rights. Agreement was reached on most issues. But gender was bracketed throughout the document for discussion and resolution at Beijing, and health issues were reserved for full conference deliberations.

Once all delegates were in Beijing, discussion took place over regional, national, religious, class, and racial differences. But dialogue also had to accommodate differences between governmental delegations at the UN Conference and attendees at the NGO Forum, which was a much more diverse, indigenous, and radical group. A publication of Unity 99, *Report from Beijing: The 1995 UN Fourth World Conference on Women and the Non-Governmental Organizations Forum as Seen by U.S. Journalists of Color*, records the difficulties in getting the forum up and running. Ostensibly, the Chinese government became afraid that the in-pouring of politicized grassroots women would have a destabilizing effect on the official UN Conference and on Chinese society in general. Prejudice seems to have been manifest by the press as well. Coverage of the conference in general was relegated to the inside pages of major newspapers in the United States; the forum was rarely mentioned. Although Hillary Clinton's address to the UN gathering was covered, her impromptu speech at the NGO Forum was largely ignored (14).

Nonetheless, delegates from the more than 1,000 NGOs in attendance had a clear effect on deliberations over the platform. A journalist attending both gatherings commented that "the value of a non-governmental organization lies precisely in the fact that it brings to government another way of thinking that comes from identification with the people and immersion in the non-governmental dimensions of society" (Chittester 88–89). She records that two prevailing concerns at the NGO Forum in Huairou were the feminization of poverty and increasing violence against women. Women at the forum kept a running tab of which items of the *Platform* were being debated daily at the UN Conference and deployed their special interest lobbyists and caucuses in response.[8]

### Controversies

Controversy arose over use of the word *universal* as a modifier for *human rights* (the winning argument being that human rights, by name, are intended to apply to all humans); over inclusion of *sexual orientation* in the list of conditional rights for women; over whether the Vatican should be part of official deliberations; over whether parental or husband rights trump human rights documents in issues of sexual alliance and birth control; and over whether cultural tradition takes precedence over international treaties in terms of violence against women, including clitoridectomy (Chittester 162–163).

Publication of an *NGO Beijing Declaration* on September 15, indicates that, in general, those in attendance at the NGO Forum found the UN *Declaration* and *Platform* to be too conservative. This NGO document is forthright in its inclusion of homophobia as a form of discrimination against women, along with sexism, racism, and poverty. (The Beijing UN document does not name homophobia specifically but adds "because of other status" to its list of barriers to full equality in paragraph 46 of the *Platform*.) The *NGO Declaration* also takes a firmer stand than the *Platform* in condemning market economies as a major cause of the feminization of poverty. It critiques the production and use of land mines, and calls for the sustained use of affirmative action to ensure the equality of women. But there is also an amazing likeness between the articulated results of the two gatherings, and there is evidence in the distinctives of the *Platform for Action* over documents arising out of preceding UN conferences for women that intentional involvement of grassroots groups in the official debate made a difference.[9]

The *Platform* is deliberately inclusive, not only of racial, national, ethnic, and religious differences, but of men as partners in the struggle. The phrase "men and women" is used continually in the document. Language in the *Platform* clearly links issues of gender and race (recognizing that over half of the world's population are non-White), although some complications are worth mentioning. In a historic action, the U.S. NGO contingent made the National Council of Negro Women its secretariat. But when well-meaning White delegates from the United States tried to lobby for inclusion of language on race and ethnicity in the *Platform*, delegates from Rwanda protested, claiming that the inclusion of such language would in itself be racist because White delegates have no authority to tell a Black country what is and is not racist. They, of course, had a point. Who speaks for whom is not a question that can easily be ignored. Yet, many in attendance felt that the Rwandan women were, in fact, defending racial violence in their country, violence that had taken a terrible toll on women and their dependent children (*Report from Beijing* 61).

The *Platform*, for the first time in any UN document, specifically names genital mutilation as a violation of women's human rights (probably because of the active participation of African delegations, making this their issue and not one externally imposed). It advises cuts in military spending in favor of social spending, calls for women to be active participants in global peace conferences, declares rape to be a war crime, speaks of "the family in its various forms," and recommends adoption of a process for enforcing the *Convention on the Elimination of All Forms of Discrimination Against Women*. It speaks actively of the role of the arts in advancing the cause of women. And it concentrates a whole section on issues for the girl child, claiming that: "If women are to be equal partners with men, in every aspect of life and development, now is the time to recognize the dignity and worth of the girl child and to ensure the full enjoyment of her human rights and fundamental freedoms" (paragraph 39). Indicating the full participation of NGOs in the work of ensuring women's human rights and full opportunities, the *Platform* designates specific actions to be taken by nongovernmental as well as governmental agencies within each area of concern.

Reservations entered into the record by a number of delegations on the last day of the conference and in follow-up meetings involved the extent of a woman's right to control her own sexuality and the extent to which a ratifying country's "fundamental laws and texts" would take precedence over specific issues in the *Platform*. Perhaps the most interesting statement of tension over international consensus and specific law came from the tiny country of Vanuatu:

> While therefore endorsing the Platform for Action of this important Conference, the Vanuatu delegation wishes to state that its endorsement of the Platform is made with full respect for the constitutional, religious and traditional principles which the sovereign State has inherited and kept for the good government of our nation. (*Report of the Fourth World Conference*, Chapter V, section 31)

Because few of us know anything at all about the interior workings of this country, it is possible to take such a statement as without guile, as a statement of (the perhaps hopeless but admirable) intention to respect local tradition and global treaty simultaneously, recognizing that neither is absolute, singular or immune to critique, but that both make claims in the name of the good.

## Notes

1. This approach can be overromanticized as well. Given that two-thirds of the world's illiterate persons are women, that girl children drop out of school

at earlier ages and larger numbers than do boys, and that in many cultures women are socialized not to speak in public debate, intracultural debates will continue to privilege educated, enfranchised male speakers for some time, and at conferences like the one in Beijing, country delegations will continue to be composed of the educated elite and take place in the privileged idiom of academia and policymaking.

2. In *The Creation of Patriarchy*, historian Gerda Lerner gives the word its "wider definition" as "male dominance over women and children in the family and the extension of male dominance over women in society in general," but she goes on to say, "It does *not* imply that women are either totally powerless or totally deprived of rights, influence, and resources" (39). In an article entitled "The 'Declining Significance' or the 'Changing Form' of Patriarchy?" Sylvia Walby asks whether the term *patriarchy* can even begin to cover the complexity and diversity of patterns of gender relations, composed as they are of interrelated structures of household work, paid work, state, violence, sexuality, and cultural institutions (4).

3. Other writers to look at on the issue of defining "woman" include Judith Butler who, in her *Gender Trouble: Feminism and the Subversion of Identity* (1990), argues, like Mohanty, for extreme caution in attributing characteristics to the "gendered self." Seyla Benhabib (*Situating the Self*) and Linda Alcoff ("Cultural Feminism versus Post-structuralism: The Identity Crisis in Feminist Theory") argue conversely that if women are no more than the sum total of particular descriptions, what can possibly be demanded in their name?

4. Cultural critic Edward Said reminds us that oppressed groups do as much to perpetuate falsely essentialized notions of race, class, and gender as do oppressors. In *Orientalism* (1978), he demonstrates how Western thinkers and writers have created a monolithic view of the East that has institutionalized the Orient, the Orientalist, and consumers of Orientalism. But in *Culture and Imperialism* (1994), he addresses the fact that in post-colonial nation-states, ideas of the Celtic spirit, negritude, and Islam have as much to do with "native manipulators, who . . . use them to cover up contemporary faults, corruptions, tyrannies" (16) as with imperial forces. Seeming to set out to prove this, Toni Morrison's 1998 novel *Paradise* illustrates boldly and masterfully that White supremacy may be mirrored in Black culture as a loathing for all but the purist blackness.

5. In a widely quoted article, "Woman Skin Deep: Feminism and the Postcolonial Condition," Sara Suleri argues vehemently with Mohanty's decentralized position on the basis that enthroning specificity turns a blind eye on radical reality as it is lived by a number of suffering women. If only a Black can speak for a Black, she argues, if "only a postcolonial subcontinental feminist can adequately represent the lived experience of that culture," then we are all caught up in an endless game of establishing subcultural credentials and giving into, rather than resisting, limits on our thinking and imagining (760).

6. In *Domination and the Arts of Resistance* (1990), social scientist James Scott likewise speaks of an uncanny ability on the part of the oppressed to act out their resistance in hidden and ironic modes of expression. Novel-writing and other forms of metaphoric exchange—jokes, folktales, songs—fit well within the purview of "hidden transcripts" speaking "behind the back of the dominant," as do other forms of subversive behavior (xii).

7. For a deeper understanding of the complexities of veiling and female self-definition in Muslim countries, see the work of Sondra Hale with Sudanese women ("Gender, Religious Identity, and Political Mobilization in Sudan"; *Gender Politics in Sudan: Islam, Socialism, and the State*, 1996; "Letter: On Nuba Women and Children in Sudan") and the novels of Algerian writer Assia Djebar (*Fantasia: An Algerian Cavalcade*, 1987, and *A Sister to Scheherazade*, 1989).

8. Adding to the diversity of participants at the NGO Forum were a number of women who came on grants (400 from Africa, 600 from India) and those who sold items at the forum in order to pay for their trips (Sears)

9. In footnote 4 to "Under Western Eyes," Chandra Mohanty critiques the earlier UN women's conferences at Mexico City and Copenhagen as "American planned and organized," places where first-world feminists proclaimed "international sisterhood" on their own terms.

# Chapter 2

## *The Novel: European Monolith or International Literary Marketplace?*

> Languages of heteroglossia, like mirrors that face each other, each reflecting in its own way a piece, a tiny corner of the world, force us to guess at and grasp for a world behind their mutually reflecting aspects that is broader, more multi-leveled, containing more and varied horizons than would be available to a single language or a single mirror.
> —Mikhail Bakhtin, *The Dialogic Imagination*

### Talking Story

Stories have always been with us—they are told in rhyme and meter, performed in public space, and read in published form. Post-colonial writers have chosen extended prose fiction, what we have come to call the novel, as their genre of most frequent choice for "telling" stories. Why? Is it the eclectic representational power of the novel, its ability to show us multiple lives and moments in a single artifact? Is it the novel's ability to appeal to an international, intergenerational audience—creating "new" worlds for perusal by residents of "old" worlds—that makes it so appealing? Or is it the ability of the novel to incorporate a multiplicity of oral story forms into written language that gives it universal appeal? And what is the special appeal that the novel has ever had and continues to have for women, both as writers and readers?

Chikwenye Ogunyemi, Nigerian literary critic, speaks extensively about the fact that if the novel has become an international literary marketplace for ideas, that marketplace is a particularly comfortable space for women, who, in developing countries, are often keepers of the material marketplace as well—a place where the "butcher, the fishmonger, the hairplaiter, the grocer, the cosmetologist, the seamstress, the fabric trader, and the food seller" all thrive as independent and interdependent agents. In many traditional cultures, all of life happens in the market, in the center of the village, in the microcosm of life where a woman can obtain economic independence and be protected against outside invaders. This is where women share narratives—where hair plaiters and their clients tell stories about husbands and village problems and where the telling itself engenders solidarity (51–52). (The Beijing women's Conference and NGO Forum seemed to offer the same kind of safe space to women from many places in the world, thus, perhaps, accounting for much of the free speech and colorful pageantry that occurred there.)

Ogunyemi claims that market mothers are knowledgeable women with influence over both material exchange and political decision making. Seeking female companionship and communication with strangers, knowing the exasperation of being cheated and the thrill of getting a bargain, these women lead vital lives that bridge the gap between private and public existence.[1] Caught in the maze of emerging national concerns, they look for ways to negotiate women's agency in bringing change. And the accessibility of crowds in the marketplace (often positioned close to palace grounds or government buildings) renders it a conducive environment for political debate (52). Market women introduce their daughters to an environment where people are relatively free and outspoken, and their daughters may, in turn, become storytellers and novelists, countering the social erasure of women through articulating their complex lives and desires (54–55).

For Ogunyemi, what begins in the African marketplace as dialogue and oral story often becomes the basis for women's written narrative, replicating the spirit of communal palaver. Ogunyemi's compatriot, novelist Buchi Emecheta, describes her personal writing style as drawing from "the way we [women] speak in our part of Nigeria" (Ogundele, 447)—as well as from more formal traditions of Igbo storytelling. Emecheta informs us that the Igbo storyteller is always called *mother*: "My big mother was my aunt. . . . I was determined when I grew older that I was going to be a storyteller like my Big Mother" (cited in Spencer-Walters 126–27).

Ghanaian writer, Ama Ata Aidoo, also celebrates this vital verbal context for the novel by calling for an oral literature to accompany written texts—not only through the preservation of orature in written dialogue and narrative style, but by "telling" stories off the page to those who cannot read or who crave the sounds as well as meanings of words. Aidoo declares that in her own work she writes for listeners as well as readers because, like Emecheta, her mother could "talk" stories and sing songs (James 23, 19).[2] For Aidoo, this has meant working in drama as well as written fiction and always keeping the speaking voice alive in written fiction; these are ways to avoid the loneliness of writing, to stay in touch with the mother's wisdom, and to capture the excitement of public exchange.

Moving from the market to the prison where incarcerated women have always exchanged experiences, shared tidbits of food, and recited life stories, Nawal el Saadawi's weaving of oral and written versions of reality is an equally remarkable example of aesthetically shaped palaver.[3] While a political prisoner in Egypt in 1981, Saadawi shared a prison cell with secular intellectuals, Islamic revivalists, and one Christian—all voicing their anger and frustration at the political system that had incarcerated them. Across the courtyard were female beggars, prostitutes, and murderers, each with a story to tell. All are recorded in Saadawi's *Memoirs from the Women's Prison* (1983).

Earlier, as a practicing psychiatrist, Saadawi had entered that same prison with the deliberate intention to hear one particular story, that of a prostitute, Firdaus, convicted of killing her pimp. In shaping this interview into written fiction (*Woman at Point Zero* [1973]), Saadawi has kept alive the fluidity of verbal "world-making." When the psychiatrist-narrator of the novel cedes center stage to the criminal-protagonist and listens to the relentless fatal rhythm of this murderer's life story, she, the professional, an expert in the semantics of cause and effect, is seduced by voice itself ("like the voices I hear in dreams"). It is the telling, much more than the content of Firdaus' tragic tale that surrounds this narrative event with emotional power. Both the physician and the readers experience the impact of the story through a reluctant yet insistent visceral desire to see Firdaus executed rather than surrender her passion and independence to a misogynist state.

In like manner, Isabel Allende, a Chilean novelist, draws us into the ending of *House of the Spirits* (1982) by having female political prisoners share personal stories and tell magical tales to the children of a mother gone mad during torture in the hope that these children would someday return such songs and gestures "to the children and grandchildren of the women who were rocking them to sleep" (427).

Recognizing the power of such mergings of oral and written narrative (of performed folktale and transcribed fiction) in the works of these writers, we should not wonder that the laws associated with print culture are often irrelevant in post-colonial cultures—in places where the flexibility of told story still generates many variations of a "text" and where copyright of products of the imagination seems as absurd as copyrighting one's children, especially when each child has many "mothers."[4] Indeed, Huma Ibrahim argues that the reason why South African writer Bessie Head calls her personal history a *story* is "that it has not been completely told before and can certainly stand to be retold" (215–16). This openness to reinterpretation, this dynamic interface of developing story and written narrative, although confounding Western publishers, also contributes to an identification of the post-colonial novel with social and political change.

Ogunyemi claims that written-down stories possessing the power of multiple audiences *and* the fluidity of oral rendering have the power to keep transformational thinking alive and dialogic. In her view, this includes transformation of the relationships between men and women within newly independent nations as well as their relationships with the outside world. Thus, many post-colonial female writers, drawing on their traditional notions of story, empowered by their exchanges with other women, and given access to the means of publication, have brought the plight of women (and often of the underclass) to world attention, voicing the hitherto unacknowledged reality of their lives (26). "As writers with a cause," Ogunyemi states, "women are playing the transformational role of the griotte as entertainer, teacher, social critic, ideologue, and wise but despised mother" (3). In this, they are foremothers and sisters of the outspoken women at Beijing, whether this relationship remains implicit or is recognized as explicit.

### Where Has the Novel Come From?

All of this seems to beg the question: Where has the novel come from? It is well and good to link African—or Egyptian, or Latin American—written narratives with indigenous oral traditions, but where did the novel as a sophisticated international medium of published fictional exchange originate? If it originated in Europe close to the time of colonial expansion, as is often claimed, can it be in any way an "innocent" vehicle of exchange? In short, can a female non-Westerner write freely in a Western art form without ultimately imitating the very racial, classist, and patriarchal forces that made it aesthetically successful?

### The Official Story

When looking for the origins of the novel, students in Western universities have often been sent to Ian Watt's classic study *The Rise of the Novel* (1967). Watt views the Western novel as drawing from a number of genres and previous forms of fiction but coming into its own as a distinct art form in the eighteenth century in Europe, out of middle-class values, including the worth of the individual and a desire in art for "fidelity to human experience" (i.e., realism). What distinguishes the novel from other fictions, Watt argues, is an "individualization of its characters and . . . the detailed presentation of their environment" (18), values that came into being with the post-Renaissance rise of the bourgeois work ethic. The burgeoning middle class demanded reader-friendly venues in both news reporting and art in order to feed "a rapid, inattentive, almost unconscious kind of reading habit" (49). Furthermore, because women in post-Renaissance Europe were becoming a larger portion of the reading class, emotional relationships were increasingly essential to works of fiction: "such relationships may be seen as offering the individual a more conscious and selective pattern of social life to replace the more diffuse, and as it were involuntary, social cohesions which individualism had undermined" (177). In the novel, the individual was reattached to life through the choice of a life-partner. Even novels themselves, according to Watt, became chosen partners, with readers surrendering themselves to illusion in the solitary act of reading (198).

Few scholars dispute Watt's account of how the novel developed in Europe. Edward Said, archenemy of naive Eurocentric points of view, fully accepts the European novel as recent, bourgeois, and entwined with Western ideas of reality and personality. In fact, he argues, "imperialism and the novel fortified each other to such a degree that it is impossible. . . to read one without in some way dealing with the other" (*Culture and Imperialism* 71). This is his very reason for arguing that scholars in the postcolonial era need to read the canonical European texts with great care, applying to them all conflicting streams of historical analysis, and exposing their ideological bias. Thus, Said views literary hermeneutics as a form of resistance to past and present imperialist expansion of Europe and to all of the rhetorical ways in which such an endeavor has been masked and mystified.

Likewise, Nigerian scholars Chinweizu, Onwuchekwa Jemie, and Ihechukwu Madubuike accept that the European novel evolved in the eighteenth century out of prose and verse epics and romances of the Greco-Roman and medieval worlds, and they lament that, subsequently, Eurocentric African literary critics have viewed African fiction writing as "an overseas department of European literatures" (3). But they resist this literary imperialism differently from Said. For them, it is not as important to critique European and Europeanized novels to unmask their "hidden transcripts" as it is to fill in the vast gaps in the history of the novel itself.

If the European novel developed in a colonial situation out of emerging middle-class values, they argue, the African novel is a "hybrid out of the African oral tradition and the imported literary forms of Europe" (8). Not denying the cultural influence of Europe on African fiction, they insist on the equal importance of orality and even of indigenous written narrative to the kind of novel that has taken shape in Africa. Africa was hardly unliterate when the Europeans arrived, they point out; there has been a long tradition of written literature in Africa and an abundance of oral narratives that have contributed greatly to the themes and techniques of the African novel, even the African novel written in English (26).[5]

Furthermore, realism is hardly the only style of representation appropriate to the novel! The mythic and magical will always be a part of authentic African storytelling, they argue, and those Africans who choose to write in English will have to bend and flex their chosen language to capture the spirit of life in a vast and animated continent (262). One hastens to add that magic realism has long been a mainstay of internationally acclaimed Latin American fiction, emerging out of a rich mixture of indigenous and European worldviews.

### Bakhtin Takes on the Canon

When we come to a literary scholar such as Mikhail Bakhtin, we find a vast thinker (long silenced by the Soviet system) who challenges the recent history and bourgeois nature of the European novel from within European tradition itself. In his 1981 introduction to Bakhtin's *The Dialogic Imagination*, Michael Holquist says that Bakhtin "loves novels because he is a baggy monster" (xviii), which is his way of saying that the novel itself is a "baggy monster" of a genre. This, in fact, is what Bakhtin celebrates about the novel—its eclectic, folkloric, multivoiced, multiclassed, disruptive, and overfull nature.

# The Novel

Bakhtin describes the novel as a hybrid genre, as uncanonic and plastic, forming itself out of bits and pieces of other genres, "ever questing, ever examining itself and subjecting its established forms to review" (39). Thus, he views it as the perfect genre for a changing, emerging world such as our own, "the leading hero in the drama of literary development in our time precisely because it best of all reflects the tendencies of a new world still in the making" (7).

Such a view of the novel welcomes its enriching "heteroglossia," its multiple voices, both social and psychic. Bakhtin claims that the novel, of all literary genres, resists monologism and, in its breadth and complexity, keeps alive the multiple discourses of a given society. It assumes all persons are internally dialogic, no groups in society are voiceless (for even if they are illiterate, their nuanced speech can be heard and reproduced), and all culture centers around multiplicity of conflict. If all points of view are heard, and this is what holds the reader's interest, there is no unitary social consciousness to be received. Characters and readers alike are in the position of discovering their own language within the languages of others, of discovering their own ideological horizons within the ideological horizons of others. Otherness itself becomes both contingent and illusory (365). Thus, the novel is, by its very nature, different from didactic politics: it is "an anti-authoritarian, democratizing art form" (56), simultaneously teasing out and ultimately trumping singularity of thought. And so it has always been, he argues.

In tracing the evolution of the European novel, Bakhtin wants to go back to the Socratic dialogues, and other serio-comic genres of classical literature, as they unfolded in the *agora*, the marketplace that Ogunyemi and others find so generative of significant story. He claims there is little laughter in the Greek epic poems, but in Greek "novels" and romances, large, often rambling and picaresque stories of the ordinary folk, he finds a comic fearlessness "without which it would be impossible to approach the world realistically" (3). Arising out of folk genres, these somewhat unwieldy narrative forms helped to spawn Roman satires and parodic works of the Middle Ages, coming to raucous fruition in Rabelais' *Gargantua and Pantagruel*, where in the creative chaos of the Renaissance world, anything could happen, and did. Through five volumes, his heroes travel and fight and love and learn, subverting social institutions as they go, and not caring in the least that they are giants in a doll-house world.[6]

To Bakhtin, a world-in-the-making is the world of the novel, and the radical restructuring of fiction drives a view of the world as malleable, reversible, developing, and renewing itself. He argues that there are no self-sufficient cultures, only a way of becoming conscious that one's culture exists among other cultures and languages (370). He claims that these languages are "like mirrors that face each other, each reflecting in its own way a piece, a tiny corner of the world" (414), leaving us to guess at and long for the world beyond, yet giving us a taste of its richness. Such reflections stand at the very center of a study of post-colonial women's novels where multiple voices of husbands, fathers, sons, magistrates, companions, daughters, and strangers continually test a woman's sense of herself and her place in a world that contains many exotic and wonderful creatures that too call themselves women.

Psychoanalyst Julia Kristeva is largely responsible for introducing Mikhail Bakhtin to Western intellectuals and eloquently applies his notions of dialogic fiction to the study of language and political–feminist fiction. Making a distinction between structuralism as a study of the static side of language and of semiotics as a study of the signifying process of language, she clearly views Bakhtin's value in his elaboration (and celebration) of the transgressive, signifying power of literary discourse. As she discerns it, Bakhtin's notion of a "literary word" is an "intersection of textual surfaces" rather than a point with a fixed meaning. That is, every literary utterance in a given novel is a dialogue between the writer, the character, and the cultural context (resulting from the author's reading of social and historical "texts" and then writing them) ("Word, Dialogue and Novel" 36).[7] Literary endeavor this cognizant of multiple voices is bound to strain at and transgress the laws of grammar and syntax and thereby remain on the side of political and social protest as well (36).

Yet, Kristeva stresses, dialogism is not anarchy. One is not free to say everything, but, through dramatic "banter," to offer an *other* imperative than that of either absolutism or nothingness. This is "transgression giving itself a law" so as to distinguish itself from pseudo-transgression ("law anticipating its own transgression") (41).[8] Thus, for Kristeva, as well as Bakhtin, the novel (polyphonic by nature) is constantly in a state of challenging codes and creating itself as a literary form. That this is happening in new ways and many places in the current literary scene argues for the well-being of the baggy monster and leaves room for feminine voices in the novel that are neither hysterical nor imitative of male reasoning and European culture.

In addition, Kristeva wants to relate the power of the multivocal novel to its articulation of the strangeness within ourselves, to its reflection of the multiple selves whose recognition can prepare us to be citizens of an estranging world ("Strangers to Ourselves"). Anyone who has ever read a novel and identified with all of the characters knows what Kristeva means; the complexity we need to respect in the world, we also need to encounter within ourselves, reminding us close at hand that much contradiction and difference cannot be reduced to linear form. Mohanty calls this our *mestiza* consciousness—a "plurality of self," located at the junction of race, class, sexuality, and politics ("Cartographies of Struggle" 36).[9]

It is the premise of this book that such multiple mirrorings of society and individuals can keep human beings cognizant of the richness of both psychological and cultural life and call them to rewrite and recreate structures of power that have become rigid and life-denying. Nowhere is this complex dynamic better illustrated than in Meena Alexander's novel of border crossings *Manhattan Music* (1996), telling the story of Sandhya, a young woman from Hyderabad, India, seeking peace and serenity through attachment to a North American man, after her politically dissident Indian lover dies from complications of his time in prison and her parents declare their intentions of arranging a traditional marriage.

Trapped by her family's expectations for her, and by limited avenues of escape, Sandhya's assumptions about the future are naive, and she experiences a terrifying maelstrom of multiculturalism in New York. At the center of this world is Draupadi, a woman whose ancestors were part of the Indian diaspora, coming to Trinidad as bonded labor and intermarrying with the African slave population, the Asian population, and—after moving into North America—native Americans and Europeans. Draupadi is an exotic woman, crafting overtly political sculpture out of bits and pieces of life, and visiting a carnival house of mirrors where she feels exuberantly at home with all of the wild configurations of her reflected self.

Unable to join Draupadi's celebration of the multiplex self, unable to feel connected or whole as her husband's wife and daughter's mother, Sandhya becomes passionately, adulterously involved with a Palestinian who, although he shares her foreignness, cannot commit to one place, or one life, and eventually turns her away. With all of these psychic and cultural crossings "tattooed" on her soul, and denied safe haven through sexual intimacy, Sandhya begins to hear the homeless voices of her despair, driving her to attempt suicide and, finally, to listen intensely. How she "reads" what she hears in these voices and how we read her story ultimately merge into awareness that life is increasingly a house of mirrors. As we learn more about the inner workings of the human psyche—even as the world grows smaller and tighter through research, immediately transmittable political dialogue, enmeshing economics, and ecological interdependence—images and voices of difference may be what we primarily know. But what do we do with this knowledge?

Sandhya's cousin, also an immigrant from India, takes her in after the suicide attempt and talks to her of the village scandal of a pregnant girl who committed suicide by jumping in the communal well rather than admit her shame. Sakhi points out that because the girl jumped is no reason why others should: "There is no reason why women should pay this terrible price. A price for having been born, for feeling passion, for bearing life." No reason, indeed! In very embodied terms, Sakhi illustrates that a redefinition of the possibilities of consciousness and action is always both contingent and immanent. What she gives Sandhya and what the novel gives us is no simple transfer of information, nor does it project a clear plan for restructuring Sandhya's life in America, but it holds up a contextualized call for resistance to despair and fragmentation that could, if approached dialogically, set off a whole new conversation about volition.

### Doody Takes on Bakhtin

As far as Bakhtin pushes our notions of the novel and its transgressive history, he is still found wanting by Margaret Anne Doody (*The True Story of the Novel*, 1997) in his failure to acknowledge the wide and disparate elements that fed into the novel's evolution as a subversive art form, and in his failure to fully assess women's role in social history as a shaping force in the development of the novel. But her first attack, like his, is on the claim that the novel as a literary form is innately connected to realism. As she tellingly argues, "when novels by admired novelists deal with barons living in trees and with girls born with green hair it is time to drop the pretense that the primary demand of a long work of prose fiction is that it should be 'realistic'" (16). She prefers to start simply, and say that a work is a novel if it is fictional, in prose, and lengthy.

Her strongest attack, however (and this would have to include Bakhtin), is on those who have ignored the vastly eclectic history of the novel that ranges far beyond Europe and far before the eighteenth century. In fact, she argues that the novel is a "foreign import" to Europe, having been produced in antiquity by people from non-Greek and Roman areas, including the Near East and Africa.[10] "The homeland of the Western Novel is the Mediterranean, and it is a multiracial, multilingual, mixed Mediterranean" (18), Doody argues. She points to an earnest but jesting delineation of this hybrid legacy on the part of Cervantes when, in the creation of the readings and antics of Don Quixote, he traces the fictional path of romance from the Arabs and Moors through Spain to all of Europe.

Her explanation for why this rich history celebrating the Asian and African dimensions of the novel was cut off from critical theory in Europe in the late eighteenth century, even as a "new" European history of the novel was being proposed, pertains to politics and ethnocentrism. As the domestic realistic novel emerged center stage, she argues, it was striking for its tendency to exclude, for its failure to acknowledge ethnic mixing in culture or fiction. This marked a domestication of the novel related to gender, class, and race. Recapitulating the orientation of writers, Doody says: "Aspiring young European writers, male and female alike, are to be told to write about what they know—what they experientially know—as if that were the sum of what is. They are encouraged to stay in the parish and not imagine Ethiopia" (292).

Asserting an intention and, indeed, "calling" to occupy foreign lands and control and exploit their peoples, the French and English found it most convenient to eschew the portion of their fiction that was owing to Asia and Africa, redefining the novel in a more specific context. Yet, Doody reminds us that a single template has never worked to define the world of story—even prose fiction of a certain length. As she points out, it is foolish to expect characters in first-century fiction to be like characters in nineteenth-century fiction, and we would be more accepting of characters in ancient "novels" if we stopped insisting that they act like Emma and Charles Bovary! (Likewise, we would be more open to contemporary characters in African and Asian fiction if we stopped trying to translate their desires and despairs into a post-Freudian psychoanalytic mind set!)

The aspects of the history of the novel that Doody finds most fascinating, and that are highly relevant for this study, are those that have to do with the participation and presentation of women. Declaring up front that, for all intents and purposes, the novel and the romance are one, she comments on the fact that early Greek novels were most likely written for an audience primarily of women, which may account for the fact that classicists have been so unwilling to discuss or "approve" such works (12).[11]

Looking at Virgil's "novelistic" account of Dido as a woman experiencing the torments of lost love, Doody suspects that he may have been one of the first epic writers to have to compete with the increasing popularity of the novel (7). In fact, one of the things most remarkable about the Dido account is how reciprocal the affection between Dido and Aeneas is (she is no sorceress with a hidden agenda, such as the women Odysseus had to break free from, but a good woman, lonely for family and tired of ruling her kingdom alone). In this light, Doody claims that what early novels brought to erotic love was the very idea of equality between the lovers.

When love is equal and chosen, rather than forced by one in power, personal control is a value and one of its most interesting manifestations, she observes, is elective chastity (71). Evidencing a countercultural sensibility, a number of these fictional works hold the male hero (not only the female virgin) to a standard of chastity, fulfilling the notion that "romantic love" is impossible without choice, including the choice of respectful purity (77, 78).[12] This is not "power-chastity," that aimed toward increased physical prowess as a result of abstinence, but that which is chosen for the sake of proving the man's desire. "The characters in these novels . . . do not and will not act in accordance with the law" (80). They go against social mores for the sake of fulfilling their own desires, in this case the desire for equity in sexual sacrifice.

A contemporary example of this dynamic can be found in Buchi Emecheta's Nigerian novel *The Bride Price* (1976), where a young Ibu girl falls in love with the prosperous son of a slave. Chike's money and education grant him some prestige in the community, but not the right to marry a "free" woman. Married against her will as the result of a brutal kidnapping (sanctioned by the men in her family), Aku-nna tricks her husband into thinking she is not a virgin and flees to Chike who is as loyal to her as she is to him. But tradition closes in on Aku-nna. Her family will not accept Chike's bride price; she is not really married; and she dies in childbirth, literally from guilt, while Chike begs her to live. This is no naive romantic story—Aku-nna is clearly a victim of patriachal ownership of a woman's sexuality, yet it offers "difference" in Chike's willingness to break the law for the sake of chosen fidelity.

In addition to elective chastity, Doody finds that ancient novels declare the right of a woman to control her own body. Women who courageously assert this right discover that they have the power to create change (88). Likewise, in the eighteenth-century European novel, women occasionally disturb dynastic proprieties by refusing to marry dreadful suitors or to marry at all (265), leading Doody to argue that perhaps all truly fascinating novel characters are always somewhat "feminine" in that they honor internal emotions and, from a position of private desire, question civic virtue (266). Because transgression of social rule is what often drives the novel plot, and because women are the most socially oppressed persons in many cultures, it stands to reason that their issues of freedom and restraint would govern much fictional discourse. It falls to the female writer, then, to make this dissident element work to the advantage of women in the audience.

Doody is convinced that social and political dissidence, as well as gender dis-ordering, has always been part of the working of the novel. The imagination itself is dissident. "There is a political dimension to imagining any kind of alternative to a present reality" (8), as the death-defying stories of Scheherazade nicely illustrate. Narrative has something of a needling quality to it and constantly tells us that things need not remain the way they are. But Doody hastens to remind us that publication and public reception present limits to radical revisionism. "A novel is better off if it can pretend that it is supporting the social virtues, without stimulating too much overt political thought on the part of characters and readers" (232). In addition to factors already mentioned, this removes fiction from the realm of the didactic and moves it toward a problematic, metaphoric re-imagining of experience and institutions.[13]

Indian novelist Anita Desai illustrates this in *Fire on the Mountain* (1977), in which a great-grandmother seeks solitude in the country after a lifetime of "doing all the right things" for husband, children, and grandchildren. Resentfully, she takes in a great-granddaughter for the summer months, a great-granddaughter as fiercely protective of her privacy as she. They learn a grudging respect and affection for one another that loosens up the old woman enough to face the fact that she has "invented" her genial father and husband, both of whom were, in reality, autocratic and cruel. Realizing the pervasiveness of her own appearance-saving fiction is, for Nanda Kaul, both a way of resisting the hypocrisy of a woman's life and an opening to re-imagine a habitable life for herself.

Obliquely reconstructive, the nondidactic novel goes far toward keeping the "difficulty in life." In their travels, novel characters meet all kinds of strangers that they must, by nature, approach interpretively. Thus, they learn to speak different "languages" and to learn the meaning and limits of multiple others. No sooner does a novel give voice to one of these "foreigners," or marginal persons, or slaves, or women, than the reader finds out that he or she too can speak and has a story to tell (perhaps a counterstory). The circle is open. In novels, good girls run away, and good boys land in jail: the unexpected happens and we learn to assess its impact.

As Doody points out, one of the most unexpected elements we face in life and in fiction is the fallout from eros. Eros is the enemy of the status quo, the enemy of the polite and predictable, particularly the enemy "of arrangements based on socioeconomic schemes" (373). What finally grabs us is the fact that we can make no satisfactory arrangements to deal with our loves and desires; they will trick us and challenge us and force us to revise our thinking (if not our very lives) over and over again. Doody uses the example of Toni Morrison's *Beloved* (1987) as a positive example of this radicality. In the novel, a child is killed because her mother cannot bear to imagine her in slavery. But the child cannot stay dead; she has to come back to live and to love, and the novelist allows her to break all the natural laws to do so. Barring the laws of both universal and culturally specific probability, no law is so strong that it cannot be broken and recreated (several times) in a well-constructed fiction.

### Where Is the Novel Going?

So we end this chapter with a look at where the novel is going, how it is moving us into new ways of seeing, particularly into new ways of seeing each other across borders. Edward Said, in keeping with his efforts to unmask and dismantle the assumptions of the European imperial novel, admits that the *future* of the novel may be *self*-critique—to challenge the "lofty independence and indifference" with which the novel itself has contributed to nation-building. Recognizing that the nation-state is in disrespect and disrepair, policymakers, novelists, and readers of all types are having to accept that the world is our home. To the extent that novelists can speak to the difficulties of this allegiance—its uneven beauties, limitations, and possibilities—without imposing absolute rules for its development, they may be the intellectual ambassadors of the future.[14]

In *The Novel and the Globalization of Culture* (1995), Michael Valdez Moses, also somewhat reluctantly, recognizes the positive power of international literary exchange. He says that the modern bourgeois novel has triumphed as an international form because traditional societies everywhere have had a singular historical destiny (modernization) forced on them, allowing them to share a common mode of written literary discourse. In his view, the novel and the globalization of culture co-exist because it is not simply the sociopolitical demands of the modern world that unify us, it is self-consciousness and its resulting narrative practices. As distinctive literary traditions are being adopted, adapted, appropriated, and merged across borders, we recognize that we cannot roll back global sociopolitical development, but we can use the literary arts to "help us correct . . . distortions of abstract philosophical theory" (xv) and empty universalisms.

The novel, with its density of detail and speculative framework, can comment on the conditions of a society and the subjective reactions of significant individuals within that society in such a way that readers both inside and outside of the context are encouraged to imagine new responses to historical change (xv). This is a way of keeping multiculturalism alive at the very point when we are forced to face its ironies, and the novel has always been very good at irony.

Take, for example, Buchi Emecheta's troubling cross-cultural novel *The Family* (1989), where, as a native Nigerian living in England, the author has risked a "new language" by making her protagonist Gwendolyn a child of Jamaica, speaking Jamaican *patois*; where she has risked the alienation of Black from Black by making Nigerian custom (an African neighbor's reluctance to deliver bad news) the cause of Gwen's vulnerability in her father's house; and where she has risked the very credulity of her English-speaking readers by allowing Gwen, victim of incest, abandonment, and madness, to celebrate the birth of her abusive father's innocent girl child.

In a final irony, Gwendolyn names the child Iyamide: "My mother is here." This disquieting act of loving and naming love goes beyond literary theory to a novelistic praxis which makes peace with (and subverts) European forms of the novel, makes peace with (and overturns) African patriarchy, makes peace with (and extends) linguistic diversity.

Taking a distinctly practical view, Martha Nussbaum sees the value of the present and future novel in its ability to keep politicians, policymakers, and general thinkers honest—that is, to keep them aware that life is complicated (definitely multivocal) and demands moral choices. By taking us on a speculative trip through dense experience, the novel prepares us for hard choices and keeps us from being naive about their effects. She argues that this is equally true for fantastic and realistic fiction, for "the very form [of the novel] constructs compassion in readers, positioning them as people who care intensely about the sufferings and bad luck of others, and who identify with them in ways that show possibilities for themselves" (*Poetic Justice* 66).[15]

More specifically, Susie Tharu and K. Lalita, editors of *Women Writing in India* (1993), focus on the power of women's novels from developing countries to challenge and change the face of Western feminism. They find that Western feminists are all too willing to move against patriarchal ideology without considering issues of class, race, or empire. Western feminists need to open up to these complicated and complicating realities; they need to become more self-conscious about their own limitations; they need to take more risks in terms of allowing themselves to be disoriented in a world they think they understand and control; and they need to be open to radical, unexpected solidarities with women quite different from themselves in education, social class, race, and style of articulation (26). They need to recognize that it is not the same essential female nature that is struggling against the same relentless patriarchy everywhere in the world.

Reading widely in women's novels can show how much these things vary. To repeat Tharu's earlier quoted words, Western women need to read novels by women from the Southern nations "not as new *monuments* to existing institutions or culture . . . but as *documents* that display what is at stake in the embattled practices of self and agency, and in the making of a habitable world" (39). The making of a habitable world is what the Beijing conference was all about. We need every story we can get!!!

## Notes

1. As an act of public disturbance in the 1970s, market women in the Nigerian state capitals of Benin and Ibadan threatened to go naked in public (forcing their children to be cursed for seeing their mothers naked!), in order to protest the government's insistence that they pay taxes before registering their children for school. Government submission was swift (Ogunyemi 54).

2. To understand Ama Ata Aidoo's insistence on the oral element of fiction, all we have to do is remember the absolute delight of story time in those years when, even if we could read for ourselves, we were not deemed so sophisticated in our literary habits that we could not be read to by teachers, parents, babysitters, and anyone else we could coax into opening a book in our presence and "talking" its pages. The increasing popularity of books on tapes says a great deal about how, as adults, we still love the sounds of our stories.

3. In the novel *Fantasia: An Algerian Cavalcade* (1987), Assia Djebar portrays the "harem"—a gathering of matrons (with young girls listening in) in traditional Arab culture—as a center of oral storytelling. Hovering somewhere between marketplace and prison, the women meet in enclosed private space

according to carefully constructed protocol, but find relief from domestic worry and abuse:

> At every one of these gatherings, they are trapped in the web of impossible revolt; each woman who tells her tale—loud exclamations of the one, rapid whispers of another—gets something off her chest. The "I" of the first person is never used; the time-honoured phraseology discharges the burden of rancour and rales that rasp the throat. In speaking to the listening group every woman finds relief from her deep inner hurt. (154)

4. Oral and written narrative interface in North American "traditional" culture in many ways. Native Americans and African Americans have always had a rich oral tradition (in the case of African Americans, of course, because it was illegal during slavery days for them to be taught to read and write). Trickster tales, slave songs, courting songs, and the like, feature widely in current written literatures of both groups. But frontier culture also had an oral–written identity. To read Mark Twain is to realize that the tall tale, the populist lecture, the medicine man's harangue were all part of oral culture and could be reproduced (in dialect) in the picaresque novel.

5. In an article exploring orality and patriarchal dominance in Buchi Emecheta's *The Slave Girl* (1977), Tom Spencer-Walters argues that the oral and written traditions have never been discontinuous or conflictual in African literature. In fact, he asserts that the ideological and social visions of African writers have always evolved out of "the conscious and skillful adaptations of oral traditions, riddles, proverbs, legends, myths, and folktales into a work of art" (126).

6. Echoing Ogunyemi, Bakhtin asserts that a good deal of the life to be found in Rabelais' sprawling picaresque novel emanates from the world of the Medieval and Renaissance marketplace where many voices could be heard simultaneously, and where "each food, wine, or other merchandise had its own words and melody and its special intonations, its distinct verbal and musical imagery" (*Rabelais and His World* 182).

7. In several places ("My Memory's Hyperbole" 9, and "Revolution in Poetic Language" 48), Kristeva speaks of this dialogue as intertextuality: "a field of transpositions of various signifying systems."

8. Pseudo-transgression is always with us, from Tom Sawyer's pretense of freeing Jim, knowing full well he is already free, to Larry Clark's feature film *Kids*, which pretends to be about the transgressive sexuality of contemporary urban kids, while it repeats all of the patriarchal sexual values of their parents' generation.

9. Mohanty takes this idea, in part, from Gloria Anzaldua's *Borderlands/ La Frontera: The New Mestiza* (1987). Anzaldua plays off of Latin American history to suggest that the *mestiza* defines a new consciousness among women, one that entertains a pluralistic consciousness and a tolerance for contradic-

tions. In "Coming to Writing," Helene Cixous celebrates the perplexity that a female author (herself), fully aware of her duplicity, creates in an audience demanding unicity of self (33)

10. Deirdre Lashgari argues that, in addition to a rich oral tradition, Senegalese writer Mariama Ba inherited a written African literary tradition extending back to the early pharaohs of Egypt ("To Speak the Unspeakable" 5).

11. Classical novels that are available for study include the following: Xenophon's *Cyropaedia* (pre-354 B.C.), *Joseph and Aseneth* (100 B.C.–100 A.D.), Chariton's *Chaireas and Kallirrhoe* (50 B.C.–140 A.D.), Petronius' *Satyricon* (66 A.D.), Apuleius' *Golden Ass* (160–180 A.D.), *Paul and Thekla* (160 A.D.), Heliodorus' *Aithiopika* (50–380 A.D.).

12. *Joseph and Aseneth*, a Jewish novel of the first or second century, depicting the relationship of Hebrew Joseph with the daughter of an Egyptian priest, depicts this value of willed chastity (Doody 78–79).

13. Describing the necessary obliqueness of the political novel, Irving Howe says:

> Like a nimble dialectician, the political novelist must be able to handle several ideas at once, to see them in their hostile yet interdependent relations and to grasp the way in which ideas *in the novel* are transformed into something other than the ideas of a political program. (23)

14. Reluctant to say that intellectual exiles and border crossers are on a par with those forced to cross by torture and hunger, Said nonetheless recognizes the role of the intellectual and artist to articulate the predicaments of "mass deportation, imprisonment, population transfer, collective dispossession, and forced immigrations," and to do that with integrity and power (332).

15. In an equally pragmatic vein, critic Jonathan White argues that because the novel seems to be outstripping and outselling all other forms of academic and personal history, because it seems to have become a source of ideas as well as entertainment, we have no choice but to take it seriously and to consider its ability to challenge history from the inside out. In fact, he argues, the novel may be an alternative way of "*doing* history and politics" such that the effects and possibilities of events are speculatively probed and evaluated (208–9). This becomes particularly significant when the "history" being exploited is that proclaimed by colonial powers, when the post-colonial novel becomes a dynamic way of "talking back" (Lashgari, "To Speak" 2).

# Chapter 3
▼▼▼▼▼▼▼▼▼

# *Choosing a Language:*
# *Neo-Colonialism or Post-Colonialism?*

Language is loaded and has the power to kill!
—Deirdre Lashgari, "To Speak the Unspeakable"

*Congolese writer Sony Lbou Tansi was raised by Zairian family members until he was sent for formal instruction to a French school in Congo-Brazzaville. There his teachers spread him with human feces in punishment for errors in French grammar. He has since become a well-known novelist and playwright in a language he has every reason to hate. (See "Topologies of Nativism" by Anthony Appiah.)*

*Chicana writer Gloria Anzaldua remembers being beaten on the knuckles with a sharp ruler for speaking Spanish during recess and sent to the corner for trying to tell an Anglo teacher how to pronounce her name. The essay in which she tells this story is written in fluent English. (See* Borderlands/La Frontera.*)*

*American Indian writer Leslie Marmon Silko tells the painful story of a rural couple who "lose" two of their tubercular children to white bureaucracy through the simple fact that the mother knows just enough letters to sign her name, but not enough to read the document of severance. (See "Lullaby.")*

*Indian writer Meena Alexander recounts the story of poet Sarojini Naidu who was locked in her room by her parents for refusing to learn English, and when she came out, would speak nothing but English to her parents. "She acquired English, the language of coloni-*

zation, via the closed room, forerunner of the prisons she was forced to inhabit as an activist in the National movement." (See The Shock of Arrival, p. 175.)

African-American writer Maya Angelou was raped as a child by a member of her family's community. She told what happened, and when the rapist was released from a short prison term, he was kicked to death. She did not speak for five years, fearing that she had murdered him by speaking his name. (See I Know Why the Caged Bird Sings.)

Both Ovid and Shakespeare tell the tale of Philomela who was raped by her brother-in-law, Tereus, King of Thrace. Because she resisted violation by threatening to tell all, he cut out her tongue, depriving her of speech altogether. When Zeus changed her into a nightingale, she never stopped singing.

## The Violence of Language

As literary critic Deirdre Lashgari declares and as the vignettes just presented illustrate: "Language *is* loaded and has the power to kill" (13). And there really is no way to escape its violence—not by refusing it and not by embracing it either. Violence is done in the name of the "master" language and it is done in the very process of naming. We are caught in violence from the moment we first speak.

Addressing this point, ethical philosopher and literary theorist Gayatri Chakravorty Spivak acknowledges that she writes with great difficulty in both English and Bengali. Thus, she has had "to recognize that neither is a natural or an artificial language." Neither provides a comfortable homeland: "I'm devoted to my native language, but I cannot think it as natural, because, to an extent, one is never natural . . . one is never at home" (37–8).

Reflecting on this discomfort, Julia Kristeva, reminds us that language is born out of alienation. It occurs in the life of the child at the point when the child realizes that he or she is different from, alienated from, the world that has given him or her sustenance so far. Even in our mother tongues, we experience the great gaps that exist between us and the world of objects, between being and the representation of being. Thus, language is both the source of our primal homelessness and the way that we seek to create and define home. We do not need to have feces smeared on us or to have someone kicked to death on our behalf to know that the world is other, even hostile, and that our attempts to tame it will ever prove faltering and inept. To speak is to seek connection and to feel estranged—from one's surroundings and from language itself.

Lashgari points out that one of the major problems we have is the very language we use to talk about difference. As an example, she uses the English word *androgyny*. In talking about the confluence of male and female traits, the term inevitably plays into an essentialist agenda that identifies maleness and femaleness as separate sets of human capacities. In order to apply, the term needs to outdate itself. Thus, she concludes that we must be "willing continually, to interrogate our own and each other's language, noticing the holes, the gaps, the distortions" (13). All of the quarrels surrounding wording in the *Platform for Action* resulting from the Beijing Conference, as discussed briefly in chapter 1, illustrate that language in and of itself is a problem, exacerbated by syntactic and political differences between languages and by who speaks them.

*Identity politics* describes the attempt to textualize an other (or a projected self) and thereby fix him or her in linguistic and political space. Thus, it brings together problems inherent in the nature of language and in the recognition of whose language it is one is speaking. Gloria Anzaldua uses the following example: If you should meet a woman for the first time who lives on the Mexican/U.S. border and who has a *mestiza* background, do you address her as Chicana, Mexican American, Latina, or Hispanic? And what might your choice mean? After all, you are still speaking in English, the labels are Anglicized, and whichever one you choose is both limiting and foreign.

Language is loaded. Ideas about identity and the words that express them draw boundaries that deny the complex reality of any one person or any one group. Yet we need to address one another as something. Language has the power to kill, but silence itself is dismissive.

### Linguistic Violence and Identity Politics

Gayatri Spivak speaks of the inaccuracy of speaking authoritatively about India. She reminds us that India is an artificial construct, mistakenly named by Alexander the Great, and restructured by the British. The only way in which the name India works is in contradistinction to another cultural construct. Although Spivak might very well identify herself as an Indian in reaction to White supremacy, she will always identify herself as a Bengali to an Indian. Although she might have to take on the mantle of the "marginalized" while in Western countries, she would never be considered "marginal" in India. As she declares, "One needs to be vigilant against simple notions of identity which overlap neatly with language or location. I'm deeply suspicious of any determinist or positivist definition of identity, and this is echoed in my attitude to writing styles" ("Strategy, Identity, Writing" 38).[1]

Theorist and filmmaker Trinh Minh-ha applies a similar skepticism to the rush to identify women writers according to their gender and ethnicity. Should a woman from Africa or India identify herself (or allow herself to be identified) as a "writer of color," a "woman writer," a "woman of color," a "third-world woman writer," or just "a writer"? Although Chandra Mohanty rightfully dismantles the phrase "third-world women" as one connoting essential victimization, Minh-ha reminds us that adding "writer" to the phrase indicates that one is seizing power (no matter how minimal). The writer always acts from a position of power, situating herself before and above the work, making it happen. Thus, "writing weaves into language the complex relations of a subject caught in the problems of race and gender and the practice of literature as the very place where social alienation is thwarted differently according to each specific context" (*Woman, Native, Other* 6).[2]

By refusing both silence and acquiescence, by choosing language (any language), by choosing to play the game of language with speculative energy, the conscientious writer finds ways to fight against stratified identity politics. In that we do not make naked contact with the world, in that we always come clothed with historical and linguistic mediations, the real quest is not to seek a nonviolent discourse, but to give into discourse generously, letting metaphors proliferate. It is thus that the internal dynamics of identity politics, the construction and reconstruction of the evolving self, can assume power.

The language(s) that we are brought into by our birthplace, gender, and education provide us with a set of relationships that must be negotiated. One of the things that language (or languages) provides is a place to locate the self, a vantage point from which to perceive others and from which to perceive the self. If the first-person singular pronoun is the capital "I" as in English (unlike most languages that have a lower case spelling of the first person), something is communicated. If the plural of "we" is masculine (as *nosotros* in Spanish), something is communicated. The self "finds" itself in the midst of such syntactic connections, but it "makes" itself by using (even bending) these connections to suit its own purposes.

Kristeva understands the ambiguity of this process to be one of a subject-in-process, a subject recognizing itself to be unstable and coming to know itself through the radical alterity of speech acts. As she views it, the exploring self supposes a frontier and imagines the crossing of that frontier almost simultaneously, and it is the sudden appearance of new signifying chains, new ways of arranging word-signs, that brings this process into practice "where practice is taken as meaning the acceptance of a symbolic law together with the transgression of that law for the purpose of renovating it" ("The System and the Speaking Subject" 29). Identity is neither given nor fixed: it results from a play of signs. In this sense, the innate violence of language is always subject to counterviolence, to the creation of metaphors that explode and shatter, reform and transform expectations (Smith 89).

So, perhaps, what is most important in establishing the integrity of literary language is the risk-taking respect that any writer holds for the practice of making new sentences, sentences that inevitably do some violence to the richness of reality, but that, in their speculativeness, also open up the possibility of new ways of relating to the world and the self.

## The Politics of Choice

On July 19, 1998, the *New York Times* reported that "while Europe has at least 15 languages, Europeans are increasingly using one: English." As Europe is uniting economically by adoption of the euro, and as American cultural influence increases, "English is the language that the Old Continent must use to communicate" (Tagliabue). The wording of the article is quite interesting in that it appears to credit the influence of a former "colony" (the United States) with the drive to adopt a single colonial language (English). The identity politics contained therein are complex. Is it *Americanized* English that will prevail in Europe? If so, what does this say about the current political status of the British? Or, more specifically, is it the English of Madison Avenue that will prevail? Because it is advertisers who "inform" the global market, and because advertising in Europe has for years brought English words and phrases into Italian and Finnish vernaculars, perhaps it is the language of "spin" that matters.

On another scale, prestige for Europeans can now be measured according to who is fluent in the "master tongue." The article hints that the motives for which Swiss bankers and journalists use English with

Germans (even though they may speak German among themselves) has to do with pride of accomplishment and desire to disassociate. In short, the "triumphal march" of commercial English now appears to be dominating Europe in the same way that European languages became the superimposed media of education and elitism in Southern nations during the late nineteenth and twentieth centuries. Language is indeed loaded.[3]

A similar hegemony occurred at the Beijing Fourth World Conference on Women. Although regional preconference and postconference discussions took place in a variety of languages, when the main conference took place, communication across borders required elaborate systems of translation and the adoption of a single language of discourse. The same scenario is true for other UN deliberations and written directives. There is an expediency to all of this—English is the language spoken most frequently in all kinds of political, economic, and academic gatherings. But is it spoken by more people than Chinese or Spanish? If the numbers are even close, what does this say about class and power issues? Language has the power to kill as well as liberate.

### Choosing the Mother Tongue

For a number of these reasons, in 1981, Ngugi wa Thiong'o, the Gikuyu writer from Kenya, wrote his "farewell to English" entitled *Decolonising the Mind*. Arguing that English in Africa has been a way of erasing pre-colonial traditions and histories, he was choosing at this point to return to Gikuyu and Kiswahili as a way of ensuring their continuance, notwithstanding the fact that he, an English speaker–writer, and the continent had changed radically in the colonial gap. One senses here an urgency to save what is left. And in doing so, Ngugi was cautioning his fellow African writers about the power of language to shape personal and cultural identity: "Language carries culture, and culture carries, particularly through orature and literature, the entire body of values by which we come to perceive ourselves and our place in the world" (16). By taking such a stand, Ngugi was flying in the face of what he has called Chinua Achebe's "fatalistic logic" that English is inevitably the unifying language of Africa, and Achebe's hope that a "new English" can be designed that will carry the African writers' ancestral values (8).

It is not insignificant that this choice took shape in Ngugi's consciousness as he, a political detainee, sat in Cell 16 at Kamiti Maximum Security Prison in 1978, thinking of how he might use novel-writing as a form of defiance against detentions of "mind and imagination." In seeking commitment to the African novel, he found commitment to African languages (71) and began his struggle with Gikuyu syntax on the only paper available, the coarse toilet paper offered to the prison population.

Knowing his target audience (now the people of his region) was largely illiterate, even in their own tongue, he utilized "readers" within extended families and in public gatherings to bring *Caitaani Mutharabaini* (*Devil on the Cross*, 1980), into the world. Thus, his written work has been reappropriated into the oral tradition (83). Yet, recognizing the continuing importance of a larger African and global audience, he has sought cross-cultural dialogue through the "age old medium of translation" (xiv).

Ngugi has set a strong precedent for maintaining multiple languages of struggle that are in danger of being swept away by the unitary language of the global marketplace.[4] Yet in his insistence on indigenous language, he may be in danger of turning the "mother tongue" into another form of patriarchal "father tongue" and failing to see the gender complications of his highly significant choice. Language can kill in many ways.

### Appropriating English and Gender Issues

Controversial Indian writer Salman Rushdie has taken a very different approach to language choice. In an essay entitled "Imaginary Homelands," published a decade after Ngugi's declaration, he discusses how an appropriation of English into "new Englishes" by post-colonial writers can become an act of resistance, forcing the colonial language to reflect indigenous and cross-cultural experience. This is never a "clean" choice, he argues:

> Those of us who do use English do so in spite of our ambiguity towards it, or perhaps because of that, perhaps because we can find in that linguistic struggle a reflection of other struggles taking place in the real world, struggles between the cultures within ourselves and the influences at work upon our societies. (17)

What he finds new and liberating about this linguistic struggle is that it insists that the "center" acknowledge the "rim" because the "rim" has begun to speak myriad versions of a language that the "center" would prefer to control ("In Defense of the Novel" 50).[5] Deirdre Lashgari describes the outcome of this process when she comments on how the increasingly wide use of English and other European languages in Southern cultures has "greatly expanded the range" of those languages, resulting in "englishes," "frenches," and "spanishes" that are capable of expressing a wide variety of cultural experiences (5–6).[6]

She reminds us that to choose not to write in Western languages means that a writer risks situating herself outside of powerful literary institutions—publishing houses, international prizes, and accessibility to talented translators (6). The latter cannot be ignored. When Ngugi wa Thiong'o chose to write exclusively in Gikuyu, he had already established a sufficient international reputation to ensure the translation of his works into multiple languages and therefore to ensure a continuing international readership. Women writing in Southern nations have received little of the encouragement from the publishing industry that has gone to their male counterparts, and should they choose the mandate of the mother tongue, might well relegate themselves to small indigenous audiences.

But, of course, it is never that simple. Nawal el Saadawi, writing in Arabic, has had a large readership, even before translation, as do many Latin American women and some Indian writers choosing Hindi over less widely known languages such as Urdu, Bengali, or Tamil. Special projects such as Susie Tharu and K. Lalita's two-volume collection of translations of rarely available works by Indian women, published and highly endorsed by The Feminist Press in New York, indicate that to write in a traditional language is not necessarily to be obscure. Yet this is still a risky choice, and the prevailing tension between cultural particularism and universalism underscores the risk.[7]

In addition, there is the issue for women writers of the patriarchal values embedded in any language, indigenous as well as colonial. Gayatri Spivak speculates that whatever language a woman writer chooses to use, she is in the difficult position of having to declare herself a "questioning subject" rather than a "defined object." This means ceasing to explain and defend who she is as a woman, and beginning to question male privilege in terms of the texts (and textuality) that her culture produces (4). To do this, a woman writer may find advantages in stepping outside of her given linguistic culture, and looking in skeptically.

One of the things such a countercultural move might protect her from is the association of guilt with women's writing (true in any culture, perhaps more pronounced in traditional cultures). Trinh Minh-ha describes this guilt as that of placing one's writing over housework, over families, and other less fortunate women. To reinforce her point, she quotes Chicana writer Gloria Anzaldua: "'Who am I, a poor Chicanita from the sticks, to think I could write? How dared I even consider becoming a writer as I stooped over the tomato fields bending, bending under the hot sun?'" (7). Few women from poor nations want to be perceived as social parasites, living the life of the cultural elite that ultimately relies on the generosity of the illiterate. To assuage that guilt by producing revolutionary literature is to risk "homogenizing the masses" (10). Yet a woman socialized as a second-class citizen (even if she herself has education and means) needs to revolt against her position to some degree in order to write anything. Is it possible that language mobility can give her perspective and cross-cultural support for her endeavors which monolingualism might not provide?

If so, this is a position that needs to be taken carefully. Nigerian literary critic Chikwenye Ogunyemi contextualizes the issues of language choice with clarity and force. For her, a Nigerian novelist choosing English is always engaged in an embattled choice. The language, as encountered, seems rigid (lacking in emotional vitality), has been used for the master's control, and conveys little of the milk of human kindness (113). For women, especially, choosing to write in English risks "the psychosocial questions raised by the centrality of liberty, equality, and sisterhood (?) in feminist discourse" (110). (Can feminism mimicking the French Revolution really help African women?) Furthermore, there is always the danger of playing into the White world's tendency to define Black experience and then appropriate it, thus erasing important differences (108).

But, with all of that said, Ogunyemi argues that a generation of writers like Salman Rushdie and Buchi Emecheta have rescued the English language and "turned it to fresh, clean use," making it "a language that alienates as it frees" (114). To follow this path, the writer must become an iconoclast like the mythic *ogbanje* figure—"the one who runs back and forth from one realm of existence to another," erasing natural and artificial boundaries in order to get a glimpse at the "possibilities of becoming" (62). But, the Nigerian writer writing in English must also become the *abiku* figure, the one born to die, the one who inevitably adopts an ambivalent attitude toward home and imitates "the free-roaming nature of a text" (69). Thus, there is great irony in nurturing the English-writing female. She may be the saving grace for oppressed women (thus greatly admired) yet threaten their cultural security (thus inviting hostility) as she "involves the outside world with the trouble within by writing about it in a foreign language" (71).

Audience is, as always, a factor in choosing a literary language. Ogunyemi laments that not many educated people in Nigeria read beyond preparation for their exams, and so, in their indifference, "kill the author" (70). An international audience, then, sought through an international language, supplies the writer with animating solidarity. To complicate matters further, whole portions of the Nigerian rural community cannot read in any language, even though they are the subjects of published story; thus a writer, even if he or she chooses the mother tongue, winds up displacing the oral storyteller without replacing her (unless an active system of "readers" is used). In inevitable betrayal, writers wind up telling another's story "to an unseen audience, national and international" (91). (This is not unlike the dilemma of "official" delegates to the Beijing Conference on Women who, although prepared to be "voices for the voiceless," inevitably betrayed the idiom of the women they left at home.)

Ogunyemi claims that in the 1980s and 1990s this was remedied somewhat by Nigerian women writers telling their own stories, rather than those of the rural poor, "in the hope that change at this level will filter down to their rural mothers" (91). But such a reach for integrity still relies on publication and eclectic audience, as well as a recognition that many Nigerian writers and readers trained in colonial schools simply have more fluency in English than their own tribal languages. Language *is* loaded!

### Women's Discourse(s)

In that women often bear the burden of double colonization—of having been perceived as second-class citizens under colonial rule and under traditional, as well as state patriarchy—it is worth asking the question of whether they can ever speak in the same fashion as their male rulers, or even their oppressed male counterparts. Answering no would force us to say that women inevitably speak and write in a different "language" from men and to trap them always in the position of other. Wouldn't one form of success, then, be to write so that no one knows if the author is male or female? To so conquer a common tongue, whether it be indigenous or European, that it becomes joint property of slave and free, female and male?

Kristeva, and others, have written extensively on these questions and approached the issue of women's discourse from many angles. Their theories sometimes overlap, sometimes apply in very different venues. Kristeva bases her analysis of women's discourse on the centrality of the mother's body to any child's relationship to the world and to that child's desire for articulation. From Plato's "Timaeus" she borrows the concept of *chora* as a creative "space" that precedes (and challenges) binary analysis of the world. In "Timaeus," Plato refers to the *chora* as a "receptacle," the "wet nurse of Becoming,"[8] a "nourishing and maternal" site where elements (fire, water) and enunciations (syllables, names) take on possibility. Applying the term to human development, Kristeva understands the *chora* as a generative state of being where bodily rhythms and drives motivate the formation of language; understandably it is associated with the mother's body as the locus where, for most of us, these drives are first mediated and discharged.

The *chora* experience is undifferentiated and prelinguistic; it "precedes evidence, versimilitude, spatiality, and temporality . . . all discourse moves with and against the *chora* in the sense that it simultaneously depends upon and refuses it" ("Revolution in Poetic Language" 35). Like the biological child who takes shape within the womb and must separate from it, but desires to revive that primal sense of connection, the "speaking child" seeks language because he or she both wants to experience the world and to re-experience intimacy between self and (m)other. This is what Kristeva calls the *semiotic* urge of language, that which begets and nourishes speech. The *symbolic* operation of language—syntax itself—is that which controls, designates, and structures primal desires and rhythms into discernable meaning.[9]

Poetic language, then, becomes the speaking individual's ability to return to the semiotic *chora*, to re-appropriate the unknowable aspects of primary experience, to reactivate repressed desire through musicality, metaphor, and linguistic play. Poetic language is a "fire of tongues," a re-energizing of discourse—an expression of deep pleasure (*jouissance*).

All persons experience this "dialectical movement between semiotic and symbolic" (24); the mother/female experiences it with a double intensity (first as child and later as maternal source), and may, therefore, lay closer claim than the father/male to poetic language, to the ability to "impose a music, a rhythm—that is, polyphony—but also to wipe out sense through nonsense and laughter" ("Desire in Language" 110).

What does this mean for a woman's writing? That "carnivalesque discourse"[10] may be her birthright (although not her exclusive right)? That she may practice "a freer and more flexible discourse" that allows her to speak about the mysteries of the body? That understanding the mastering aspects of language, she may yet prefer the diffuse? That she may write on the edges of controlled text and find there an amorousness that defies or disrupts categorical analysis (or power politics)?

It is of interest that having been born in Bulgaria and educated in eastern Europe (albeit by French nuns), Kristeva chose to write in French because, as she says:

> Despite the xenophobia, antifeminism, or anti-Semitism of one person or another, I maintain that French cultural life, as I have known it, has always been marked by a curiosity, discreet but generous, reticent but essentially receptive to nomadisms, oddities, to grafting and exogamies of all kinds. ("My Memory's Hyperbole." 6)

Thus, despite its role as repressive father tongue to many colonized persons, French provides Kristeva with freedom to re-inscribe the semiotic within the symbolic, to write as a feminist, even as she warns against the unicity of the term *feminism* and is quick to admit that all those submitted to social marginality have a claim on the disruptive elements of "female language" ("New Maladies of the Soul" 359).

Helene Cixous, a "Jewoman," raised in Algeria (speaking German at home and English at school), but also electing to write in French, carries this flirtation with the margins and origins of syntax into celebration of outlaw language. In her understanding, male syntax favors the law: "it lays down its familial model, lays down its conjugal model, and even at the moment of uttering a sentence, admitting a notion of 'being,' a question of being, an ontology," is seized by a masculine desire for philosophical discourse ("Castration or Decapitation?" 482). From this legalistic viewpoint, the female is perceived as hysteric, as outlaw, the one "outside the city, at the edge of the city" (484). She is fond of wandering, of excess, of risking the unexplainable, the unforeseeable. And she, like Kristeva's writing woman, is carnivalesque. Having been left out of the legal discourse, having lived "an-arche," she has learned to like being the awe-ful hag, the dangerous one, the woman who "un-thinks the unifying, regulating history that homogenizes and channels forces" ("Laugh of the Medusa" 738). She is the "wild ass" woman, who will not be silenced, loves her body as the source of life (regardless of whether she gives birth or not), and breaks up the "truth" with laughter.

In speaking of her own coming to writing, Cixous admits that she learned to speak French in a garden setting from which she was constantly on the verge of being refused, because she was a Jew. In short, she came to the French language as a cultural outlaw and has come to revere this position. At one point, she advises: "If you do not possess a language, you can be possessed by it; let the tongue remain foreign to you. Love it like your fellow creature" ("Coming to Writing" 23). She has come to love being possessed by her words, not owning them, and to define women's discourse—the discourse of those perceived to be outside the law—as that which has "abundance" and "drift," a bit of the wild.

In short, she has come to associate exile—lack of secure placement, of access to the law—with the desire for language, and to see that extinction of voice may generate its opposite. One step ahead of the "gramma-r wolf" who devours foreignness, the alien speaker (the woman, the outlaw, the witch, the one positioned at the edge of public discourse) can still admire difference and play with migrant sounds.

Working out of an anthropological understanding, Elaine Showalter, North American critic, speaks of women's discourse as being distinctly that of the wild zone, but a wild zone that always overlaps with the dominant masculine culture and thus produces a double-voiced discourse. Like writers from the colonized world, women writers everywhere have learned how to speak the dominant language of public dialogue, but they simultaneously cherish their "muted" stories, those that can only be told in the "harem," or in the women's steam bath, or wherever the "colonized" gather to kibitz, critique, and fantasize. Although she argues against "feminist fantasies of a wild zone of female consciousness or culture outside of patriarchy" ("Feminism and Literature" 191), she very much believes in a wild zone within the patriarchal circle, carving out and celebrating its own mysterious crescent.

### Women's Palaverous Discourse

Where Chikwenye Ogunyemi wants to go with this consideration of inside–outside language is her notion of *palava*, the marketplace discourse that takes in multiple voices, multiple points of view, and that can render the colonial language (much as Kristeva did) both familiar and critical of male privilege. The source word here—*palaver*—is itself an inside–outside, muted–dominant term. Webster defines *palaver* as "a long parley usually between persons of different levels of culture or sophistication." As such, it was a major dynamic in the circuitous negotiations by which Europeans shaped African (and Asian and Latin

American) geopolitics. Furthermore, as the colonialists spoke only with White male leaders, and silenced colonized women, the term is doubly suspect. So Ogunyemi claims that international palaver is "at odds with the aim in indigenous palavers to find out the truth of a case by meticulously examining all sides of a subject orally and aurally, to effect a resolution" (97).

Yet, as she points out, a UNESCO publication in 1979 entitled "Sociopolitical Aspects of the Palaver in Some African Countries" builds on the indigenous concept of palaver to articulate its positive use in conflict resolution. At its best, African palaver "emerges as critical discourse—serious as well as trifling, logical and rambling, orderly and haphazard, written and spoken, a celebration of the contradictions of life with the principled use of word power for communal good" (98). Ogunyemi claims that this is the very same discourse that defines women's wild, transgressive and relational marketplace talk. So what was palaver (idle or manipulative talk) for the British became palava (transgressive critique) for Nigerians, and what has been a way to arrive at moral equilibrium for Nigerian men has become counterdiscourse for women as they factor themselves into the talk. Palava thus becomes a complicated counter-identification of Nigerian women with a master's voice, moving beyond how the "Nigerian situation is perceived by the dominant forces" to "how things are run as seen from a woman's more inclusive perspective" (102). This is women's discourse with a complicated history and circuitous effect.

If palava is the rich, multivocal discourse that takes place in the marketplace around issues of gender, religion, elitism, graft, and so on, Ogunyemi claims that *palava sauce* is the attempt to make these issues accessible metaphorically and textually. It is also a way of tracing their international ramifications. If writing in English puts Nigerian women writers into an international women's network hung up on gender issues, they hardly enter this world passively. It is their palaverous discourse that works to complicate gender matters—to question how "men can be emancipated from the careless, self-serving ideologies of masterhood," how women can "be reinstated so their voices can once again be heard and respected," how women and men can "resolve the socioeconomic crisis to advance together into the twenty-first century" (103). Such inclusive discourse models the transgressive possibilities of English (or any language) for all who have a muted story to tell.

For women, almost universally shut out from, or only tentatively invited into, public discourse, transgressive language becomes a way of staying true to silenced event, even while being openly understood. And story is the best place of all to "practice" such subterfuge.

## *Mestiza* Consciousness

The language struggles of Indian writer Meena Alexander as recorded in her memoirs entitled *The Shock of Arrival: Reflections on Postcolonial Experience* (1996), embody almost all of the issues of choice and language diversity discussed so far. Born in Allahabad, Alexander learned Malayalam as her mother tongue, Tamil as the language spoken by her friends, and Hindi as a regional Indian language. She learned English from a Scottish tutor in India and at the Diocesan School for British children in Sudan. At the Diocesan School, education was strictly administered, and students were kept distant from Arabic or Malayalam or French, or even from the English they spoke with their parents, in order to perfect their (British) English skills. Commenting on her later struggles to write in English, Alexander says that "it was as if a white skin had covered over that language of accomplishment and I had to pierce through it, tear it open in order to make it supple, fluid enough to accommodate the murmurings of my own heart" (4).

She laments that she never learned to read or write in Malayalam; Malayalam works must be read to her. But she wonders if she has never taken the time to become literate in her mother tongue in order to hold tight to her early experiences of orality through nightly recitations from Malayalam epics. She remarks that her mother tongue remains for her at the level of speech and childhood dreams, and she takes pleasure in the fact that those who know the language, recognize Malayalam patterns of sound, alliteration, and assonance in her poetry (39).

She has *chosen* to write "in the script of a colonial language, which I must melt down to my own purposes" (38). This has not been an easy choice for her, for "her own purposes" have seemed highly antithetical to this "rough basement" of a language, as William Blake once referred to English. She speaks of her writing as a tearing apart and restitching of English syntax so that taking on her anguish and joy, it can lead her back to the body of her thought (48). This is a recognition of the counterviolence needed to correct the violent enclosure of English as it was taught to her, and that she feels might be necessary to correct the violent enclosure of any learned language.

In a chapter entitled "Translating Violence," she faces this recognition directly as a gender issue. She wonders what the murmurings of multicultural feminism can mean if, in fact, women are universally other in the dominant languages of the world, if they exist outside of the "canonical rigors" of classical literatures, whether Arabic, Sanskrit, or Tamil. She concludes that writing or acting for a woman means being willing to fracture both the "patriarchal mold" and the "marginality of female existence" as she knows it (83). This is an occupation inviting exile, and, for some women, can only take place in the language of exile, which Alexander seems to have chosen for herself.

Reflecting Bakhtin's notions of the heteroglossic qualities of all culture and language, she celebrates what writing in America gives her—"a rich, vivid sense of space, a welter of experience that cannot be easily held together in a single language" (128–29). Recognizing with Salman Rushdie and others that "to try and reduce our world to homogeneity spawns terror" (130), Alexander has embraced the complex world of the crosscultural traveler, and, at odds with both her mother tongue and the colonial language she has chosen for her literary struggles, she is far from letting anyone's desire for homogeneity rule her effort to transform violence into (at times strange) beauty.

Thus, she is leading the kind of hybridized life that Gloria Anzaldua writes about in all of her essays describing Central American speakers, for if we look at what has happened to Spanish in the last 500 years, we find a colonial language so abrogated and appropriated that it has become, on the border of Mexico and the United States, a renegade tongue fighting for space from the class dominant, "new" master language English. In the process, it has been forced into such heteroglossic possibilities that Anzaldua can list at least six "spanishes" that exist in her context (standard Spanish, standard Mexican Spanish, North Mexican Spanish, Chicano Spanish, Tex-Mex, and Pachuco or calo) (*Borderlands/La Frontera*). Each has different pronunciations, different words, different anglicisms, different variations of pronouns—and this doesn't even touch the varieties of spoken Spanish that exist away from the border and deep into Latin America, where a variety of indigenous languages have so tightly woven with colonial Spanish that *mestiza* cultural manifestations are encyclopedic.[11]

Recognizing the identity politics played out in such an environment where Chicanos may not speak Spanish to Latinos for fear of censure, but rather stumble on in flat English, Anzaldua nonetheless revels in the metaphoric possibilities of such a linguistic mix. As a "border woman" trying to keep her "shifting and multiple identities" intact, she urges cultural and self-reconstruction through "dialogic polyvocality, transformative crossings, and affirmative indeterminacy" (Reuman 306).

For her this means writing in several languages, including English, and retelling the hard, muted stories that have been miscast or erased in the past (a way to e[r]ase her guilt-as-writer as well). In Anzaldua's terms, *mestiza* consciousness, at its best, reveals a "tolerance for contradictions," and her choice to remain intentionally multilingual seems to be a way of remaining the "outlaw," avoiding entrapment in any one politicized discourse.

To take any language seriously—that is, to pay attention to its conflicting voices, and bend its recalcitrant laws—is to avoid entrapment. Nawal el Saadawi, fluent in several languages, writes almost exclusively in Arabic, as does Lebanese novelist Hanan al-Shaykh. (Neither has had trouble attracting talented translators.) Meanwhile, many African and Indian women have chosen to write in a colonial tongue. In the Spanish/"spanishes" speaking world of Latin (and North) America, Julia Alvarez writes in English; Rosario Castellanos chose Spanish, and Claribel Alegria has been translated from Spanish to English by her husband. Integrity seems to be less the choice of a language (or languages) than honesty about the violent nature of language and identity politics, along with recognition of how that violence can be subverted and rewritten through desire and a dialogic (dare we say feminized) imagination.

## Notes

1. The ultimate warning against giving in too easily to the language of identity politics is Edward Said's book *Orientalism* (1978), in which he relentlessly and skillfully deconstructs the idea of Eurocentric "Orientalist" studies—those that join all persons of an Asian origin into a single nameable, analyzable entity. Ghanaian philosopher Anthony Appiah presents a similar critique of "nativism," turning his analytic razor against Afrocentric scholars who contend that a clearly defined and unbroken stream of African oral tradition exists. Recognizing that these scholars rose up to challenge the Europeanization of African literature, Appiah still laments that "railing against the cultural hegemony of the West, the nativists are of its party without knowing it" (952).

2. In recognition of the extremities of identity politics, Trinh Minh-ha comments on the fact that in South Africa there are nine distinct racial categories, determining where one may live and work, in which an individual can be registered. These designations can only be changed if the individual can "prove" that he or she has been put in the wrong group. In one given year, the House Affairs Ministries announced that although only nine Whites had "become" colored, 506 coloreds had "become" White and 666 Blacks had "become" colored ("Not You/Like You" 374).

3. There is common speculation that English has become the international language because it contains more words and is therefore more nuanced than other Indo-European languages. But where did this extensive vocabulary come from, if not from the appropriation of terms from appropriated territories?

4. Ghanaian philosopher Anthony Appiah respectfully calls into question Ngugi's declaration of linguistic nativism by noting that he openly acknowledges the influence of film technique on his 1986 Gikuyu novel *Matigari ma Njirugi* (956). Has Ngugi eschewed Eurocentric bourgeois culture, only to find himself unwittingly incorporating its effects?

5. In a similar vein, Bill Ashcroft, Gareth Griffins, and Helen Tiffin, in their seminal study *The Empire Writes Back* (1989), explore a two-step process by which Southern writers in a post-colonial world might transform English into a variety of culturally flexible "englishes." The first step is *abrogation* where the linguistically embedded normative categories of imperial culture are refused. And the second is *appropriation* where language is "utilized to express widely differing cultural experiences" (38–39).

6. Despite his own "farewell to English," Ngugi wa Thiong'o is not about to overstate the power of European linguistic hegemony. Despite the domination of English, he claims, "African language and African/English pidgins have been kept alive in the daily speech, in the ceremonies, in political struggles, above all in the rich store of orature—proverbs, stories, poems, and riddles" (23). Daily speech itself involves digressions, inventions, and dramatic illustrations (76). Thus, even he would admit that a resistant heteroglossia is alive in English African discourse.

7. Nigerian writer Molara Ogundipe-Leslie takes a highly pragmatic view of language choice by stating that she writes in either Yoruba or in English depending on whom she is trying to reach (116).

8. See footnotes 12–14 to "The Semiotic and the Symbolic," found in Kristeva's "Revolution in Poetic Language."

9. Kristeva's specialized use of the terms *semiotic* and *symbolic* needs to be differentiated from the common use of *semiotic* to refer to the science of signs and *symbolic* to refer either to signification in the broadest sense or to a particular type of poetic trope.

10. This term is used to suggest Bakhtin's notion of linguistic *bricolage*, Ogunyemi's notion of palava, and Webster's definition of carnival as "a traveling enterprise offering amusement." As Kristeva argues in "Revolution in Poetic Language": "Magic, shamanism, esoterism, the carnival, and 'incomprehensible' poetry all underscore the limits of socially useful discourse and attest to what it represses" (30).

It might well be argued that the carnival-like spirit of the NGO Forum, exiled ("outlawed") to Huairou, accounted for much of the open, exploratory debate at the Beijing Women's Conference in 1995—that it, indeed, kept justice "in play."

11. In the title article of *An Other Tongue* (1994), Alfred Arteaga also discusses the linguistic hybridization and cultural *mestizaje* that define life on the Mexican/U.S. border:

> Hybridized discourse rejects the principle of monologue and composes itself by selecting from competing discourses. . . . It is born of the struggles for discursive dominance and relates within itself and with other discourses according to the principal of dialogue. It is dialogic because it is so multivoiced. (18)

# PART TWO

# WOMEN'S NOVELS AND WOMEN'S ISSUES

# Chapter 4

## *Naming the Mother: Reproduction and Domestic Labor*

> [J]ust the thought of anyone getting pregnant make me want to cry.
> —(Celie) Alice Walker, *The Color Purple*

> She had never experienced the joy of motherhood. Why then did the women worship her?
> —(Efuru) Flora Nwapa, *Efuru*

Celie, the protagonist of Alice Walker's best-known novel *The Color Purple* (1982), is a poor, Black American girl child who is stripped of every vestige of her self-respect by both stepfather and husband. She is raped and beaten as a child; her children, the result of rape, are taken from her; and she is rendered barren by premature sex. Uneducated, she is given to her future husband with the dowry of a cow. Her new husband beats her "like he beat the children," his children, that she is expected to care for.

Motherhood is hardly romanticized in Walker's novel. When we first meet Celie, her mother is about to die "from all of these children" (11). And, some two hundred pages later, Celie admits "just the thought of anyone getting pregnant make me want to cry" (224).

What are we to make of such bleak realities?

### The *Platform for Action* and Issues of Mothering

Admitting to a foundational asymmetry between the constructed roles of males and females in culture, anthropologist Michelle Zimbalist Rosaldo, as has been seen, writes that "men have no single commitment as enduring, time-consuming, and emotionally compelling—as close to seeming necessary and natural—as the relation of a woman to her infant child" ("Woman, Culture, and Society" 24). What does such a recognition say about who women are and how they should be talked about, written about, treated by family and state? The *Platform for Action* arising out of the Fourth World Conference on Women had to deal with such questions within a context where some participants argued that using motherhood to define femaleness does an injustice to the full range of capabilities for women, whereas others, recognizing the centrality of mothering to women's experience, argued for careful articulation of the medical and economic rights of mothers.

Articles 22, 27, and 29 of the *Global Framework* for the *Platform* lay out key issues for assessing the needs and rights of mothers. They remind us that one-fourth of households worldwide are female-headed and that these are often the very poorest of households because of gender-based barriers to fair labor (Article 22). Even within two-parent families, economic necessities and life choices are bringing increasingly more women from exclusively reproductive work into paid productive work. Yet, men are not accepting greater responsibility for domestic tasks, including child care (Article 27). In the larger context of women's total caregiving—their role in the welfare of the extended family and the community—Article 29 speaks to the necessity of all nation-states recognizing "the social significance of maternity, motherhood," while not allowing such roles to "restrict the full participation of women in society."

The spirit of these articles is to establish the value of domestic labor—indeed to protect it where necessary—but also to resist the restriction of women to the domestic sphere and to resist discrimination against women in the productive labor market. A set of practices not specifically mentioned in the *Global Framework* but relevant to its stated issues is a tendency, especially in affluent circumstances, to "commodify" the mother.[1] Wet-nursing the children of the rich by poor mothers commodifies the breasts of women.[2] Hiring surrogate mothers on behalf of childless couples commodifies a woman's womb. Advertising for young egg donors with high IQs and beautiful bodies commodifies the reproductive potential of women. Such "labor" is, at times, well remunerated; at other times it is economically exploitative. In all cases, it participates in an area of identity politics that restricts the female to maternal function.

Although these actions are not specifically addressed in the *Global Framework*, paragraph 93 from section C: "Women and Health" of the *Platform for Action* does highlight the commodification of maternal potential in young women through forced early marriage and early pregnancy, which "continues to be an impediment to improvements in the educational, economic and social status of women." Where preparation for marriage involves genital cutting, the health risks for adolescent girls increase as well. So, although many cultures in the world celebrate motherhood through elaborate religious and cultural rituals, the fact is that motherhood itself, when forced, or imposed on the young, works against the physical, economic, and intellectual well-being of women.

As partial answer to forced or risky pregnancy, paragraph 94 speaks to the need for increased attention to sex education (for both men and women) and health care. Declaring that it is the right of couples to decide when and how often to reproduce, it calls for their "access to safe, effective, affordable and acceptable methods of family planning" and for "right of access to appropriate health-care services that will enable women to go safely through pregnancy and childbirth." Paragraphs 95, 96, and 97 remind us that reproductive rights "embrace certain human rights that are already recognized in national laws, international human rights documents and other consensus documents"; these rights include the right to reproduce free of coercion and discrimination.

Through her character, Celie, Alice Walker shows what havoc the lack of such rights can wreak. Yet, Celie's experience also illustrates that when the need for nurturance is not mandated, when compassion is called for in the community, women often respond with empowering generosity. Celie cares for the ill and decimated singer Shug, bathing and dressing her as she would her own daughter (57). Later, Shug nurtures Celie's sense of self and allows her to cry over her abusive history like a young child (108). When Sofia has been beaten to a pulp by the police, Celie goes into her cell to wash and tend her broken body (87), then she shares the mothering of Sofia's children with other members of the community (96). Celie's sister, Nettie, mothers Celie's children in Africa, and the sisters come to speak of Olivia and Adam as "our children." This is what a number of third-world women have come to refer to as the power of *other mothering*, taking motherhood out of the exclusive realm of biological fact and placing it within the realm of a multiplicity of social and community factors.

Walker never makes these gestures seem simple or sentimental. Near the end of the novel, when Celie and her once abusive ex-husband are sitting on the porch talking like old friends (a clear example of "transformed partnership" which the *Platform for Action* calls for), they begin to discuss whether Shug and Sofia can be described as "womanly" and decide that it is just too difficult to say. The categories of "womanly" and "manly" won't hold still for them in an absolute sense, and they are left with the slipperiness of gender relations rather than a succinct gender war. Defining The Mother and her needs may turn out to be equally complex.

## Defining the Mother versus the Mother as Definition

How does a woman get to be a mother? Literary theorist Elaine Showalter says that all ideas about women's bodies have to be interpreted "in relation to the social contexts in which they occur" ("Feminist Criticism in the Wilderness" 70). These ideas may be quite different in the United States and Canada than in Nigeria or Bangladesh, although correspondences between cultural systems are always part of significant social analysis.

Nancy Chodorow is a common reference point when it comes to defining the mother in the West. Her theory is that women learn to be mothers by being mothered. This is not a matter of instinct, she argues, but an extension of lactation and pregnancy functions that, in hunter–gatherer societies, simply made it more *efficient* for women to perform the primary care-taking (17). Subsequently, mothering has reproduced itself cyclically. Women with mothering capacities produce, through gender and psychic identification, daughters with mothering capacities. "These capacities and needs are built into and grow out of the mother–daughter relationship itself" (7). (On the contrary, sons, who must separate from their mothers to establish "gender" and thus come to recognize their otherness from the mother, repress nurturant capacities.) All of this is culturally reinforced so that the daughter who relocates herself as mother is likely "to get gratification from the mothering relationship" (206) and to find that her choice is validated (even expected) by those around her.

Playing off of Julia Kristeva's idea of the *chora*, the creative space that exists between the body-as-biology and the body-as-social reality, Alice Adams, in *Reproducing the Womb* (1994), says that the constructed role of mother is inevitably bound up with (although not limited to or dependent on) biological realities. Of particular interest to our study of women's novels, Adams, like Kristeva, connects the role of mothering with the birth of language and, thus, the written word. As discussed in chapter 3, Kristeva designates the *chora* as a prelinguistic, prematerial "pregnant" space, "unnamable, improbable, hybrid, anterior to naming, to the One, to the father, and consequently, maternally connoted" ("From One Identity to Another" 1167). When originary unity with the mother is broken, otherness comes, speech comes, identity comes, alienation comes. For Kristeva, it is poetic language that reminds us that our speech comes out of and still participates in the rhythmic, instinctual world of the mother's body, a world that rational, scientific discourse may hide (1168).

Separation from the mother and emergence into language and communication systems are experienced by everyone, regardless of gender, but Kristeva and Adams suggest that only a woman can re-experience the entire process, only she can re-experience "the original physical unity with another body, the rupture of that unity and the (re)birth into language" (Adams 27). This gives her a way of understanding the undecidability of language and of laying claim to the writing life itself!

### Issues of Procreativity and Creativity

So why then has women's creativity as well as their procreativity so long been a matter of patriarchal control and exclusion? Addressing the control of women's procreativity by medical practitioners, medical anthropologist Emily Martin explores imagery stemming from a Cartesian model of the body as machine. In Western medicine, which is increasingly making its way into the developing world, a "typical" birth has become predictable. Contractions can be measured and assessed as either efficient or inefficient. The mother makes successful progress through definable states of labor, or she is chemically or surgically "assisted." According to Martin's analysis, the uterus has come to be seen by the medical profession as a machine that produces a product; the mother is the laborer, and the doctor the foreman who controls her labor.[3] A Caesarian delivery that requires the most management and the least labor is considered to produce the best product (63).

Women worldwide resist such language, calling attention to the many variations in labor, promoting the practice of midwifery, learning to understand and cooperate with the rhythms of their own deliveries, and transforming the imagery with which birthing (unalienated labor) is described. They are writing poems and stories about the experience of mothering, and they are insisting on the right to control the number of children, if any, they bring into the world.

Likewise, they are finding ways of resisting attempts to control and exclude their creativity—attempts that have included the assumption that procreativity (domestic labor) is creativity for women, the assumption that women are better suited to inspire poetry than to create it, and forced "sterility" through the exclusionary politics of publication. As the proliferation of first-world and third-world women writers are demonstrating, these politics can change.

Still, there is the complication of whether "mother" and "writing woman" are to be liberated as a unit. In an article entitled "Writing and Motherhood," Susan Suleiman points out that Western Victorian critics were far kinder to mothers than to childless writers, with the assumption that mothers would wait until their children were grown in order to work. A mother who broke this cultural "law" and wrote while her children were young might be thought "abnormal," but a childless woman, artist or not, was distinctly, "unnatural." Working off of the thought of French feminists Luce Irigaray and Helene Cixous, Suleiman refuses to distinguish between the feminine and the maternal, stating that being a woman (with or without children) means that one is "never far from the *mother*," and will, as writer, contribute significantly to culture because of the "force of reparation and nourishment that is fundamentally 'other' in relation to the desiccated rationalism of male discourse" (370).

### Recognizing the "Other" Mother

Nigerian literary theorist Chikwenye Ogunyemi argues the same point but from a different cultural context and with different effects. Because of the way that mothering weaves into and with all other aspects of a woman's life in Africa, Ogunyemi argues that mothering must be the central trope for a literary theory of women's novels:

> Motherhood/mothering engenders numerous connecting threads, resulting in an intricately woven *lappa* with patterns replicated with slight variations. . . . The slight deviation in uniformity (difference) stimulates interest to the keen eye without upsetting it too much, since the project is still grounded in the familiar—that which is repeated and modified. (9)

She remarks that the covers of African women's texts often depict women "wearing" children on their backs as essential items of clothing, clothing that shelters the mother from physical isolation and from harsh exposure to cultural critique. Yet, the childless woman is "covered" as well, in that all Nigerian women of a certain age are "mummy," all are someone's mother.

To illustrate this pervasive presence of the mother, Ogunyemi discusses the diversity of motherly features embodied in African female deities. The first of the mythic embodiments of the mother she presents is Osun, primary mother "bringing up her son single-handedly, a role which prepares her to become the mother-at-large, caring for the world" (10). Mammywata is the childless mother who cares in a motherly fashion for her devotees, epitomizing "the childless woman who mothers the community at large, since she has the resources for such a purpose" (31). Mammywata is the appropriate model for the childless woman in the Nigerian novel, the woman who, although successful in other ways, mourns her barrenness within a culture that still perceives the childless woman as a tragic, even witchlike, enigma. Chi is the divine mother lodged within, and who, in the case of women writers, can come to stand for their storytelling foremothers as well as present muses. Omunwa/Iyalode is the political-economic mother, inhabiting the marketplace where market women resist the restrictions placed upon them. Ogbanje/Abiku, the risk-taking, networking mother (as discussed briefly in chapter 3), stresses possibilities for the child (or the text). Under the influence of Oganje, each child takes on multiple mothers, forming a corps for communal parenting (just as readers, critics, librarians, and teachers corporately parent and nurture a text).

African women writers, aware of these possibilities for writing about the mother and for mothering/authoring their own texts, clearly are breaking free from restrictive definitions of what these roles might mean and be. Likewise, their use of the term *womanism* (also used by African American women) opens up and complicates notions of Western feminism and motherhood. Fearing the separation of women's issues from those of men and children—especially because colonial policy involved strategic divisions between tribes, classes, and genders—African womanists seek productive co-existence with men and cautiously accept the power that motherhood bestows on them. That power is both interrogated and revised, yet it is ultimately claimed in the name of the community at large. In Ogunyemi's words, "motherly and daughterly power . . . exhibits strength and responsibility toward the needy who appear in its orbit" (61), regardless of gender and ethnic origin. Ironically, then, biological infertility for African women may become a "strategy" toward more inclusive public power (Stratton 97). Recognizing that only a poor strategist would give up a culturally reinforced power that she already possesses, African women are interested in finding ways to extend and exploit that power in the body politic. Ogunyemi describes womanist writings as those with "a maternal disposition, a steadfastness of purpose, and an all-inclusiveness," those written by "round women" (119).

Yet the political extension of mothering through "other" mothering is hardly restricted to African or African American women's writings. Isabel Allende's *House of the Spirits* (1982), beautifully captures (and complicates) the many faces of the mother, including that of political resister.[4]

In this novel, childbirth is generally seen as horrifying. Esteban Trueba, like many patriarchs, is afraid of the biological power of pregnancy (62); the child Miguel is horrified by his surreptitious witnessing of a birth (264); but the ultimate horror is reserved for illegal abortion (238ff). And yet, the miracle of childbirth is what cements the lifelong relationship between Blanca and her peasant lover, and prenatal communication between mothers and daughters proliferates, often continuing into life and empowering both mother and daughter.

Perhaps even more significant, the "other mother" becomes a source of survival and renewal—but not without a dark side. Esteban's sister, Ferula, "mothers" her mother and younger brother out of strong cultural/Catholic imperative and so turns herself into a bitter, self-martyred saint (152). In her loneliness, she longs for motherly affection herself (95) but projects that need into her choice to mother Esteban's wife Clara (97ff). Jealous of this attention to his wife, Esteban throws Ferula out of the house. In death only is Clara able to attend to Ferula with loving reciprocity.

The most moving reciprocity, however, occurs in prison when Alba, Esteban's granddaughter, has been arrested for helping political dissidents escape military death squads. After her torture, Alba is cared for by fellow prisoner, Ana Diaz. Most redemptively of all, Alba, who has no children, mothers the children of Adriana who has gone mad at the hands of her torturers and rapers:

> I . . . sat with a child in each arm and told them magic stories from the enchanted trunks of my Great-Uncle Marcos until they fell asleep, and . . . in the meantime I thought of the fate of the children growing up in that place with a mother who had gone mad, cared for by others, unfamiliar mothers who had not lost their voice for lullabies, and I wondered as I wrote, how Adriana's children would be able to return the songs and the gestures to the children and grandchildren of the women who were rocking them to sleep. (426)

Although the physical and economic risks of mothering remain great in many parts of the world, so do the value and the power, that which needs to be protected by national and international policy and that which is, inevitably, probed and preserved by women novelists.

## Flora Nwapa Faces the Mother

There are many novels that could be used to illustrate how the world's women are defining and redefining the roles and risks of mothering. A writer who comes to mind immediately is Flora Nwapa, because of her relentless focus on the plight and accrued power of the childless woman.

Ogunyemi consistently refers to Nwapa as the fertile mother of Nigerian women's fiction: "In her role as public mother, or *omunwa*, this personable woman graciously encouraged other men and women with a support system grounded in her publishing business and her attitude" (131). Her faith in Black men reinforced a womanist political stance, and her willingness to explore and transform the shameful role of the barren woman established "other mothering" as an act of liberation. Yet, in one interview after another she declared that she wrote simply because she loved to listen to and tell stories. If she was political it was through the role of the *griotte*—entertainer, teacher, trickster, "big mother."

A binding thread in her novels is the presence of Uhamiri, a fictionalized version of the female water deity who combines qualities of Osun (primary mother) and Mammywata (the childless mother), and who is presented by Nwapa as the Ugwuta Woman of the Lake, "the woman-who-is-not-a-mother-but-is-the-mother-of-all" (139). In Nwapa's fiction, Uhamiri is not a fixed idea, mirroring Ugwuta practice or belief, but an imagined figure who offers alternatives to the "Nigerian obsession with childbearing and carelessness with childcare" (142). As Sabine Jell-Bahlsen comments, Nwapa's Uhamiri manifests a flexible fluid side of the universe, in contradistinction to "the static side expressed in ancestral male traditions" (79). Unlike the distant government, Uhamiri is interested in the well-being of her people—not just the bare essentials of their lives but their sense of justice and joy as well (Ogunyemi 143). Nwapa creates female protagonists, followers of Uhamiri, who cannot get pregnant with biological children but who have beautifully fecund minds. She shows us ways in which these women work through the harsh strictures of their societies and discover a larger maternal world, often in and through the "palaverous" marketplace. Thus, she is able to recreate Ugwuta tradition and cultural heritage within "a woman-centered discourse" (Umeh 46).

### *Efuru*: The Joys of Motherhood Tested

*Efuru* (1966) was Nwapa's first great success. In this novel, as well as *Idu* (1970), which follows, the women "are types of Ugwuta women she knew when she was growing up, women of her grandmother's generation" (Ezeigbo 59). These women are excluded from many forms of tribal power, but have their own significant spheres of influence as market women and as worshippers of the lake goddess Uhamiri. Both works center on the Nigerian woman's reproductive struggles.

Efuru is childless and must deal with the personal and cultural pain of that condition, including the betrayal of two husbands who love her but cannot accept her barrenness. Eventually, she comes into publicly recognized power through her refusal to be demeaned by that condition and by choosing to "mother" a wide variety of others.

When Nwapa took this first novel to Chinua Achebe, the "father" of modern Nigerian fiction, for his advice, she was admitting that African men and women are in a shared "cultural bind and, therefore, are mutually dependent" (Ogunyemi 135). Part of that cultural bind, it would seem, is a perceived need to obtain status and economic security through the production of offspring.

The power of motherhood, and the necessity of producing offspring *for* the husband, is present throughout *Efuru*. So attuned are women characters to this power and this necessity that Ajanupu, Efuru's mentor, smells that Efuru is pregnant, long before she is told, and is surprised that others have not noticed. Efuru is considered to be more beautiful when pregnant, a proper subject for female pampering and praise. After delivery, she blesses herself saying "I have had a baby; I am a woman after all" (31).

But the girl baby dies, no other comes along, and she is plunged into the pain of childlessness. She fears that not being able to reproduce will make her a man, and so she goes along with her mother-in-law's suggestion of a second wife. Barrenness is clearly a far worse pain than her husband taking a second or third marriage partner.

Yet, in an interesting development of events, it is Efuru's very childlessness that becomes her resistance against cultural prejudice and her means toward significant voice in the community. The reader is led to anticipate Efuru's social significance by the fact that she is introduced with the words "Efuru was her name. She was a remarkable woman" (7). Later in the novel she is marked as a "woman among women" (87). Much of this transformation comes through her gradual identification with the goddess Uhamiri, herself childless, who undergirds and cares for the community at large. Like Uhamiri, Efuru's most important care-taking takes place outside of biology and has a distinctly political–economic edge. Motherless almost from birth, Efuru has had a number of other mothers herself. The village doctor's mother, an educated woman, saw to Efuru's education early in life, giving her a distinct social advantage. Her mother-in-law, Ossai, and her mother-in-law's sister, Ajanupu, become other mother figures, the latter more effective than the former. (Ajanupu has eight children of her own but always supports Efuru's nontraditional actions, and openly, aggressively defends Efuru when she is falsely accused of adultery.)

Acting as other mother, Efuru brings the servant child Ogea into her life as an intimate companion and apprentice: "The little girl had grown to love her mistress. She regarded her as her mother and called her mother. She defended her anywhere she heard people say ill about her" (90). Then, once she has left her first marriage, Efuru begins to care for many members of the community. She arranges medical services for the old woman, Nnona, and for Ogea's father, Nwosa. She feeds the hungry children who hang around her home, in one instance making guests wait for her attention until she has seen to these young charges. Having always sympathized with her first mother-in-law's hard life, she nurses her in death, overlooking the awkwardness of their earlier parting and risking village gossip.

But Uhamiri brings economic success and status to Efuru as well as a generous spirit. Always the successful trader, it is Efuru, rather than her husbands, who understands trading and economic exchange, and it is she who raises the money to pay her first dowry. Although she has endless problems collecting money from her debtors, she lends without interest, often to those who have been plagued by the extortion of "professional" money lenders. She is particularly generous to Ogea's parents who have no talent for managing money whatsoever.

Ultimately, Efuru's power in the community comes from an unsentimental but compassionate response to the needs of others—her economic skill, social status, and political power are used on their behalf, which in turn increases her power among them. Thus, Uhamiri, through Efuru, brings *shalom* to the community, despite the fact that Nwapa has created the river deity as a reverse image of the cultural value for women: She is childless and her worshippers tend to be as well. Efuru's dreams about Uhamiri illustrate these complexities and, in a further ironic twist, link her spiritually with her own mother who, like Efuru, had only one child and worshipped the goddess.

The story ends with the childless Efuru dreaming of Uhamiri and asking, "She had never experienced the joy of motherhood. Why then did the women worship her?" (221). The answer may be found in the maze of Efuru's own life—a barren social pariah, yet educated more than most women, she resists abuse, and turns the power of that resistance outward to the community that has shaped her. Listening carefully to the foreign-educated doctor to whom she has freely confided and who urges her to return to her second husband, even after he has falsely accused her of adultery, she politely but firmly refuses, saying, "It is not possible. Let day break" (221). In *Efuru*, we find the African woman novelist embracing her tradition and reversing it simultaneously.

We also find her embracing the "idea" of the novel and reversing it simultaneously. Efuru's development propels the story but it is hardly a linear progress. Nwapa allows Efuru's mind free play over uncanny ideas, odd bits of narrative from the persons she meets in the marketplace, village gossip, children's songs, performed story, and seeming contradictions in her own culture. The style is palava at its eclectic best and the novel accrues its meaning by nonlinear "spending," by irregularities of speech and thought, by anecdotes only obliquely connected to Efuru's fate.

The reader is rendered an eavesdropper. All that he or she knows comes through overhearing the dialogue, gossip, and digressive storytelling that makes up Efuru's world, and by which Efuru makes her indirect way through unwomanly disgrace to mythic power. Very little is narrated, all is surmised—from the family palaver that "dances around" the uncomfortable fact that Efuru has married without dowry and has upset the social hierarchy by marrying beneath her, to the euphemistic way that her circumcision is spoken of as a "bath" (12–13). We sense the pain involved in this latter practice from the reactions of those around Efuru; we intuit her spirited response to the pain from marketplace banter that accompanies her return to trade following a month's postcircumcision feasting (16–19). We sense her robust spirit again as she mediates the rift between her father and her husband's family over the unpaid dowry. Although effusive flattery (another form of palaver) covers over this break in protocol, Efuru quietly slips her husband the money for the required conciliatory gift and then kneels down to receive the gift itself (23–24).

No analysis is given of these events. We watch and listen from the sidelines as all the right and traditional things are said, but as Efuru's social skill controls the outcome.

Palava circumscribes Ajanupu's collection of debts. She lets her debtor (and us) know that a given encounter has bite by responding to "It is well today that you have come to my house" with "It is well *but not very well*" (italics added, 46). Likewise, when Efuru's mother-in-law inquires about the strain in her marriage to Adizu, Efuru nuances her response with "It is bad but not very bad" (50); yet she marks the statement with a hiss. We enter the deep pain of Efuru's marital struggle through internal palava as she sorts through the possibilities of Adizu's inattention to her (54), each scenario seeming as possible as the next. When she goes to Ajanupu's house to talk over her options, the squabbles of Ajanupu's children are as present on the page as Efuru's decisionmaking, reflecting once again that few important choices are made outside of a complex context that refines, redirects, and interrupts rational process. Efuru's decision to marry Gilbert is likewise surrounded by banter, play and "talking around" (117–19).

Perhaps one of the most playful demonstrations of palaverous indirection in the revelation (or obscurity) of plot occurs when Efuru and her father encounter the *dibia* (shaman) who is in an unusual mood to talk and must be heard out before they can get to an interpretation of her dreams of Uhamiri (151–54). Even (perhaps especially) prophecy must give way to the circumlocutions of life. This happens again when Ogea's parents attempt to articulate the tragedy of their being robbed of the loan Efuru has made to them. All present share stories of thievery, relevant or not, and Nwabata's fear of receiving sympathy, as well as Efuru's embarrassment over having loaned money to irresponsible persons, is eased (177–78). All is said, and nothing. We who have ears hear.

Connected to Nwapa's skillful and oblique use of palaverous speech to bring us inside of Efuru's world is her direct use of orality. Characters express pain or surprise or even irritation with the untranslatable but eminently communicative "Ew-o-o" or "Weo-o." They hiss to express anger and repeat incantations in moments of deep fear, such as when Efuru's one and only baby daughter is dying: "Evil forces leave my child, evil forces leave my daughter. It will not happen. It cannot happen in my presence. Our ancestors fight against them. Our ancestors fight against death, don't let death defeat you" (67). On a moonlit night, they remember the meaningless words of children's songs (115) and the wonderful verbal rhythm of children's games: "If you give us yam, / Igbemgbele,

Ocho-ockwuoo, Igbemgbele, we shall take. / Igbemgbele, Ocho-ockwuoo, Igbemgbele" (102–3). Emeka the storyteller is invited to tell his stories for their own mesmerizing sake (105).

Perhaps the most stark use of indirection in this work is Nwapa's insistence that we learn key facts from overhearing and sorting through gossip. Efuru is a successful trader, which makes her initially the envy of many others in the village. When she seeks a maid to help with her baby daughter so she can go to market, her friends "narrate all the atrocities of maids," chiding her that money has less value than children (37). Efuru dismisses their banter and hires Ogea. Her daughter, Ogonim, dies, seeming to affirm the gossips. But Ogea has had no part in the death and turns out to be the loyal "daughter" Efuru lost. At what point does Efuru trust her own intuition? At what point does the reader? Is such trust ever absolute?

We learn about the closeness of Efuru's second marriage to Gilbert through the jealousy of village gossips (137–39). Gossips poison Efuru's second mother-in-law against her (160ff). Gossips judge the infertility of Efuru's marriage to Gilbert (175) and reveal that Gilbert has had a son with another woman (chapter 14). And it is gossips who introduce the idea that Efuru is ill because she has cheated on Gilbert (215).

Some of these things are true, some false, some factually true and in need of compassionate analysis. Ajanupu's total refusal of the story of Efuru's adultery marks her as a discerning hearer and primes us to rejoice in Ajanupu's bold confrontation of Gilbert. It also prepares us to welcome Efuru's subsequent refusal to return to a suspicious husband, choosing instead to focus on her worship of Uhamiri, the goddess who had no children but mothered them all. Would the reader have felt so positive about these actions without Ajanupu's indigenous hermeneutic?

Is such a skillful use of strategic indirection characteristic of "woman-centered discourse"? Helene Cixous describes women's discourse as "*female libidinal economy,* a regime, energies, a system of spending not necessarily carved out by culture" ("Castration or Decapitation?" 488). Furthermore she says it takes the metaphorical form of wandering, of a voice that enters by the ear but reaches the "most intimate point" (489). It can be part of culture, but doesn't have to be. It can be utilized by men, but often isn't. It reflects the outlaw nature of a woman like Efuru, loyal to her father but defiant when she wants to marry a man without means of dowry; loyal to Adizu, but willing to leave him when he does not return for her only daughter's funeral; loyal to Gilbert, but unwilling to confess an adultery she has never entertained; and above all, loyal to Uhamiri, even if that involves sailing on uncharted waters. Nwapa has placed Efuru in a text bearing her name, surrounded by all of the enigmatic voices that would challenge and, in a few cases, accompany her course of action. So the novel ends, appropriately, with a question. As Efuru dreams of Uhamiri, the woman of the lake, she ponders: "She was happy, she was wealthy. She was beautiful. She gave women beauty and wealth but she had no child. She had never experienced the joy of motherhood. Why then did the women worship her?" (221). Why indeed?

Acknowledging the provocative nature of the ending, fellow Nigerian novelist Buchi Emecheta entitled her most famous novel *The Joys of Motherhood* (1979), some thirteen years after *Efuru* appeared. In both stories, the protagonists are dependent on well-meaning and generous fathers after the early deaths of their mothers. Both protagonists are rejected by their first marriage partners for the stigma of barrenness. Both are skilled market women. But, whereas Efuru pursues life in the rural village and becomes a celibate worshipper of Uhamiri, Nnu Ego emigrates into Lagos, basically loses her tie with religion except for occasional references to her chi and participation in nominal Christian ritual, and, after producing eight children, dies abandoned and alone on a country road. It is said after her death that although women pray to her spirit for children, she, having been so well endowed, grants none. The truth is that, except for the fierce pleasure of her "productivity," mothering has brought Nnu Ego little joy. Two of her sons have abandoned her for study in the Western world; two of her daughters marry well but are attached to their husbands' households; her remaining children are aimless, and her husband, Nnaife, has turned into a bitter man. She herself has been so caught up in the feeding of her children and maintenance of her household that she has become fearful, stingy, and isolated from others, hardly a mother to the larger community. In short, she has been devoured by motherhood, and dies a thin dry stick of a woman. Thus, one text invents another, and the dialogue continues to decenter and problematize our idea(s) of the mother.

### Subsequent Fictions: *Idu, One Is Enough, Women Are Different*

Flora Nwapa's mother-centered works following *Efuru* develop related themes—themes of women's identity, of reproductive choice, of the restriction of women's value to the domestic sphere, of the opening up of economic opportunity for women and its impact on mothering, and finally, the theme of other mothering as a source of community involvement. Theodora Ezeigbo quotes Nwapa as having said, "'Sisterhood will survive if we women pay less attention to men and marriage'" (65). Although this seems to fly in the face of her womanist agenda, it could well be an attempt to open up dialogue, urging women to give up their obsessions with traditional notions of domestic femininity for the sake of new models of reciprocity. At another point, Nwapa told Ezeigbo that she believed that African women's history had to be recreated in African women's fiction (58). *Idu* could well be seen as one of those recreations in which marital reciprocity takes precedence over traditional notions of motherhood.

In the novel, Idu and Adiewere are joined in a love match but suffer the anxiety of childlessness. Adiewere reluctantly agrees to a second wife but, when Idu becomes pregnant, turns all of his attention back to her. She produces a son and some years later becomes pregnant with another child. But during Idu's second pregnancy, Adiewere dies suddenly and, against all tradition, Idu declares that she is going into death with him, regardless of the child she has produced and the fetus she carries. Appearing depressed and anorexic, she cloisters herself and literally starves herself to death. People in the village are horrified and confused, as have been critics ever since.

Nwapa's *One Is Enough* (1981) moves the action to Lagos, where postindependence dynamics, including rampant corruption, flourish, and where issues of the mother become ever more convoluted. Amaka leaves her childless rural marriage at the point when her husband takes another wife and chooses to test her commercial skills in the "modern" city. Encouraged by her mother (who has always valued motherhood over her own polygamous marriage) to seek children, Amaka eventually takes up with a Nigerian priest. He seems safe. He is devoted to his church work and hardly likely to interfere with her vow that one husband is enough:

> She neither wanted to be a wife any more, not be a mistress, or even a kept woman. She wanted a man, just a man and she wanted to be independent of this man, pure and simple. In that case, she was perfectly all right. Rev. Fr. Mclaid would never, never, want marriage nor would he claim her child. (100)

But when twin boys are born, the priest, who has spent considerable energy fighting traditional prejudice against twins, feels an indissoluble commitment to this woman and her children. Amaka, eschewing marriage, is in a tight place, but Father Mclaid finally reassesses his position, and they part friends. The novel ends (in a fashion that shocked many) with Amaka saying, "I shall forever remain grateful to him for proving to the world that I am a mother as well as a woman" (154). She's not exactly equating the two, but it comes close.

A further complication is that as Amaka becomes prosperous in Lagos, she also gives quite generously from her new wealth. In that sense she qualifies as a worshipper of Uhamiri—prosperous in trade and willing to nurture (other mother) the community through her largesse. The novel allows for no easy moralizing.

The oddities of generosity in prosperity continue into *Women Are Different* (1986). In this novel tracing the stories of four young Nigerian women, educated together in colonial school and taking radically different routes in the post-colonial period, Rose, the childless one, is once again the poignant center of the work. These women, Uhamiri's daughters, wrestle with all kinds of relational, vocational, and mothering issues as they move from mission school to the wider world of Lagos. They have been trained to be independent by their teachers, but the world of Lagos is not prepared for European ideas of individual rights. Ultimately, their experiences illustrate the collapse of Nigerian marriage—whether arranged, polygamous, or monogamous—and the collapse of the domestic ideal for women. All of the women must work as well as care for children and home; few have male companionship and help for more than a temporary period of time. So, in the end, when Dora, accepting her profligate husband home again, introduces her lover to Rose to at least give Rose the possibility of motherhood, it is perceived by both Rose and the lover as a generous gesture—impossible but generous.

Is a woman to be defined through her maternal behavior? Does that only include biological children? Does a woman get to decide how these expectations will be realized? Nwapa prepares dilemma tales, allowing her readers to engage the dilemmas. As she has said, "'I show it and people will make their own judgments'" (Wilentz 145). Gay Wilentz argues in many places that "Afracentric writers displace the binary oppositions encoded in [global] debates and problematize rather than reify women's position in both traditional and contemporary cultures" (145). In terms of issues of the mother, Nwapa does this with relentless energy, but also with grace for what happens in the margins.

## Complications of the Colonial/Biological Mother: Jamaica Kincaid

The novels of Caribbean novelist Jamaica Kincaid introduce us to issues of the mother directly related to colonial power and to the exile's search for identity. As Moira Ferguson argues in her persuasive study *Jamaica Kincaid: Where the Land Meets the Body* (1994), the relationships between mothers and daughters in Kincaid's fiction are always mediated by the realities of life under colonial rule: "That doubled articulation of motherhood as both colonial and biological explains why the mother–daughter relations in her fiction often seem so harshly rendered, a fact that has constantly unsettled reviewers" (1). A further disturbance to readers and reviewers is that the daughters, seeking to escape claustrophobic mothers who have internalized European criteria for "good girls," flee to the very countries from which those same repressive powers have emanated.

Perhaps the impulse to leave the mother, only to return (in real or symbolic terms), is universal. If Kristeva is right about the origins of language, poetic language can only return us to our primary connection with the mother if we have first experienced radical disjunction, that is, if we have first learned to speak from a distance. Biddy Martin and Chandra Mohanty discuss this journey as the search for "home," that which can only become a significantly safe place if one has experienced exile. Arguing that secure places are often "purchased" through exclusion, denial, and blindness, they assert that exile breaks open the possibility of recreating both self and community (a product of work and struggle), and thus allows for creative return. In their view, healthy community is inherently unstable: "it has to be constantly re-evaluated in relation to critical political priorities; and it is the product of interpretation, interpretation based on an attention to history, to the concrete" (308).

This is to say that although Kincaid depicts daughters stifled and violated by their mothers' preference for static appearances over vital realities (i.e., for "proper" English over island Creole), the other mothers these daughters choose, whether geographical or personal, never provide comfortable alternatives. Instead, they stimulate self-evaluation and critical understanding, in this case, of the multiple complicating effects of colonial hierarchy. It is also to say that when originary mothers are rejected in Kincaid's fiction, they are simultaneously loved, for they too have had to survive under colonial rule, and they too have resisted in their way. But the daughters' resistance cannot passively mirror the mothers'. If the daughters would learn to speak truly, they must leave the space of the mother, turning it into articulated memory. In her own life as writer, Kincaid has made this journey with strength and compassion, leaving home and circling back in numerous ways.

*A Small Place* (1989) is an anti-colonial polemic, unmediated by fictional play, and the cause of Kincaid's official exile from her Antiguan home in 1989. In it she has done the unacceptable, she has violated the female role of passivity and voicelessness prescribed by both colonial and post-colonial culture (Byerman 92). She mocks first-world tourists, deplores the colonial past of Antigua, and presents a blistering critique of post-colonial corruption. "The narrator underscores the notion of lost innocence, of a young child who grows up in a paradise—or so she thinks—only to realize that more than one abandonment lurks around the corner" (Ferguson 93). The most complicated abandonment is, as always, that of the mother. In her own voice this time, Kincaid expresses her love for and distance from her biological mother who, by a string of complicities (including collusion with a foreign doctor on matters of forced cleanliness), becomes indistinguishable from the colonial "stepparent." Yet in one beautifully complicating vignette, Kincaid comes upon her mother putting up political posters that expose the corruption of neo-colonial Antiguan rulers, and she must acknowledge their strained solidarity.

### Fictional Exiles: "Girl," *Annie John, Lucy*

There are many ways that the conflicts articulated in *A Small Place* enter the fiction of Jamaica Kincaid and force us to confront the physical and metaphoric complications of naming the mother. The short story "Girl" from *At the Bottom of the River* (1978), plunges us into the anger of an island mother, fearful that her daughter will defy the set of Eurocentric values she herself has so ardently adopted. The story is a monologue—better yet a harangue—a set of instructions for the daughter motivated by the mother's fear and shame. The mother in this short fiction has forced herself to be "a good girl"; now she wants to write her daughter's script, making sure she avoids the greatest threat of all—becoming a "slut." Yet such avoidance would require the daughter's denouncing her budding sexuality. The mother suspects a rebellion coming on and almost fatalistically warns against its inevitability:

> [T]ry to walk like a lady and not like the slut you are so bent on becoming; don't sing benna in Sunday school; you musn't speak to wharf-rat boys, not even to give directions; don't eat fruits on the street—flies will follow you; *but I don't sing benna on Sundays at all and never in Sunday school;* this is how to sew on a button; this is how to make a button-hole for the button you have just sewed

on; this is how to hem a dress when you see the hem coming down and so to prevent yourself from looking like the slut I know you are so bent on becoming. (3–4)

If both family and state prosper from the control of female sexuality, and the "proper" response is for women to keep their sexuality hidden, then the "Girl's" open sexuality will be a shameful offense and a challenge to assumed power.[5] Well might the mother, the cultural initiator of the daughter, teach her these things. Yet this is the very kind of unexamined enculturation that Kincaid protests.

*Annie John* (1983) and *Lucy* (1990) are autobiographical novels that continue to explore these issues. As young Annie John becomes increasingly alienated from her beautiful mother, she longs for their early, uncomplicated connection:

> With love for her mother apparently draining out of Annie John's body, she then thinks of food—of nurturance, of her womb relationship, of times when her mother would chew up hated carrots to make them more palatable for her daughter. She attempts to maintain a feeling of union but the rift is too wide. (Ferguson 49)

She remembers bathing with her mother, dressing like her mother, living without thought in the security of her mother's love. What is hardest to take is that the mother initiates their separation.

If this separation ultimately marks Annie John's rebellion against legalisms, it also marks her recognition that the laws of the father (including the rules of the colonizers), are always mediated through the mother, she who must become "other" for the daughter to develop. Annie John flees to England where she believes that the other can be truly other. But is that possible?

*Lucy* picks up the story as a female immigrant from the islands takes up residence in the North American home of Mariah and Lewis and is clearly "other mothered" by the American woman she both admires and resents. Refusing to open any of her own mother's letters, Lucy watches Mariah and her friends closely, picking up clues about women's sexuality. She becomes the slut her mother feared, openly meeting her body's needs, but she is not as fiercely condemned in this new place as at home where the same Puritan values had been more stringently applied. Nonetheless, the liberation offered by life with Mariah and Lewis is deceiving. Lucy is encouraged to be free as long as she will allow herself to be loved and defined according to their fashion. (She will now be colonized by their love for the exotic.)

Finally, Lucy knows she must distance herself physically and metaphorically from this relationship. The separation begins with the gift of a camera. Now Lucy can frame her perceptions of the world; she can stand back and interpret the stories she is told by Mariah, by her lovers, by her best friend. As a result of this framed analysis, Lucy renames herself Lucifer, identifying with a kind of pre-colonial fierceness and post-colonial defiance; she answers her mother's letters tersely; and she moves into a new space in her life that is yet to be filled.

The love–hate relationships that Kincaid's protagonists have with their mothers are clearly the product both of normal developmental conflicts and of the painful ambiguities brought on by colonial rule. More than that, they seem to express the difficulty we currently face in deciding what kinds of powers to ascribe to the role of mother itself.

### Refusing Motherhood: *Autobiography of My Mother*

The protagonist of Kincaid's latest novel, *The Autobiography of My Mother* (1996), engages in a lifelong attempt to assess and evaluate the role of a mother who died at the moment of her daughter's birth. In fact, the simple statement, "My mother died at the moment I was born," begins the novel and becomes a kind of mantra throughout, reminding the reader that fierce self-reflection is the only thing available to the motherless child. Caught by the mother's absent presence, the protagonist believes that she alone can create her place in the world: "No one observed and beheld me, I observed and beheld myself; the invisible current went out and it came back to me. I came to love myself in defiance, out of despair, because there was nothing else" (56–57). She refuses to have a child—there is no place for that in her construction of self—submitting to risky abortions in order to avoid such a reality. She indulges in wild and desperate sex (enacting the colonized body) but, almost nunlike, marries a man she does not love and lives in seclusion both with him and after he dies.

This chosen despair has everything to do with the nature of language and with the false rhetoric that makes up colonial discourse. The protagonist's mother was a Carib woman, which meant that she was extinct before she actually died. "The Carib people had been defeated and then exterminated, thrown away like the weeds in a garden," whereas "the African people had been defeated but had survived" (16). The mother, herself an orphan, was, in the protagonist's words, a "living fossil," someone who shouldn't have been, and left no proof of her existence other than her self-creating, self-doubting daughter. The protagonist never heard her mother speak.

She does hear her father speak and does not trust a word he says. The father, of African descent, but named after Alfred the Great, the English king, "a personage [he] should have despised" (109), never arrives at a clear sense of himself, or at least not one the daughter can trust. He is a policeman and speaks perfect English, except when angry, at which time an instinctive *patois* takes over. He believes that he loves his daughter, without realizing that he cannot love (113); he believes that he is honest, brave, and freedom-loving, while remaining oblivious to the thief, liar, and coward his daughter senses him to be (54). His smile is a taut mask that keeps underlings at bay and invites his betters to come close (185). In short, as the protagonist reflects at the end of her "autobiography," the victor and the vanquished exist together in her father, and he, of course, chooses "the mantle of the former, always the former" (192). She tries to imagine his love for the extinct Carib woman who was her mother and can find no reason to trust her own conception.

So she never trusts her own existence. Never having separated from her mother—or having known only the most radical separation—she mourns the absence of relationship between mother and daughter and knows that this lack is the "central motif" of her life (225). The result is that she seeks separation from all and, in solitude, creates herself: a self that is decidedly Carib, decidedly outlaw, outrageously sensual, and fiercely unlovable. As she realizes early on, in the company of her stepmother, "Love would have defeated me" (29). How could she attach in a meaningful way who had never understood her detachment? And, in this, she may well reconfigure the colonial self. Born into the cultural vacuum created by the extinction of her mother's people, she assumes the arduous task of trying to see past the death reflected in the face of her father's English-speaking wife, and fails.

For her, language as communication is suspect. There is no "mother tongue" to return to through poetic language because she has had no experience with the mother, and because she has never known the mother, she has never come outside of longing for her. Having never experienced, then, the full significance of a dialectical relationship between the biological and social worlds, she can only really speak to herself, in the comforting rhythms of the imagined mother's body that are very like the rhythms of her own female body. "I spoke to myself because I grew to like the sound of my own voice. It had a sweetness to me, it made my loneliness less, for I was lonely and wished to see people in whose faces I could recognize something of myself" (16). The truth is that these faces scarcely exist: the mother's Carib people are all but gone, and the father has adopted the persona of the oppressor.

In a period of dire loneliness, when she has depersonalized herself through mindless labor, speaks to no one, and has desexed herself through workman's clothes and a shedding of hair, she can only validate life through her own reflection in a "still pool on the shallow banks of a river" (99). She memorizes the hardness of her features and takes comfort there (100). Likewise, she takes comfort in the pungent smells and sharp sensations of her body. Here she finds reality, here she identifies with the bodily sensations that may very well have been her mother's. She revels in the forbiddenness of physical self-love, of the pleasures she can receive from men she does not love. This is narcissism written in blood, defining the self against abject loss.

All speech circles inward, because there was never an outward sensibility. Mainstream language is suspect because of how it defines and commodifies life. She has never learned to separate experience into discrete words and phrases, "Defeat is not beautiful; it is not ugly, but it is not beautiful" (65). And so she uses the outlaw *patios*—"the made-up language of people regarded as not real" (30–31)—when she can, talking outside of the official language, and happy with the muted mysteries that infuse her version of reality (the young boy who drowned while swimming to meet a fruit-laden river goddess, the poisoned necklace given to her by her stepmother which killed the family dog, the spell that kept Mdm. La Batte barren). Her story is for herself. It includes long lyrical sentences and mnemonic repetition. To the failure of her father to understand the story of the young boy's drowning she says, "he pointed his brownish-pink, pinkish-brown finger at me and said that I had not seen what I had seen, could not have seen what I had seen, did not, did not, did not; but I did, I did, I did" (50).

Such immediate recreations of oral speech are not surprising. The first printed words she was taught to read were "British Empire" (14); her first and only recorded attempt at writing were the early letters she wrote to her father from school, bleating out "the plaintiff cry of a small wounded animal" (19), only to have them appropriated and completely misinterpreted by her teacher. Internalized storytelling is far better—it leaves no trace.

So she tells her story, which is the undifferentiated story of herself, her mother, and all of the children she never had—creating herself, creating the thoughts and speech of father, sister, brother, and eventually husband.

Most of all, she creates her own thoughts, reminding herself of what it is to feel as if the "silent, soft, and vegetable-like" self that is her center of consciousness must constantly be reinvented through sounds, sights, and especially the strong smells of her own female body. One comes to wonder if she was ever born at all, ever "had" a mother, ever had anything beyond a rich instinctual urgency pushing her into the anticipation of meaningful connection with what comes after, but refusing connection at the same time.

And so she invites fecundity, but refuses to give birth. Where Efuru, Idu, and a whole string of fictional characters have lamented the plague of childlessness within cultures that equate womanhood with motherhood, this protagonist refuses to be mother in a remarkably oblique fashion:

> I had never had a mother, I had just recently refused to become one, and I knew then that this refusal would be complete, I would never become a mother, but that would not be the same as never bearing children. I would bear children, but I would never be a mother to them . . . I would bear children in the morning, I would bathe them at noon in a water that came from myself, and I would eat them at night, swallowing them whole, all at once. (97)

The cannibalism here is hyperbolic (solipsism consumes otherness). In fact, she uses no birth control but abortion, while pursuing her sexual desires freely and openly. What are we to make of this invitation–refusal? At one point, she claims that the child in her will never be still enough to allow her to have a child of her own (57). At the time of her first violent abortion she acknowledges the narcissistic danger of her choice by confessing, "I had carried my own life in my own hands" (91). Near the end of her narrative, she explains that the very absence of "that attachment, physical and spiritual, that confusion of who is who, flesh and flesh" (199) between her mother and herself has been "so profound an abandonment" that she is not able to rear children—neither children of flesh nor of signification. By marrying a man she does not love (a Scotsman at that), she has made a nonromance of her life and will make no romances in words.

And yet the text of the "autobiography" exists. Claiming to have abandoned public discourse for hidden desire (the symbolic for the semiotic, in Kristeva's terms), the protagonist has nonetheless given us a memorable account of the maternal body—its desires, swellings, rejections, and recreations. Her mother, the Carib woman, is declared extinct, yet is powerfully present in her self-reflections and post-colonial ruminations. Motherhood is denied and obsessively analyzed simultaneously. This is profoundly complicated. As the protagonist herself admits in speaking of the impossibility of speaking to her husband (and us, the outside readers?), "Truth would have undone him, the truth is always so full of uncertainty" (223).

This is a double-voiced narrative, "turning . . . crisis into a *work in progress*" (Kristeva, "Tales of Love" 177)—a work in progress in which the speaking self creates wild, resistant subjectivity and the writing self creates mimetic text. As in Ruth Prawer Jhabvala's *Heat and Dust* (1975), Kincaid's female narrator interprets "the meaning of another woman's life from the fragmentary data found in personal documents," insisting "on the reflexive nature of this enterprise" (Abel 147). It is a consuming task, involving confrontation with the personal and colonial past, insisting on the embodied nature of any linguistic act, as well as asking questions about what kind of future is possible when all familiar ideas of the mother have been erased.

Kincaid asks questions about redefinition in the most stark fashion possible. We should thank her for that, for no amount of nostalgic fantasizing about "the joys of motherhood" can release us from the painful reality that women and their dependent children make up 70 percent of the world's poor and more than 80 percent of the world's refugee populations. Mothers die in childbirth at alarming rates and are forced to have more children than they can nurture. If redefining motherhood, the rights of mothers, and the need for policies that protect the health and opportunities of all women is to take place, it must be in the cold light of day, without false sentiment. It must recognize that redefinition of anything requires a linguistic exploration that explodes the limits of rational syntax. It must recognize the effects of a variety of systems of power on the behavior of mothers, and it must hold women accountable for their passive complicity with those systems of power (Mdm. LaBatte, and the stepmother are compelling examples of complicitous diminishment of the female). Ultimately, it must pass beyond the sterile cynicism of Kincaid's narrator who has felt that no space was safe enough to complete her own birth, as well as that of her mythic and actual offspring, into full, celebrative self-hood.

Let it be the case that women (and men) can provide this space for one another through nurturing the development of multiplex persons, communities, myths of success, and cross-cultural connections. This cannot happen through the over-easy conflation of any two entities (problems, practices, or policies), but only through separation and reconnection, through dialogue across difference. Beijing made this kind of tenuous connection possible within concentrated political discussion; novelists do it one life, one case, one wild "heteroglossic" story at a time.

## Other Novels to Consult for Themes of the Mother

Buchi Emecheta's experience as a single mother of five on her own in London, making her way through the welfare system and university at the same time, is captured in her autobiography *Head Above Water* (1986) and is fictionalized in her early novels *In the Ditch* (1972) and *Second Class Citizen* (1974). Tsitsi Dangarembga's *Nervous Conditions* (1989) portrays problems of mothering (and socializing daughters) in the transitional period in Zimbabwe from the colonial to post-colonial eras. Also, dealing with complications of mothering in the transitional period, J. Nozipo Maraire's *Zenzele: A Letter for My Daughter* (1996) reproduces a long letter from a Zimbabwaean mother, party to the struggle for independence, to her daughter about to leave for America to study. Kamala Markandaya's classic *Nectar in a Sieve* (1954) captures the fears and struggles of rural poverty in India, including ironies surrounding the conventional wisdom that many children will bring peace and prosperity to parents in their old age. Isabel Allende's *Paula* (nonfiction novel; 1996) depicts the death of the author's daughter from a mysterious illness, woven together with the story of their relationship and the equally complicated and puzzling history of Chile in the post-colonial period. Rosario Castellanos' *The Nine Guardians* (1957), while telling the story of the Indian uprising in the 1930s in rural Mexico, also tells the tragic story of the physical and class separation of a young girl from Nana, her only true and "other" mother.

## Notes

1. See Gerda Lerner's *The Creation of Patriarchy* (1986) for a full discussion of how the commodification of the mother can be taken as the source of patriarchy.
2. See Mahasweta Devi's short story "Breast Giver" as a bold statement about the commodification of women's body parts.
3. See Anais Nin's powerful story "Birth" for a depiction of one woman's unwillingness to have her labor (in this case, to produce a dead child) controlled by an impatient physician.
4. The Mothers of the Disappeared, active in many countries of Latin America where husbands and children have been killed and imprisoned

for political reasons and without due process, are an interesting example of political power arising from the collective role of the mother.

5. Jamaican writer Michelle Cliff makes a similar point when she comments on Jean Rhys' rewrite of *Jane Eyre*, *The Wide Sargasso Sea*, which focuses on the role of Bertha—the mad first wife, the woman of unbridled passion:

> It took a Caribbean novelist, Jean Rhys, to describe Bertha from the inside, using the lens of the colonized female questioning colonization, keeping Bertha's "humanity, indeed her sanity as a critic of imperialism, intact," in Gayatri Spivak's words. . . . What a fine phrase, *critic of imperialism,* to describe the character we all encountered as girls—our hair plaited, our bodies uniformed, our minds trained on the mother (*sic*) country—as the madwoman in the attic, uncontrolled and uncontrollable, the worst thing a woman could become. (67–68)

# Chapter 5

## *Resisting Arrest: Violence Against Women and the Fight for* Human Rights

> I take myself back, fear.
> You are not my shadow any longer.
> I won't hold you in my hands.
> You can't live in my eyes, my ears, my voice
> my belly, or in my heart my heart
> my heart my heart.
>
> —Joy Harjo, "I Give You Back"

Mahasweta Devi's devastating short story "Draupadi" describes a woman violated in a thousand and one ways. She is a dark-skinned tribal guerrilla, in opposition to the Indian military, partnered with a man eventually martyred to the indigenous cause, and the namesake of a goddess with four arms, five husbands, a fiery spirit and the anonymity of political exile. When Draupadi is apprehended by the army, their commander interrogates her without touching her, then goes to dinner giving his men leave to "make" her—to shame her, to reduce her dignity as a woman, to subdue the primal wisdom with which she refutes the reasoning of his army handbook. And they do. They tie her arms and legs in a spread eagle formation and rape her over and over again like relentless machines, biting her breasts until they are raw: "indeed, she's been made up right" (281). Finally, she is thrown onto the straw inside a tent, a cloth tossed casually over her. She's been put in her place as woman, as tribal outcast, as political enemy, as other. How are we to live in a world where such things happen to women (and disenfranchised men) on a regular basis?

## Facing Violence Against Women

The *Platform for Action*, section D, defines violence against women as "any act of gender-based violence that results in, or is likely to result in, physical, sexual or psychological harm or suffering to women, including threats of such acts, coercion or arbitrary deprivation of liberty, whether occurring in public or private life." This definition came directly from the *UN Declaration on Violence Against Women* drafted by the UN Commission on the Status of Women in 1992, and adopted by the General Assembly in 1993.

Specific manifestations of violence against women, as cited by article 2 of the *UN Declaration*, include battering, sexual abuse of female children, dowry-related violence, rape (marital and nonspousal), female genital mutilation (and other traditional practices harmful to women), harassment and intimidation at work (and elsewhere), trafficking in women (i.e., forced prostitution), and violence perpetrated by the state and military (Heise 3). Added to that list would have to be fear of violence, perhaps the most debilitating manifestation of all. As the *Platform for Action* states, "The fear of violence, including harassment, is a permanent constraint on the mobility of women and limits their access to resources and basic activities" (paragraph 117).

Avoiding essentialist arguments based on unequal physical strength, section D of the *Platform* attributes the cause of gender-based violence to the "historically unequal power relations between men and women, which have led to domination over and discrimination against women by men and to the prevention of women's full advancement" (paragraph 118). It goes on to say that these unequal power relations between men and women often create a cultural climate where women are shamed for reporting acts of violence, where women do not receive adequate legal protection, where they do not have adequate access to legal information, and where media images promote misogyny.

Reinforcing the notion that the cause of violence against women is more likely to stem from structural relationships of power than from biological differences, the World Bank Discussion Paper *Violence Against Women: The Hidden Health Burden* (1994) quotes Cheryl Bernard, director of Austria's Ludwig Boltzman Institute of Politics, as saying that violence against women in the home "takes place because the perpetrators feel, and their environment encourages them to feel, that this is an acceptable exercise of male prerogative" (Heise 29). That is, violence against women in many cultures is so much a part of how women are perceived and how they are treated day to day that it is construed as normal, therefore even natural. The World Bank study goes on to say that male sexual behavior is often predatory, "not because male 'sexuality' is aggressive, but because sexuality is used to express power relations based on gender" (29–30). Tying domestic and sexual violence to cultural and state violence, the study claims that violence against women is especially prevalent in places where force is commonly used to resolve conflict among persons and groups of persons.

Feminist writer Robin Morgan, and others, would argue that religious fundamentalism can be a particularly vehement cultural system that perpetuates and condones domestic and state violence against women. Morgan asserts that when women make particular strides toward equity and influence, fundamental religious systems often engage in conservative backlash; furthermore, when religious fundamentalism is on the rise, women are often the primary targets ("Our Bodies, Our Souls"). Fear is a tactic in each of these actions.

It is significant then that in Mahasweta Devi's story of Draupadi, the turning point of the story occurs when, having been raped and mutilated, she refuses fear and turns it back on her torturers. After her night of horror, the military commander calls for Draupadi (or Dropdi, as her more human self is called) to appear before him, hoping to establish once and for all the proper relationship between those who have no power and those who seem to have it all. But she refuses to wash or to dress. "She pours the water down on the ground. Tears her piece of cloth with her teeth" (282). Then with her head held high, she walks toward the commander, in full sunlight, in the presence of his men and says, "You asked them to make me up. Don't you want to see how they made me?" She walks toward him until her bloody breasts touch his uniform, sending him reeling backward, "and for the first time Senanayak is afraid to stand before an unarmed *target,* terribly afraid" (282). In a moment, she has reversed the power–fear equation, and she knows it. This reversal gives *her* the power to avert shame and expose gender violence for what it is—a way of staying in charge at the expense of others. As the title of this chapter suggests, and this is the essential point, women worldwide are finding ways to resist being arrested and diminished—either physically or developmentally—and this resistance is taking shape in both political and literary discourse.

### Battering and Rape as Prototypes of Violence

Domestic abuse is the first thing most people think of when they hear the phrase "violence against women," probably because it is so very ordinary. In the United States, wife battering is believed to be the most common cause of women's injuries, "accounting for more trauma than all rapes, muggings and automobile accidents combined" (Neft and Levine 153). In Morocco, a husband is permitted to beat or murder his wife if she is found with a lover; in Latin America, such a crime may be called a "defense of honor." The Nigerian penal code allows a man to beat his wife if his "correction" does not leave a scar, and, in Mexico, if her injuries heal within 15 days (154). Papua New Guinea provides one of the worst-case scenarios. The majority of wives have been beaten by their husbands as reported by both spouses, and the statistics vary little between rural and urban families, between low-income families and moneyed elites (Bradley 11).[1] The incidence of domestic violence is so high, in fact, that it is considered by many to be a normal part of married life, causing members of Parliament to question legislation restricting the practice by asking: "If the majority of the people accept it, why should anything be done about it?" (13).

In addition to the pain and disability of physical injury, domestic abuse in Papua New Guinea (and other places) impedes the economic development of women. Women often stay away from community development meetings because of threats from their husbands; if they engage in income-generating projects, their money can be forcibly taken from them and used for nonessential items, including alcohol (Bradley 19).[2]

Yet, it is acts of violence against women's sexuality that probably leave the deepest scars and whose healing cannot be measured in days or outward signs. Six separate studies that inform the World Bank Discussion Paper *Violence Against Women* indicate that between one in five and one in seven women in the United States will be the victim of rape in her lifetime (Heise 5). In Pakistan, it is not unusual for a woman who reports rape to find herself charged with "unlawful sexual relations," which can carry a penalty of death by stoning (Neft and Levine 156–57). Worldwide, the burden of proof in a rape case is on the victim, who must produce medical evidence and proof of resistance, both of which can be hard to produce based on factors of cultural shame, availability of forensic physicians at the time of crisis, and the common socialization of girls and women to be passively subordinate.[3]

In addition to individual rapes, there is the "rape-for-profit" industry, whereby increasingly younger women are being coaxed or sold across borders to serve in the international sex trade as indentured slaves. As the *Platform for Action* declares, this traffic has become "a major focus of international organized crime" (section D, paragraph 122). According to Human Rights Watch, more than one million women and children work in Indian brothels; many of them come from Nepal (1).[4] At least 400,000 are under the age of eighteen (Neft and Levine 160).[5] Israel has become a typical destination of young women from Ukraine, transported by the infamous Russian mafia. The *New York Times* quotes Michael Plazer, head of operations for the UN's Center for International Crime Prevention as saying, "The earnings are incredible. The overhead is low. . . . Drugs you sell once and they are gone. Women can earn money for a long time" (Specter). Typically, it takes years for a young girl to buy her way out of sexual slavery; by that time she is most likely infected with AIDS.

### Militarism as Violence Against Women

Strategic mass rape, as part of military campaigns, is one of the most debilitating kinds of sexual violence that exists. According to Slavenka Drakulic, a Croatian political writer, women have been raped in almost every war "as retaliation, as damage to another man's 'property,' as a message to the enemy" (180). Yet, she asserts that what happened to women in Bosnia and Herzegovina in the 1990s is unprecedented in the history of war crimes. According to the World Bank, more than 20,000 Muslim women were raped in Bosnia between 1992 and 1994, many of them in rape camps where they were violated repeatedly and forced to give birth to Serbian children (Heise 19). During the ethnic cleansing in Rwanda, thousands of Tutsi women were raped and forced to bear Hutu children, rendering them social pariahs in Rwandan society. These women cannot easily remarry, often have AIDS, and show signs of depression, nightmares, and violent fantasies against their "children of bad memories" (McKinley). According to Elizabeth Royte, a writer for the *New York Times Magazine*, rape was relatively uncommon in Rwanda before the civil conflict that broke out in the early 1990s, but during the genocide, women became clear targets of strategic violence. Even before the killing began, Tutsi women were portrayed in the media as arrogant and lewd. "Rape, then, was committed not as a personal act of violence but as a political one, used to terrorize entire communities" (38).[6]

There are other ways that women are targeted during military campaigns. In section E: "Women and Armed Conflict" of the *Platform for Action*, it is clearly stated that "Violations of the human rights of women in situations of armed conflict are violations of the fundamental principles of international human rights and humanitarian law" (paragraph 131). Such a statement is in keeping with the *Geneva Convention* of 1949, the *Additional Protocols* of 1977, and the *Vienna Declaration and Programme of Action* from the World Conference on Human Rights. These documents contend that special protection for women and children during times of armed conflict is clearly warranted both by the fact that women and children increasingly outnumber combatant casualties, and by the fact that women often function as caretakers for both injured combatants and civilians (section E, paragraph 133). Women and children make up more than 80 percent of war-related refugee populations (paragraph 136). Women living in rural poverty have the added and long-term danger of coping with land mines and often bear the burden of maintaining social order when communities collapse during war (paragraphs 137, 139).

In addition to all of the above, women are often objects of sexual torture in times of war and military dictatorship. In a study of the torture of women in Latin America, anthropologist Ximena Bunster-Burotto notices a difference between violence against women as part of the generalized violence in certain Central American regimes, as over against the torture of specifically targeted women in countries of the Southern Cone where military governments have often been entrenched for decades. Here political women are identified as enemies of the state, or as women in "dangerous liaisons" with men active in resistance movements and therefore susceptible to the terrorism aimed at their partners. In either case, systematic torture is the vehicle of punishment and interrogation, and the immediate goal of the torture is to violate a woman's sense of herself through sexual attacks.[7] The ultimate goal is to "teach her that she must retreat into the home and fulfill the traditional role of wife and mother" (166).

Finally, there is the complicity of the sex trade with military training. Writing about the sex industry that services military bases in the Philippines, Mary Soledad Perpinan comments that although degrading forms of sexual exploitation make up the trade—female boxing, oil wrestling, the designation of Filipina prostitutes as "little brown fucking machines"—the ultimate effect is loss of respect for life. "Denigration of women leads to the desecration of life: it makes it easier to pull a trigger or push a button to annihilate the living" (151).

In *The Demon Lover: On the Sexuality of Terrorism* (1989), Robin Morgan generalizes this argument. Men have historically operated, she believes, according to the principle of *thanatos*—a love of death that is perpetuated by a belief in the necessity of violence. Women, she thinks, have more often operated according to *eros,* but that love of life has been co-opted by death both in the obvious ways discussed above and in more implicit ways. For although women may not share the "phallic excitement" that accompanies military campaigns, they are vulnerable to the political and social power that validates this excitement, and they pay their allegiance through culturally sanctioned erotic desires. The hardened hero, in pursuit of his cause and vicious to his enemies, is not only envied by men, he is desired by women. This object of desire may be "demonic" in his acts of aggression, but he also promises safety. So, whereas war imperils women in countless ways, they still line the parade routes to cheer for their men in uniform. This complicity perpetuates state violence and compromises liberation movements where women are promised the world and make the coffee.[8]

### Human Rights and the Courage to Resist

Section I: "Human Rights of Women" in the *Platform for Action* discusses all of the aforementioned as transgression of inalienable, integral, and universal human rights. Why does something like that even need to be said? The history of the association between women's issues and universal human rights is traced in chapter 1, but focusing on the *basic right to freedom from violence,* Charlotte Bunch further notes that "significant numbers of the world's population are routinely subject to torture, starvation, terrorism, humiliation, mutilation, and even murder *simply because they are female*" (italics added, "Women's Rights as Human Rights" 486). This alone requires a reiteration that women are fully human and that violence against women cannot be viewed as a "private matter."[9]

In their resistance against personal and systemic gender violence, women are clearly refusing to remain in the private sphere. There are many evidences of this resistance to be found, from the Beijing Conference itself, to more concrete and localized actions. In arguing against sisterhood as "shared victimization," bell hooks suggests that women's rage, an appropriate response to injustice, "can act as a catalyst inspiring courageous action" (*Killing Rage* 16).

One could well argue that righteous rage inspired the Afro-Indian women of Belize to surround the houses of men beating their wives and make sufficient noise to publicly shame them. That same rage may have inspired the women in one community in Peru to organize a neighborhood watch and to wear whistles with which they could summon a group of women if attacked (Heise 39). It took some amount of rage for Muslim women to craft a document entitled "Claiming Our Rights: A Manual for Women's Rights Education in Muslim Societies" and to distribute it for discussion in six different language groups (Crossette, "A Manual on Rights of Women Under Islam").[10] And it certainly takes rage for women to fight rape, in all of its manifestations. As Sharon Marcus reminds us in a powerful article entitled "Fighting Bodies, Fighting Words," rape proceeds out of the culturally inscribed notion that men have power, whereas women must live in fear.[11] To expand notions of power beyond physical power and fear beyond traditional forms of intimidation requires rewriting the "rape script," not an easy task but one that many women are taking up.

As one example, two documentary filmmakers, Mandy Jacobson and Karmen Jelincic, have made a piece entitled "Calling the Ghosts" in which they tell the story of two professional women who survived the Serbian rape camps and who were willing to expose their pain in order to "make sense of what happened" *and* to shame their torturers within the arena of international media (Miller). These women, subjects and filmmakers alike, are truly daughters of Draupadi, but so are all of those writing women who will not shut up, even when exiled, and who speak to us through the complicated and transgressive worlds we call novels.

### Resisting Battery and Rape: Nawal El Saadawi

Nawal el Saadawi is an Egyptian physician-psychiatrist-writer who began to publish novels simultaneously with entering the public sphere as a prophetic political voice. Serving as the minister of health in Egypt from 1958 to 1972, she was dismissed for (among other things) writing *Women and Sex* (1969), an honest portrayal of women's sexuality (Malti-Douglas 11). Placing herself under self-imposed exile, Saadawi spent most of the next decade working for the UN, returning to live in Egypt in 1980. In 1981, she was arrested and imprisoned under Egyptian president Anwar Sadat as part of a general roundup of political activists and intellectuals accused of sowing dissent. A year after her release, she founded the Arab Women's Solidarity Association, which was shut down in 1991.

From 1958, when her first major novel *Memoirs of a Woman Doctor* was published, Saadawi wove fiction into her world of medical practice, political activism, and socialist commentary. It is all of a piece. As Fedwa Malti-Douglas comments, "in el Saadawi's discourse the scalpel is never far from the pen" (12), and the pen may be engaged in a multiplicity of activities, all of them rewriting the "official story" for women. Part of that rewriting of repressive tradition has involved arguments about what it means to be a progressive Middle Eastern woman. Feminism in the Middle East is associated with Western thought, whereas socialism is considered anti-West. So, although leftist politics retains the rhetoric of liberation for all persons, it maintains a deeply ingrained hostility to movements that seek genuine equality for women (13).

Through all of this, Saadawi has kept a consistently open and complex identity. She writes all of her books in Arabic; if they can't be published in Cairo, she takes them to Beirut. Only then are they released to be translated for the wider world. She maintains a socialist perspective, giving ample attention to a Marxist critique of class issues and neo-colonial policies. Yet she persistently asserts that women's issues are central to issues of power relations in Egypt, and although she participates in most of the UN-sponsored international debates on women's rights, she continues to hold that women's oppression must be fought in context—for her, the Middle Eastern world. So, acknowledging that accusations of Westernization, commonly imposed on Arab feminists, allow those in authority "to expel from the tribe" the persons they do not want to hear (whether those in authority are from the conservative right or the oppositional left), she has refused to leave Egypt for more than occasional periods of time. She writes about Egypt, in Arabic, while refusing to be cowed by an anti-imperialism that serves those in power, even though she herself finds much to critique in Western imperial thought. In this, she is truly "writing back" to the systems of power, whether they be international or national, and so has modeled the need for global feminists to seek the well-being of women within each separate society (16).

**Prison Memoirs**

The memoirs that Saadawi wrote out of her experience of arrest and imprisonment in 1981 establish a framework for understanding the honesty and resistance that lie at the heart of her novels. In fact, in that the first-person narrator of the memoirs weaves her past and present stories with those of the many political and criminal women that she encounters in prison, the work takes on a semi-fictional, clearly multivocal quality. Truly, this narrator is remembering, recording, and reciting stories as a means of preserving life. In this, Saadawi has much in common with her legendary sister Schahrazad and, like Schahrazad, works her magic at night.

*Memoirs from the Women's Prison* (1983) is all about systems of power and their attendant violence. First there is the forced ostracism of the woman activist. Saadawi records how her "uncalled-for boldness" (112), her efforts to integrate issues of "women, society, medicine, literature and politics" (2) in the Egyptian scene, have rendered her estranged, even blacklisted, in her own country. When arrested, she finds herself up against an all-male judicial system—no women "in the police, nor in the army, nor among the judges or legal guardians or religious officials" (21). Her arrest itself on September 6, 1981, is conducted with a gratuitous show of violence. Police surround the building, crash down the door to her apartment, circle her with their rifles raised, and envelop her "like an iron chain" (7). In prison, all women are subjected to verbal attacks on their sexuality: "'Bitch, whore, daughter of a whore' . . . oaths directed to all women's body parts" (34). And political prisoners are held indefinitely in filthy cells, without trial or clear charges—only the vague accusation of participation in "sectarian rift."

But beyond physical denigration and systemic injustice, she suffers the slow torture of incessant noise and crowding (129), of escalating doubt in her own judgment (136), and the remembrance of violations of the past: her father's verbal abuse of her mother that made Saadawi abhor rulers and authorities (117); the cultural expectations that forced her mother to marry at seventeen, produce ten children, and die at forty-five (119); and the religious fundamentalism that has permeated her experience as an Egyptian woman. Fundamentalism presents itself within the prison cell when Bodour, the religious zealot, and Fawqiyya, the political zealot, square off in a horrifying display of how women internalize patriarchy. Both refuse the refuge of laughter, one because it is shameful and the other because it is lacking in gravity (126). But the cruelest words come from Bodour's mouth. Imprisoned for vague and ambiguous reasons, she nonetheless attacks a beaten cellmate with the accusation that "God could not possibly expose you to pain or torture or prison or beating without a sin on your part" (131).[12]

Within this catalog of violations, the reader senses a theme common to Saadawi's writing—that all violations of women through the vulnerability of their constructed gender roles are, in fact, analogs of rape. The breaking down of the door during arrest, the sudden interruption of Saadawi's work on her novel, the intrusive and stupid interrogations to which all prisoners are submitted, the language of sexual assault hurled at incarcerated women, the physical beatings to which some are subjected repeat over and over the truth that women can be "taken" at will.

But the essential value of these memoirs is not that such practices are unmasked and named for what they are, but that they are exorcised through the self-preserving counterpower of metaphor itself. Saadawi writes back to the architects of the prison system by writing against the rules, penning her stories in the middle of the night on toilet paper. Through such activity, her pen becomes a weapon. Although it is compared to a pistol in one scene, its real likeness is to the hoe with which Fathiyya, one of the criminal prisoners, supposedly killed her husband after finding him raping her daughter. As Malti-Douglas comments, "Fathiyya's killing hoe permits Nawal to turn her pen into a killing instrument" (165). And as Saadawi herself says, "My hand, as it grips the pen, is like her hand when she took hold of the hoe and struck the blow" (116). One woman's resistance inspires another's, and with that pen, Saadawi strikes her blows, describing her arrest and prison experience with stark metaphors that truly return protest for violence, that explode and shatter the smooth surface of "normal" experience.

As Saadawi tells it, the police who came to arrest her "attacked the flat like savage locusts, their open mouths panting and their rifles pointed." Their noses were curved like "the beaks of predatory birds" (7). At the Courts of Inquisition, "Their long and sharply pointed rifles and bayonets reminded [her] of the needles which used to be plunged into the bodies of witches in search of the mark of the devil. Their eyes were like bits of glass" (23). The electric light in her cell stares "like a strangled, bulging eye" (28). As writer, she is Draupadi, walking boldly into public space to expose sequestered violence. Unlike Draupadi, Saadawi has the support of a homosocial prison world where women, crowded into an assaulting environment, have forged risky solidarities across class, educational, political, and religious borders, all the more remarkable in that they were each arrested for promoting "sectarian rift"!

### God Dies by the Nile

In earlier novels, Saadawi prefigures much of what appears to be politically explicit in her prison memoirs. *God Dies by the Nile* (1974) is such a prefiguring novel. The rural setting, with its strangely eclectic collection of characters, contains every possible form of violence—political, racial, class, religious, familial, geographical, and, most pervasive, gender-based. But, as in all of Saadawi's work, it is the stark resistance to violence and misuse of power that occupies the reader's memory.

Political violence based on class difference enters the village of Kafr el Teen primarily through the frustrated ambition of its Mayor (always capitalized), a well-educated, half-English city man who chafes at his rural posting, while his brother reaps high success in Cairo. Jealous of his brother's power, the Mayor allows, in fact demands, that he be treated on a par with Allah. As the village barber admits, "We are all God's slaves when it's time to say our prayers only. But we are the Mayor's slaves all the time" (53). Later, Sheikh Hamzawi, the keeper of the mosque, admits that the people do not fear God in their hearts; "What they really fear is the Mayor" (106). This gives the Mayor sinister and absolute control over the lives of the poor and disenfranchised.

When he impregnates Nefissa, a young village girl who abandons her baby on the street and runs away, he covers his tracks by picking his own scapegoat—a quietly impious but respected farmer named Elwau. Having arranged for the murder of the "culprit," he accuses the girl's father of this "crime of honor," and sending him off to jail, paves the way for seduction of the younger daughter Zeinab. All lives are in his hands, and one young child fantasizes that the Mayor's big house with the iron gates houses not Allah but the devil.

His power turns traditional village leaders into sycophants, which may be one of his most seditious acts. The head of the Village Guard, the sheikh of the mosque, the village barber—all fawn on the Mayor, cheating their own people on his behalf and panting for any sign of favor. Even when his cronies sense that the power structure he has built is breaking down—that "people have started to open their eyes much more than before" (126)—they help to frame Galal, Zeinab's young husband, for robbery and thus watch another one of their own race unjustly hauled off to jail. Their corruption is an irreparable violation, one common to all political systems, but greatly exacerbated by the colonial enterprise.

Religious violence, often a theme for Saadawi, appears in this work as inextricably bound with political violence. Sheikh Hamzawi's greatest pleasure, a petty one to be sure, is making the Mayor and his underlings do his bidding during prayer services. Sheikh Zahran, head of the Village Guard, insists that Nefissa's father Kafrawi beat her into submission when the mayor requests her presence in his home, accusing Kafrawi of refusing the good of Allah. Haj Ismail, the village barber and quack doctor, contrives a false oracle from Allah to send Zeinab into the Mayor's bed.

Fatheya, a young woman of Khar el Teen, is beaten into submission when Sheikh Hamzawi, a man old enough to be her grandfather, requests her as his fourth wife in order to prove his manhood and to maintain his power over the prayer life of the village. The sheikh submits her to endless tyrannical sessions of memorizing the Koran, but ultimately sacrifices both her and their adopted son (Nefissa's child by the Mayor) to the seething vengeance of the villagers who, without true religious guidance and clear political analysis, suspect this "demon" child of causing their economic ills. Religion serves power in this tale, and none escape.

Familial violence also raises its grotesque head, not only in multiple acts of domestic abuse, but in the Mayor's verbal cruelty to his wife and in the childhood rape of Haj Ismail by his overbearing cousin (51). There is little safety to be found in a climate of violence, where power is supreme and the very idea of violent competition—as in a cock fight or the "defrocking" of Sheikh Hamzawi—is exciting. In such a world, private as well as public violence is "the peculiar pleasure that men experience watching a violent struggle between opposing parties" (110).

When Zeinab and her ailing aunt, Zakeya, make their way into town on religious pilgrimage, they are beset by violent pornography: "a huge picture which showed a naked woman lying on her back with her legs open, and three men pointing their pistols at her" (86). This public display is shocking to them, yet horribly familiar to their situation at home where all women—particularly those without means—are vulnerable to violence all their lives. Women are beaten into submission, subjected to hard work, scorned when they bear female children, punished when a male child dies, and raped with impunity.

As in many of Saadawi's works, rape is the prototypical act of violence against women (and powerless males), the one that best expresses the misuse of power directed at difference. Power of position allows the Mayor to have any woman he wants, so he takes both Nefissa and her sister Zeinab into his home as servants, using them at will. When Sheikh Hamzawi is stripped of his power, his wife, Fatheya, is fair game for gang rape. Zakeya, like many women, was regularly raped in her marriage. But the cruelty of the male gaze also is a form of rape in this novel, reinforcing everyone's awareness that a woman can be taken at will.

Once he has used and disposed of Nefissa, the Mayor "has eyes" for her younger sister, Zeinab, and winking at one of his lackeys, says, "But the youngest is always the most tasty" (14). Watching her walk by, his possessive eye selects out the desired parts of her body: "He could see her firm, rounded buttocks pressing up against the long galabeya from behind. Her pointed breasts moved up and down with each step. Beneath the tail of her galabeya two rosy, rounded heels peeped out" (14). The surveillant male gaze strips Zeinab of all privacy. Later, she says that she can feel the Mayor's blue eyes "singe her back." They gaze at her "fixedly, inflexibly, cruelly cutting through her dress, feeding on the beauty of her legs" (66). So it is no surprise to the reader that he has his way with her, or that the men of the town gang rape Fatheya as much with their eyes as with their genitalia: "Male eyes gleamed with an unsatisfied lust, feeding on her breast with a hunger run wild like a group of starved men gathered around a lamb roasting on a fire. Each one trying to devour as much as he can lest his neighbor be quicker than him" (115). Whether this savage event would have occurred without the complicating patriarchal presence of the half-English Mayor is, of course, a matter of conjecture clearly invited by Saadawi, who is no naïf in terms of the violence inherent in traditional family and religious life, but who well knows the corrupting influence of foreign rule.

As evidence of traditional violence, the reader encounters the ravaging of female sexuality by the village *daya*, an asexual "woman" named Om Saber who cuts the flesh between young girls' legs and tears the virgins' hymens with her finger at their weddings. That she also helps women with abortions and sprinkles chicken blood on the sheets of nonvirginal brides complicates her role.

As has been seen all along, some kinds of gender violence come in disconcertingly paradoxical forms. Fatheya is confused by the uncleanness that she is made to feel every time she gets her period. After all, Om Saber came to her as a child to cut off the "bad, unclean part" (32). Yet, she is still treated like a leper, "as though there [is] something corrupt or bad about her" (33). This kind of cure-less cultural loathing renders any woman vulnerable to violence. When Zeinab finally leaves the village to follow her husband to prison, she accepts, almost as a matter of course, survival sex, becoming a prisoner of "rape for profit" because that is, at least, something that a woman can do.

Zakeya's seizure, when she "dreams" in vivid images of all the violence that has been done to her in the course of her life, reveals all of these connections. In this dream she revisits her own savage circumcision and the husband who "kicked her in the belly when she was pregnant"; regularly raped her, "pressing harder and harder down on her flesh"; and who "beat her up with anything he could lay his hands on" whenever a male child died or a female child was born (69). When she awakes, it is with prophetic clarity that all of this violence has had a tragic history: "She opened her mouth wide and started to scream and to wail in a continuous high-pitched lament, as though mourning the suffering of a whole lifetime suppressed in her body from the very first moment of her life when her father struck her mother on the head because she had not borne him the son he expected" (75).

But, for all of this, it is Zakeya who stands at the center of resistance to violence in this work, who insists in her own inscrutable way that the future can be different. Interestingly, this is a resistance that defies language. Poor villagers like Zakeya are illiterate, yet they know very well that language has power, dangerous power. They know the vulgarity and corruption that emanates from the idle talk of the Mayor and his garrulous sycophants. They know that once Elwau's name is spoken in connection to Nefissa, his fate is cast. Zakeya chooses silence, powerful and brooding silence, rather than speech. And Saadawi, refusing to put words in her mouth, refusing the cheap empathy of making up thoughts and words for a nonlinguistic majestic presence, leaves her in the shadow world, a world where smells are intense and intuition absolute.

Zakeya begins in shadow. She walks onto the set "gaunt, severe, bloodless" (1). Her pace is rhythmic, her look set, the thud of her hoe relentlessly steady. Returning from the field, she sits immobile at the entrance to her house, "her eyes staring into the darkness as though fixed on something" (4). Her one happiness comes from the remembered smell of her mother, a smell of dough and yeast, causing her face to soften for just a moment (5). But the mask rarely cracks. Her one living son has been taken from her to serve in the colonial army. She fears for her nieces. She sits and stares wordlessly at the Mayor's iron gates.

The novel begins and ends with Zakeya's silent presence. She cannot be the center of consciousness; that would require extended linguistic activity on her part. Rather, Saadawi lets the many voices of the village play into and around events that lead Zakeya to an awful climax that seems to have been waiting for her all along. Yet Zakeya's elemental power permeates the story such that mysterious, hidden forces (both demonic and transformational) shape empirical events. For example, although Elwau's name is more thought than spoken as a "suspect" in the violation of Nefissa, it spreads throughout the village in an instant of evil solidarity: children are found singing "Camel driver, camel driver / It's Nefissa and Elwau," even before the suggestion has become articulated idea. When Fatheya and her adopted child have been torn to pieces by the mob, her body cannot be lifted until the dead child is restored to her arms, at which point it becomes "light and easy to carry" (116). In the end, when the truth of the mayor's complicity in all of the violations of Zakeya's family become clear—the rapes of her nieces, the false arrest of her brother Kafrawi and her son Galal—it does so in an inscrutable and elusive fashion. Zakeya merely says, "It's Allah," and then with total deliberation brings her hoe down on the head of the God who has tyrannized her, the Mayor himself. He's dead in a single blow.

While the unctuous underlings babble on with their flattering nonsense (in this novel the palaver is that of quick-talking con men), Zakeya refuses all but the most necessary language. Instead, dreams and remembered sensations, many of them painful, form her conscious and unconscious awareness. And it is her eyes where this concentrated, prescient reality manifests itself. Zakeya's gaze and that of her nieces—perhaps angry, perhaps defiant, perhaps both, but always proud—confronts the powers that seek to crush and grind and manipulate them. This is their emphatic return of the power gaze (usually a male gaze) that is such an important part of resistance everywhere, but particularly poignant in a country where "looking women over" is a common form of intimidation and control.

African American cultural critic bell hooks supplies a cross-cultural understanding of this dynamic. Hooks remembers being punished as a child for staring confrontationally at grown-ups, which was a way of "talking back" through looks that defied authority. She comments that the "gaze" has always been political in her life as a Black woman in North America, for slaves could be severely punished for looking, and Blacks are still expected to lower their eyes in the presence of Whites in some places in the South. Yet just as she, as a child, stole rebellious glances, so she knows that the slaves looked and that there is power in looking (*Reel to Real* 197–98).

It was Michel Foucault who theorized the surveillant gaze as one of severe power in *Discipline and Punish* (1977). Where the dark dungeon used to be the ultimate instrument of control, he argues, now surveillance—full lighting and "panopticism"—keeps the people in line. From the Inquisition to the camera eye, we have institutionalized "ruthless curiosity." Yet as bell hooks rightly points out, there is play in the syntax of even this system, for "relations of power" always leave gaps where agency can be discovered and activated. There are "spaces of agency" for black people (and all colonized people) where they can not only "interrogate the gaze of the Other" but also gaze back (199).

Zakeya knows this on some profoundly intuitive level. So she sits across the street from the Mayor's iron gates and refuses to look away from the source of her pain and fear. In fact, Sheikh Hamzawi, in one of his self-aggrandizing confidences to the Mayor, says, "It's a well-known fact that the womenfolk in the Kafrawi family have their eyes wide open and are quite brazen, your highness" (17). On the day when they take her son into custody under false arrest, Zakeya's eyes stare "into the night with a terrible anger like the anger of some wild beast being hunted down" (134);

when she receives her "revelation" of the (un)true order of events, she becomes the hunter, and her eyes are wide open with fierce intention. As she executes the Mayor with her tool of her backbreaking labor, she does so with unblinking eyes. As for him, he looks "into her eyes, just once," and from that moment he is "destined never to see, or feel, or know anything more" (137). Zakeya does continue to see, however. Even after her arrest, her large black eyes are wide open, and in a flash of truth-seeing/truth-telling, she recognizes that she has killed God (the most controlling power of all) by the Nile.

Like Zakeya, Saadawi too has brought her weapon down on the head of corrupt powers, those who abuse the poor and disenfranchised through means designed to control and subordinate women. By writing such a novel she has both recognized and refuted such power; she has "opened the grammar" of surveillant politics. She has interrupted/disrupted the master('s) narrative. As Madhuchhanda Mitra comments on this story, linking language, silence, and look: "It is as though the institutions that control the villagers' lives have effectively silenced them, but cannot forcibly close their eyes" (147).

Yet the defiance that Saadawi represents here is more than mere reversal of gender and political hierarchies, it is beautifully complicated by the fact that as Zeinab and Zakeya's son Galal exchange a gaze of love and mutuality, the male gaze itself is rewritten: "When their eyes met he would feel his legs go weak under him . . . he would be seized with a strong desire to carry her away from under the watchful eyes to where he could close a door on her and hold her in his arms" (123). There is still the desire to enclose here, but the motive is protection from surveillance of an invasive sort, and the power is one of mutual desire. True, Zeinab and Galal are tragically separated in the end—he is in prison, she selling herself to stay alive—but for one brief moment, the power hierarchy is not only reversed, it is reconciled.

One could hardly accuse Nawal el Saadawi of being a romantic. The novel is stark, moving swiftly and without digression to an end written in the first line. There is no playful storytelling, no redeeming ritual exchange. Yet there is solidarity, trust in peasant intuition, and an odd celebration of the life of the senses. Like the narrator of Kincaid's *The Autobiography of My Mother* (1996), the protagonist of *God Dies by the Nile* seems to predate her own birth, knowing things that go way beyond the personal, perhaps by going so deeply into the personal that they cannot be spoken in ordinary discourse, but only in the universal discourse of the experiential, reactive body. Having the skill to make this private reality public, in this case, lies with a third-person narrator-author, who has the exquisite ability to love without pity and to tell the terrible truth with hope. In becoming the "voice of the voiceless," she (Saadawi) has both used and refused the violence of speech.

## State Violence, Ethnicity, and Latin American Women's Novels

### Julia Alvarez's *In the Time of the Butterflies*

State violence has a long history in Latin America, as we have already seen through the work of anthropologist Ximena Bunster-Burotto. Women are targeted by this violence both in their own right and as a means for extracting information from and coercing the loyalty of their male partners. Julia Alvarez's historical novel *In the Time of the Butterflies* (1994) looks at several aspects of gender violence through the assassination of three sisters in the Dominican Republic during the repressive regime of General Trujillo. The fourth sister, the survivor, narrates events leading up to their ambush and murder. As she and Alvarez collude with history on the intersecting stories of these already legendized Mirabel sisters, we discover diverse ways that women become implicated in politics. Minerva is the sister who loves political action for its own sake, who right from the beginning resents Trujillo's dictatorial powers and sets out to thwart his desires for absolute control. Patria enters the political arena through her role as mother. While attending a religious retreat, she is witness to military action that kills a young anti-regime guerrilla. As the life drains out of his body, and he merges in her imagination with her own stillborn son, Patria declares, "*I'm not going to sit back and watch my babies die, Lord, even if that's what You in Your great wisdom decide*" *(162)*. Maria Teresa, the youngest of the sisters, falls in love with a political activist and enters the movement as his partner. Regardless of differences in motivation, all three are judged to be dangerous by the regime.

In that Alvarez starts from historical personages, writes her novel in English, and reacts to the patriarchal tyranny of Latin American dictatorship, one would not expect to find immediate connections with the work of Nawal el Saadawi in *God Dies by the Nile*, yet there are a number of interesting intersections. The vulnerability of young women in the face of corrupt political powers, the need for young women to be accompanied and supported by other mothers, the shameful jockeying for power that takes place among male sycophants hoping to befriend important holders of office are all there in both works—as is the self-congratulating and ominous identification of dictatorship with deity in the thoughts and practice of ruler and subjects alike. Everyone knew the Mayor of Kahr el Teen ruled with the power of a god; the narrator and Zakeya know he died as a vile, power-hungry deity. Trujillo shares in this blasphemy.

Rafael Leonidas Trujillo Molina ruled the Dominican Republic from 1930 to 1960 when he was assassinated by jealous underlings. He held the country in his absolute power through legitimate means as president (1930–38 and 1942–52) and through a series of puppet presidents that he controlled as feudal lord. He centralized popular support by forcing virtually every man in the Republic to serve him in some way, by disseminating favors in an arbitrary manner, by charming and seducing countless young women, and by building a large cadre of secret informers that spread throughout the land. These agents were eventually charged with the murder of the Mirabel sisters. As John Barlow Martin, former U.S. ambassador to the Dominican Republic, comments:

> Except that it lacked an ideology, his was a true modern totalitarian state, complete with racism, espionage apparatus, torture chambers, and murder factories. Trujillo's spies, or informers, were everywhere. And fear was everywhere, a sickness on the land. (33)

For all of its "modernity," however, his rule had many things in common with colonial rule, including a distorted association with the divine. As Alvarez, whose father was forced to leave the Republic for anti-Trujillo activity, tells the tale, *Dios y Trujillo* (God and Trujillo) was common graffiti and chant during his regime. In a marvelous example of the manipulative power of language, she writes how his birth was described as a miracle in the schoolbooks: "God's glory made flesh in a miracle. Rafael Leonidas Trujillo has been born!" (24). The role of *el jefe's* assistant, Manuel de Moya, as observed through the cynical eye of Minerva, one of the sisters in *Butterflies*, is to convince young girls that bedding down with the "Benefactor of the Fatherland" is to "follow the example of the Virgincita" (94). Even to Maria Teresa, a Mirabel, but the youngest and most romantic, the President is like God in his surveillance watchfulness over the political and social "sins" of his subjects (39).

In Alvarez's fictional account, the most disturbing aspect of this popular identification is how it permeates the consciousness of the devout, even those critical of the regime. Patria is the perfect embodiment of this ideological conflation. When her sisters have been released from prison but her son, Nelson, and her husband, Pedrocito, are still being held, Patria, always faithful to the Catholic Church, finds herself unconsciously praying to the portrait of Trujillo required to be on display in each household. Unclear how she got started in such a bizarre practice, but knowing that she wants something important from *el jefe*, that he holds all the power and that "prayer [is] the only way I [know] to ask," she finds herself murmuring: "*Hear my cry, Jefe. Release my sisters and their husband and mine. But most especially, I beg you, oh Jefe, give me back my son. Take me instead, I'll be your sacrificial lamb*" (203). The injustice and gender violence here are unmistakable.

They are also inevitable. Patria is the religious sister, the one vulnerable to connections between God, Father, Fatherland, Priest, Patriarch. She comes close to worshipping her son and still asks her husband's permission to travel, even after she has joined the opposition, been to prison, and taken care of family business while he remains incarcerated. Deference is a kind of habit for her. But it is a distorting habit. If the devil can be "the devil even in a halo" (219), it is no wonder that Patria hears Trujillo's voice as "a godly voice" (226). This is a god who controls the inner life as well as the outer life, emotion as well as politics, and who ritualizes that control in spiteful and torturous ways.

Like Saadawi's Mayor, Trujillo lives behind iron gates and exercises iron will. His petty anger keeps everyone at a party long after they want to leave; his "razor-sharp smile" cuts questioners down to size; and always the suspicious listener, he "tortures meaning out of the words he hears" (99), using that meaning any way he chooses. Like the Mayor, he watches young women with greedy eyes—"Everybody knew that with each passing year the old goat liked them younger and younger" (223)—takes them at will, and "keeps his favorite of the moment" in a special mansion.

Yet the violence perpetuated by Trujillo and his henchmen is state violence, not merely local or personal violence, and has more likeness to the regime that imprisoned Saadawi herself, than the petty tyranny of her fictional Mayor. As state violence, it acts on many levels, and on men and women alike, but ultimately "feminizes" those it attacks. There is the violence of forced submission. All are required to attend and often participate in "patriotic" marches. Citizens are forced to write flattering letters to *el jefe* (120); Minerva is forced to praise him in public in order to get permission to attend law school; young men are forced to "join" the army (153).

At several points, state violence becomes a violation of human consciousness. Patria's religious loyalties are twisted and subverted. Minerva's memory of her father's death is obscured by the family's need to have a hero (179). At one point, Dede prefers madness to trying to think through the torturous arrests of her sisters (198).

The worst violation of all, however, may be the perpetual presence of fear. As Maria Teresa says from within prison: "The fear is the worse part. Every time I hear footsteps coming down the hall, or the clink of the key turning in the lock, I'm tempted to curl up in the corner like a hurt animal, whimpering, wanting to be safe" (227). Imagine the fate of a male prisoner who might admit to the same whimpering fear!

And that intimidation, of course, is what physical torture attempts to achieve. "Disappearances" disorient all citizens. Prison is a nightmare of noise pollution, abusive sexual language, deprivation, incessant interrogation, and torture intended to break the subject. Male politicals are tortured by threat to their female partners, and, in Maria Teresa and Leonardo's case, by the male partner watching his beloved being raped (254–56). Even mother church is raped while the priest looks on impotently: prostitutes are paid to desecrate communion (207), and the church is filled with human waste (208). All of this leads up to the actual murder of three of the Mirabel sisters as they return from visiting their husbands in prison and to the most insidious torture of all, telling the husbands about their wives' deaths: "This was going to be a special treat, by invitation only, a torture session of an unusual nature, giving the men the news" (309). What sheer diabolical pleasure to watch them whimper in grief! "God" gloats at his triumph.

But resistance forms here as well as in Saadawi's rural and prison contexts. When sent to prison, Minerva and Maria Teresa form surprising community with political and nonpolitical prisoners (thieves, prostitutes, murderers) alike (228). They sing the national anthem together, tell stories, organize classes in literacy and political education. The politicals refuse pardon as a protest against never being charged (pardoned for what?) (236), and refuse to eat as a protest against prison conditions. Minerva is known for her "crazy courage" in talking back and upholds the prisoner's "laws" at all times: "Never believe them. Never fear them. Never ask them anything" (234). When Maria Teresa loses control, Minerva crawls into bed to hold her (231) in a significant act of resistant other mothering.

Perhaps most surprising, it is Maria Teresa's journal that records the prison experience and becomes the actual naming of the wrongs; it is

Marie Teresa who "aborts" her baby rather than letting it be taken and given to some "childless general's wife" (240); it is Maria Teresa who endures rape with an electric rod and even comes to see forgiveness as a form of resistance (241). It is Maria Teresa who carries messages in the hair she is always combing and braiding, who takes the risk of befriending (co-mothering) a bisexual woman in jail for attempted murder, and who admits upon leaving prison that she "can't imagine the lonely privacy of living without [her cellmates]" (253).

Outside of prison there is both overt resistance and subtle everyday resistance as well—proof that the systems of power always leave room for hidden transcripts and creative assertions. While the *guardia* surrounds and spies on the Mirabel house, the women play endless jokes on the "secret" contingent, pouring the baby's bath water on their heads, repeating the nightly mantra "*Viva Trujillo!*" so often and in so many voices it becomes ludicrous (263). Caught in a compromising interview with an officer of the Guard, Patria offers to pray for him. When he asks why, she answers, "Because it's the only thing I have left to repay you with" (217). His knowing that Patria means this with all of her heart, and would die rather than offer sexual favors, only serves to increase the irony.

As always, the weaving together of stories offers a profound form of resistance—exposing the perverse entanglements of dictatorial power and celebrating its equally complicated erosion from below. By composing the novel as three inseparable accounts, joined together by the painful memories of the surviving sibling Dede, Alvarez resists any kind of unitary political consciousness. Militarism and its targeting of women has no simple causality, no single effect. Activists, mothers, lovers—all have their pain, their resistance, their way of participating in women's discourse.

Dede's narrative frames the story. She bears the burden of the survivor; she is the one who has had to articulate the story a thousand times to a thousand different audiences and interviewers; she is the one who has had to get it right. Yet for all of her familiarity with the facts and the interpretations given to facts, she still—like many Dominicans of a certain age—jumps when she hears gunshot sounds, even the slamming of a car door. Her articulation is always, to some degree, semiotic (motivated by desire), never completely symbolic (satisfyingly meaningful). So she controls it the best way possible. She uses third person (minimizing the subjective) and refuses to spare herself (or us) the hard truths of how she betrayed Minerva by burning her first lover's invitation to become a political renegade with him (83), of how she used her husband's *machismo* concern for women to protect her sisters, and of how she wanted to die with them rather than bear the martyrdom of survival (308). Her struggles with her own social and political cowardice—her inability to join the "butterflies" in their various quests for freedom and transformation—form the core of her credibility and join private agony to public debacle in such a way that the legend can never be fixed or complete. She is the embodiment of "writing beyond the text," articulating a present that questions the sacrifices of the past—"Was it for this, the sacrifice of the butterflies?" (318)—yet positing simultaneously that it is the sweetness of these deaths "that makes them burn" (320).

The three martyred sisters tell their portions of the tale (three sections each) in first person but with very different voices. Minerva's is a self-assured self-narrative. She knew from the time she encountered Sinita in boarding school and heard this girl child narrate Trujillo's secret (he was killing everyone, including Sinita's three uncles and brother), that the world as she knew it was a freak show and needed to be made right. When Trujillo spots her beauty and tries to seduce her at a state party, she refuses his language of conquest—"I'm afraid I'm not for conquest" (99)—and resorts to her own language of counterviolence, slapping his face when he thrusts his pelvis at her in a vulgar fashion.

Minerva has the most linear language. She eschews emotive language for the sake of categorical analysis, arguing with Maria Teresa in prison that sometimes you have to sacrifice friends for the sake of the larger cause, in this case, a helpful prison guard for the sake of exposing human rights abuses in prison. Maria Teresa, who has been through the worst torture, does not understand this kind of reductionist thinking. Neither does Minerva, ultimately. Leaving prison, she becomes depressed, confused, surprising herself by desiring life as a traditional wife and mother over political activism. Yet she tries, at all cost, to keep this problematic self-division from her husband Manola—"Outwardly, I was still his calm, courageous *companera*. Inside, the woman had got the upper hand" (267)—and is delighted when political necessity quells the alienating "demons" and sets her back on course. Yet the reader cannot help but love her for this break, for this proof that clarity of mission is not always enough, that public grammar has its private abyss where language and commitment come to doubt themselves.

Patria's first-person accounts are much more intimate in style and content. She talks obsessively about her life as an embodied creature—about her early sensualism (begging Minerva to brush her hair for the sheer pleasure of it), her sensuality with Pedro, the visceral pleasure of carrying her children before their births, and afterward, especially in times of their suffering. The visceral connection she experiences between the young guerrilla she watches die and her own son, born dead thirteen years before, resurrects an earlier conviction that her stillbirth enabled her to understand the pain of families whose loved ones were "taken" by that more erratic God Trujillo. Patria's thinking, no less persuasive than Minerva's, is centered in the maternal body. So we are not surprised at how she reaches out to the reader in intimate conversation: "You'd think there was nothing else but the private debates of my flesh and spirit going on, the way I've left out the rest of my life. Don't believe it!" (50), and later: "But Pedrito was still wanting to celebrate. *And you know him . . .*" (italics added, 150). When Patria invites the revolutionaries to come in from the yard and do their work in the security of her kitchen, two worlds merge, but it is important that the public-political enters the private-domestic space, rather than vice versa (167), and that she speaks of her house becoming the "motherhouse" for the cause.

Patria holds nothing at arms length—neither Pedro, nor children (in fact she often takes in the children of her sisters while they are on mission), nor God, nor political reality, nor reader. That all of us get somewhat entangled is no surprise or insult. This is the way new birth comes.

Maria Teresa almost seems to be the extension of that new birth. Born nine years after the other Mirabel girls, she records her account of things in a set of girlish, digressive diary accounts, complete with cartoon drawings. It appears to be babble at first, a kind of baby talk, language in the making. She accepts the given whether it is political fact, social expectation, or her own emotions. Minerva calls her her "petit bourgeois" (124) and she is that, following her sisters by course rather than self-reflective choice, and choosing to join the movement because Leandro/"Palomino" is beautiful and her instincts tell her to follow him.

Subsequent experience writes itself into her, until she is using her diary to sort through her feelings for Magdalena (her bisexual friend in prison), through the implications of Magdalena's story as an abused domestic, through her own reasons for refusing what Minerva says is a necessary castigation of the prison guards, and through her strong sense of solidarity with the women in prison. Maria Teresa did not join the movement for ideological reasons, or to protect her young, but because the world as she experienced it seemed to make such a choice right and satisfying. And we can trace that surprising consciousness (as surprising to her as to Minerva and us) in diary entries as candid as they are believed to be private.

Alvarez provides a collective portrait of female political consciousness that defies unitary voice/analysis in the name of political, gender, or literary theory. And the fact that November 25, the day of the Mirabel sisters' murder, is observed in many Latin American countries as an International Day Against Violence Towards Women, acknowledging all of the forms such violence can take, goes a long way toward validating such an honestly problematizing effort.

### Sisters to Alvarez

In 1982, Isabel Allende, cousin to the deposed progressive leader of Chile, Salvador Allende, wrote *House of the Spirits*, where she also weaves together political, gender, and family violence within the Latin American context. What begins as the rape of a peasant woman by her *patron* ends with the violent military torture and rape of the *patron*'s beloved granddaughter by no one less than the illegitimate offspring of that original rape. Gender violence appears to have escalated in intensity, political significance, and potential for damage by the time it reaches the granddaughter Alba, yet the work ends with an uncanny act of forgiveness on Alba's part—one that seems to anticipate Dede Mirabel's obsession with just how hope is supposed to take shape for the survivor in a climate of violence. (Is Alba a complete fool? Or are we facing reconciliation here that staggers the imagination?)

An even earlier precursor of Julia Alvarez, equally concerned about state and gender violence, but intrigued by the relationship of both to ethnic violence, is the Mexican writer Rosario Castellanos, daughter of privilege, born into a family from the landowning oligarchy of the southern state of Chiapas where most of the inhabitants were Mayan. When her family moved to Mexico City in 1941, as a result of land reforms initiated by President Cardenas, they moved out of overt privilege into prosaic middle-class life. But she never forgot the tensions of those early years where she forged intimate relationships with her Mayan nanny and her servant-companion Maria, but where she was also taught to treat young Maria as a toy and never questioned the injustice of her illiteracy (O'Connell 15).

In 1956, Castellanos moved back to Chiapas to serve in the Instituto Nacional Indigenista, working without pay and giving away the land she had inherited (21). Unlike others in the *indigenista* movement, however, she worked hard "to understand and represent how gender is at work in the deployment of difference and in the struggle between competing visions of national identity" (3). For this reason, Joanna O'Connell has entitled her 1995 book on Castellanos' work *Prospero's Daughter*. Like Miranda, Prospero's daughter in Shakespeare's play *The Tempest*, Castellanos is the offspring of the masters, the landowners, those "who hold the magic books" (1), yet as a female, she cannot occupy the center of power, and so forges alliances with the disenfranchised "natives." This is not to say that Castellanos promotes an easy identification of women's oppression with that of indigenous people, but that she is willing to explore intersections of gender and ethnic violence in resisting the political and social effects of colonialism. Ultimately, "what her fiction attempts is the reimagination of her society's 'conflictive heterogeneity'" (46) whereby all voices can be heard and respected.[13]

In this light, O'Connell refers to Castellanos' first novel *The Nine Guardians* (1957) as a palimpsest, a text that has been written on several times but where the older writing is still visible (86). The action takes place during the 1930s, when Cardenas had first instituted radical land reform, and tells the story of a young girl from a landowning family who struggles with the familial and political confusion swirling around her. The girl provides the center of consciousness for Parts 1 and 3 of the novel. Part 2 records many different narrative voices. But even when the young girl's point of view predominates, her voice is played off against the voices of all of those who instruct and form her world. This is both heteroglossic and linguistically hegemonic, for, although Mayan influence is felt in every part of the novel, and although few Mayas speak Spanish (in fact, it is considered arrogant for them to speak Spanish, the medium of commerce, education, law, and all other forms of privilege), the novel is invariably written in Spanish. Even where Mayan documents are used as fictional sources of collective memory, they have had to be transfigured into the master tongue. Thus, the violence of choosing a single narrative language renders ironic Castellanos' very attempt to "tell the whole story" about Mexican identity.

In *The Book of Lamentations* (1962), Castellanos looks at how distortions of power create distorted rebellions against power in the lives of both "Spanish" and Indian women. And ultimately she laments that there seems to be no mechanism by which the oppressed Mayan peasant and the "kept" Spanish woman might see that they share (aspects of) a fate. Hope is a long shot for Castellanos, who is intent on stressing the fact that as long as structures of power can keep their subjects isolated from one another, from sympathy with one another, attempts at resistance are bound to be short lived and fatal. One might say that all of her Chiapas fiction makes this point: "To acknowledge to each other their connection, the change they desire, [would mean] burning down the house" (O'Connell 171).

This is a hard truth, but pervasive. Truly addressing issues of violence against women entails dismantling the whole architecture of violent control over those identified as without and undeserving of power. In different cultures, the constellation of oppressive powers might look quite different, but the necessity of confronting them—anywhere—cannot be met without the free and empathetic exchange of violated persons. Although the *Platform for Action* and other human rights documents recognize this need for open exchange, while the Beijing Conference and NGO Forum modeled it to some degree, the storytellers, those who construct the multilayered, sometimes self-destructive, sometimes triumphant lives of particular persons, often make it a provocative reality. Writing (and reading) the intimate lives of persons renders their suffering palpable and oddly familiar.

Resisting imprisonment and torture (both material and metaphoric), post-colonial women writers are looking back, talking back, writing back, and fighting back against the misuse of systems of power, and, in the process, holding out to us, their readers, the possibility of surprising alliances between oppressed persons. Such alliances—ones hoped for, requiring work—could lead to the reconstruction of whole sets of assumptions about force, fear, and the right to live in a secure world.

## Other Novels to Consult for the Theme of Violence Against Women

*Destination Biafra* (1982) by Buchi Emecheta and *Never Again* (1975) by Flora Nwapa are both novels that deal with post-independence civil conflict in Nigeria and the ways in which women get caught by that violence. In *Destination Biafra*, a young woman is torn between traditional roles for women, her initial desire to join the army (until she is raped by fellow officers), and the cause of the rebel forces, who turn out to be as corrupt and violent as the Nigerian military. *Never Again* deals with the breakdown of national palava into empty political rhetoric and the search of women to find their role in a society devastated by seemingly meaningless war. Also dealing with the ravages of civil conflict on women and children is *Cracking India* (1991) by Bapsi Sidhwa where the religious-social-political chaos of persons living on the fault line between India and Pakistan at the time of separation is explored. *The Story of*

*Zahra* (1986) and *Beirut Blues* (1992) by Hanan al-Shaykh study the fates of two very different women caught in the conflict between Arab and and Israeli forces. Zahra is a self-conscious young woman who finds that all notions of women as objects are exacerbated in time of war, while Asmahan fights for her sanity in war-torn Beirut by writing letters, some of them addressed to the war itself. Saadawi's *Fall of the Imam* (1988) tells the age-old story of women killed by the men in power who have used them, whereas *Innocence of the Devil* (1996) narrates the abuse of women for the sake of male honor from inside an insane asylum. Bessie Head's *A Question of Power* (1973) also deals with madness, in this case resulting from a refugee woman's exposure to political, historical, and sexual violence. Emecheta's *Kehinde* (1994) explores the ravages of polygamy when it is pursued in secret and compromises the economic and personal security of the first wife. Other novels that explore this form of cultural violence include Mariama Ba's two novels, *So Long a Letter* (1981), in which a recently divorced woman "writes out" her anguished response to her husband's betrayal of her with a young wife, and *Scarlet Song* (1986), in which a "progressive" African male betrays his French wife for the sake of a self-serving liaison with a second African wife. Mahasweta Devi's collection of stories entitled *Imaginary Maps* (1995) explores violence against tribal peoples in India. "Douloti the Bountiful" is a moving and stark portrayal of prostitution as the economic and sexual enslavement of tribal women.

## Notes

1. These dramatic statistics are repeated and corroborated by Lori Heise in the World Bank Discussion Paper *Violence Against Women: The Hidden Health Burden* in a comparative chart of country findings (6–10).

2. According to Heise, women's groups in both industrialized and developing countries report that abuse within relationships tends to escalate over time (15). Alcoholism is often part of this scenario.

3. In most countries in Latin America and Asia, only forensic physicians can collect evidence on rape, and they are often located in cities where their offices are closed on weekends and evenings (Heise 32).

4. This is a conservative estimate. Neft and Levine report that there are close to two million prostitutes in India (160).

5. Human Rights Watch admits that there is no way to verify statistics of child prostitution absolutely, but they assert that there are clear indicators that the average age of Nepali girls recruited into the Indian sex trade is significantly lower than it was ten years ago. They report that a nine-year-old girl was discovered in one Bombay brothel (13).

Often the girls are recruited out of Katmandu carpet factories (24). Yet the practice of moving prostitutes from one area to another is varied and has a one-hundred-year-old history. The royal family of Nepal recruited concubines from the northern provinces as early as 1846. The opening of borders with India in the 1950s, along with the Indian demand for young uninfected prostitutes in the AIDS era, has furthered the trade and spread it to all castes and ethnic groups (6).

6. Clearly, sexual violence took place on both sides of the Bosnian and Rwandan struggles, but because the discussion here is of rape as military strategy, the use of violence against women as policy by Serbian and Hutu extremists is the issue.

7. In cultures with a conservative view of women, this kind of sexual abuse forces a woman to undergo "a rapid metamorphosis from madonna—'respectable woman and/or mother'—to whore" (Bunster-Burotto 158). Thus, the "cult of virility" (*machismo*) crushes the "cult of feminine spiritual superiority" (*marianismo*), and a woman's whole socialization is turned against her as shame.

8. As with domestic abuse, Morgan feels that this kind of cultural violence has become so common it escapes critical notice; "power *over*, as distinguished from power *to*, is now so enmeshed with world culture as to be thought human nature" (61).

9. Issues of the individual versus community and of the sovereignty of the home versus state culture inevitably enter here. In section I, paragraph 227, the *Platform for Action* recognizes that women have so often been relegated to the domestic sphere that they are unaware of their basic human rights and therefore make no claims for safety from violence, reproductive choice, and other self-affirming volitions. African American attorney Patricia Williams addresses the individual versus community issue by stating that Black women perceive rights-assertion as a matter of both individual freedom and solidarity, finding the self in relation to others (Dutt 9).

10. In an endorsement accompanying this document, Abdullahi An- Na'im, from the Emory University School of Law, says:

> The Manual provides the necessary conceptual and practical resources for human rights activists to confront the claims of cultural and contextual relativism, without attempting to evade or simplify the difficult issues raised by challenges to the universality of human rights, and the rights of women in particular, in Islamic societies.

11. As Marcus argues, a man's ability to rape a woman stems from how he positions himself in relation to her socially, rather than his supposedly superior musculature. Above all, he believes he is stronger than her, and that belief gets operationalized.

12. At one point, defending her piety, Bodour declares "'Woman lacks intelligence and religion.'" When asked if she is not a woman herself, she says an emphatic "'No!'" (Saadawi, *Memoirs* 132).

13. bell hooks speaks to complications of gender and race when she says:

> as long as the misguided assumption that patriarchal power compensates black males for the trauma of living in a white supremacist society and experiencing the trauma of perpetual racist assault is accepted without question, then the reproduction of sexist thinking and action will remain the norm in black life. (*Killing Rage* 94–95).

Castellanos studies the opposite—what happens when gender violence spawns racism in its victims?

# Chapter 6
▼▼▼▼▼▼▼▼▼

## *Pen and Paper: Son Preference, Colonial Models, and Education of the Girl Child*

> Why all said "Ah, only a girl!" to Alice Ogbanje Ojebeta and her husband Jeremy Nwabudike Emecheta when a little girl was born to them was understandable.... But the girl child did not die. Instead she started to raise hell.
> —Buchi Emecheta, *Head Above Water*

Nawal el Saadawi's first novel, *Memoirs of a Woman Doctor* (1958), written in her 20s, at a time when she had read no feminist literature or consciously engaged in the women's struggle, nonetheless captures a primal sense of disenfranchisement on the part of a young woman who, from girlhood, chafes under her brother's "natural" privilege. In the first pages of the story we find that his hair is short and free, hers long and bound. He leaves his bed in the morning as it is, she makes both her bed and his. He gobbles large pieces of meat and slurps his soup noisily, she must hide her longing for food and eat silently. He plays rough games and turns somersaults, she cannot allow her skirt to "ride as much as a centimeter" up her thighs. He expects an education, she must choose it against all odds.

About to dissect her first male cadaver as a medical student, she muses, "Why had my mother made all these tremendous distinctions between me and my brother, and portrayed man as a god whom I would have to serve in the kitchen all my life" (25)?

### Defining Son Preference

Section L: "The Girl Child" of the *Platform for Action* defines *son preference* in terms of socialization: "Girls are often treated as inferior and are socialized to put themselves last, thus undermining their self-esteem. Discrimination and neglect in childhood can initiate a lifelong downward spiral of deprivation and exclusion from the social mainstream" (paragraph 260). But more than self-esteem, discrimination can effect the very survival of the girl child. As paragraph 259 notes, son preference can result "in female infanticide and prenatal sex selection."

Other manifestations of son preference include gender imbalance in domestic and subsistence chores for children (paragraph 263); gender imbalance in the kinds of economic and political opportunities offered to young persons (paragraph 265); and discrimination against the girl child in terms of nutritional, physical, and mental health services (paragraph 266). Most important, as section B: "Education and Training of Women" points out, son preference can result in gross inequities in education. If education is to be construed as a human right, along with freedom from other forms of discrimination against women and girls (as argued in paragraph 267 of section L), then this inequity should be a major cause of concern worldwide.

According to the *Platform*, 60 percent of the children missing from primary school education are girls (paragraph 70); two-thirds of the world's illiterates are female (paragraph 70); young women drop out of school in higher numbers than their male counterparts to undertake heavy domestic work (paragraph 71); curricular and teaching materials remain gender-biased in many places in the world (paragraph 74); lack of gender awareness by educators at all levels undermines girls' and young women's self-esteem (paragraph 74), and female students are still concentrated in a limited number of fields (paragraph 76). Yet the authors of the *Platform* and most development experts consistently equate the education of girls and young women with major breakthroughs in the quality of life for all family members.

Education is certainly the "way out" for Saadawi's young protagonist in *Memoirs of a Woman Doctor*, but in unexpected ways. Early on in life she creates myths of power for herself: "I created an imaginary private world for myself in which I was a goddess and men were stupid, helpless creatures at my beck and call" (14). Out of these musings comes her decision to eschew early marriage—"I hated the word husband just as I hated the smell of the food we cooked" (14)—and to enter the faculty of medicine. Even if medicine conjures terrifying images for her of penetrating eyes peering out of steel-framed spectacles, she recognizes that it also inspires "respect, even veneration, in my mother and brother and father" (23). So she pursues the "god of science," with all of its frightening stereotypes, and becomes a practitioner, enjoying the vengeful power it affords her, and, only after much soul-searching and many regrettable physician–patient exchanges, learns to be a healer. What she has discovered is that merely being educated in a "man's field" is not enough; she must learn to shape that knowledge into a mode of thinking that allows her to perceive her patients (and herself) as whole persons.

There are no easy solutions to deeply ingrained prejudices, especially those which have taken on the aura of natural inclinations. And so it will never be enough to register young girls in school; the education they receive must respect their intelligence and diversity. As has been argued in each chapter of this study, rewriting myths of success and resistance is an essential part of making the world a habitable place for women and other disenfranchised persons. Storytellers and storywriters will always be part of that process, and, hopefully, myths of female empowerment will make it into the academic curriculum as well as the literary marketplace.

## How Son Preference Works

### Missing Girls

There are very few cultures in which daughters are actively preferred. A number of studies indicate that in the United States "females and males both think it is preferable to be male and to have male children" (Sohoni 18). More North American mothers suffer postpartum depression after giving birth to girls (18), and when a boy child dies, he is more intensely grieved (21). Such gender preference is hardly an isolated phenomenon: "Anthropological and sociological evidence from cultures and countries around the world corroborates a parental reluctance to have girls" (7).

The reasons for this preference are diverse and widespread, ranging from sons being perceived as economic social security, to the male child bearing the genetic imprint of the family line and the continuity of the family name. In Korea, "only a son can perform the crucial rites of ancestor worship" (22). Thus, giving birth to sons grants a woman increased status. The importance of social status can never be ignored. In radically male-centered cultures, the birth of a female child can so lessen the status of both parents, that suicide, separation, divorce, bigamy, abuse of the mother, and abandonment of the female child may result (23). Even the status of the midwife can be affected; in Bangladesh she may receive up to 66 percent more remuneration for a male child (22)!

Such intricate entanglements of economic and status factors, often exacerbated by poverty situations and state programs of population control, have led to alarming gender demographics in the last two decades. As early as 1991, the *New York Times* reported the findings of global economist Amartya Sen that more than 100 million females are missing around the world (Kristof). The 1995 UNDP *Human Development Report* and another UN-produced publication, *The World's Women 1995*, help to put such statistics into context. If no deliberate intervention takes place, there are from 93 to 96 female births for every 100 male births. But in that more males than females die at all ages, this discrepancy evens out by the time people are in their 20s or 30s, and, in that life expectancy is higher for females than for males, there should be more females than males in the later years. Yet, in India, the ratio of women to men has been below the norm for the last two decades, and although China, the Republic of Korea, and Pakistan were at the predicted ratio in 1982, they have been falling relatively rapidly ever since. Especially alarming are changes in birth rates.

*The World's Women 2000* reports that unnatural "imbalances in the reported sex ratio at birth might be explained by increased availability of technologies that facilitate sex-selective abortion, underreporting of female births and female infanticides" (6). Statistics from 1990 indicate that in one province in China, 1,006 female fetuses were aborted after 2,316 ultrasound tests. In this same year, China reported 36.2 million more males than females; for every 100 girls born that year 113.8 males were born. Although the government has ordered a stop to elective ultrasound tests, these procedures have proved far too lucrative for private physicians for the law to be effective (Sohoni 25).[1]

**Underfed Girls**

As one would expect, such prejudice at birth carries over into health care and nutrition. The UNDP *Report* records that in thirteen countries around the world, more girls than boys die at a young age, which reverses the normal trend. The writers of this report conclude that the cause is "discrimination against the girl child in the provision of health and nutrition" (35–36).[2] Studies conducted in Asia, Africa, and the Middle East indicate that more male children are immunized and treated in hospitals than females; girls are weaned earlier; and girls are often given a more diluted weaning diet (Sohoni 24). A mother may wean her daughter early hoping to become pregnant immediately with a boy. If a closely spaced second birth is male, this may increase the daughter's nutritional neglect (92). In many cultures, the fact that daughters eat after fathers and sons alone accounts for impaired nutrition.

One of the most devastating scenes in Saadawi's novel *Woman at Point Zero* (1973) is one where a hungry young Firdaus reaches out for a piece of food from her father's plate and is struck with a sharp blow:

> I was so hungry that I could not cry. I sat in front of him watching as he ate, my eyes following his hand from the moment his fingers plunged into the bowl until it rose into the air, and carried the food into his mouth. His mouth was like that of a camel, with a big opening and wide jaws. His upper jaw kept clamping down on his lower jaw with a loud grinding noise, and chewed through each morsel so thoroughly that we could hear his teeth striking against each other. His tongue kept rolling round and round in his mouth as though it also was chewing, darting out every now and then to lick off some particle of food that had stuck to his lips, or dropped on his chin. (19)

In this scene, the novelist has taken a cultural reality and made us experience its grotesque pain from the position of the girl child. But lest those of us who never (voluntarily) go to bed hungry or fail to feed our children enough feel safe from the impact of such deprivations, we have only to look at the statistics on anorexia and bulimia among young women of privilege to realize that food and gender are connected in many complicated ways. If young girls in poor populations go hungry in deference to their brothers and fathers, young girls in economic privilege deprive themselves of food in a paradoxical effort both to diminish themselves and to win the approval of fathers and "valued" brothers or other male peers.

There is not room here to consider all of the complications of eating disorders as practiced in the West, in traditional culture, and as part of the "nervous condition" of the post-colonial "native," as discussed by psychiatrist Frantz Fanon in *The Wretched of the Earth* (1968), but it may be worth commenting that as mothers in cultures all over the world are encouraged to be self-effacing, food is one of the concrete ways that their self-diminishment manifests itself. The mother passes on to her daughter, either through imbalanced disbursement of limited resources, or through notions of demure attractiveness, that the "good girl" does not consume food in a greedy, self-satisfying fashion. Taking the "smallest piece of chicken" may be a product of self-effacing motherhood, or gender hierarchy, or gratuitous dieting. The result is often the same—malnutrition, and psychological or physical death.

### Girl Brides

Not only are many girls absent from statistical accounts of population, adolescence as a stage of life is missing for many females, due to the desire of their families to marry them off at a young age. *The World's Women 2000* reports that although early marriage is declining "in three of five countries in Southern Asia and in 11 of 30 countries in sub-Saharan Africa, at least 30 per cent of young women ages 15 to 19 have been married" (23). The reasons given for early marriage of females include the need for early and uncomplicated bonding between the girl, her husband, and his family; assurance that the bride will be a virgin; and the desire of the bride's family to "hand over an economic liability."

In a 1997 article in the *Washington Post*, early marriage for girls in Ivory Coast was ascribed to the overall desire for social stability "cementing ties between clans and preventing promiscuity" (Buckley). As one father admitted, he preferred marriage to education for his daughters because educated girls "argue with their parents. They start asking questions. They want to have a say in everything in their life," and they don't marry until 19 or 20 (Buckley).

### Girls in School or Girls at Work

Part of the reason why girls are underrepresented in education and overrepresented in early marriage in many places in the world is that schooling costs money, families are poor, and educating a daughter is perceived to be a waste of money if she will be living and working in her husband's household and doing primarily domestic and subsistence work. *The World's Women 1995* records that the reasons rural parents give for keeping their daughters out of school include:

> fear of too much freedom, lack of a birth certificate . . . the need for girls' household or agricultural labour, a preference for investing limited resources in their sons' education with a view to parental support in old age (where daughters move out of their parents' household to become part of their husband's fam-

ily) and general control of women's wages by their husbands, better job prospects and wage rates for men, traditional stereotypes of women's roles and customary patrilineal inheritance systems. (89–91)

One of the ultimate ironies here is that study after study indicates that in many parts of the world "it is the woman's schooling that is the crucial factor in lifting her family out of poverty" (Neft and Levine 29). It enables her to find an income-producing job, encourages her to take better care of herself and her children, facilitates the education of her children, and often leads to the dissemination of knowledge among members of the community (29). Nonetheless, about two-thirds of all children who drop out of school in the first four years are females (Neft and Levine 33). And because their gender socialization begins before birth, many young girls have so internalized their parents' reasons for higher spending on boys' educations, that they drop out "naturally" and pick up the lion's share of domestic and subsistence chores for the family. Often, this is reinforced by curriculum materials where women are shown to be passive and retiring and men are depicted as managers and leaders.

Gender imbalance in home chores is almost universal. As *The World's Women 1995* reports, in southern Asia women and girls spend three to five more hours per week in subsistence work than men and boys, and twenty to thirty hours more per week in unpaid housework (108).[3] In Java girls spend 33 percent more hours per day in home and market work than boys. In Australia, sons do two-thirds the amount of unpaid household work that daughters do, and, in the United States, boys are more likely than girls to get paid for household work (Sohoni 27–28).

## Modes of Resistance

The more that the education of women is touted as a fairly inexpensive means to the improvement of families and communities, the more energy there should be for making sure that young girls are in school, that curriculum materials break gender stereotypes, that girls are encouraged to think about fields beyond teaching and health care, that boys are encouraged to share household chores, that girls marry later and plan their lives more intentionally. There is no news in this logic. But is it actually happening?

There are a number of international, national, and grassroots efforts to educate girls equitably worldwide (see Herz, Subbarao, Habib, Rainey;

Velis). Enrollment numbers at all levels indicate some level of success (*The World's Women 1995*, 92; *The World's Women 2000*, 86). UNESCO's Non-Formal Education Intervention in Nepal, which blends international interest and local commitment, is a notable initiative. Nepal is an interesting country in which to test a program for education of girls and women because 82 percent of Nepalese women are illiterate and girls are expected to participate in domestic labor and child care from an early age. Only 30 percent of school-age girls are, in fact, in school; in some districts it dips as low as 13 percent. Even when enrolled in school, Nepalese girls' attendance is 50 percent of that of their male counterparts (Leonard and Landers 176).

UNESCO's emphasis on literacy for adult women, using relevant materials, has produced good results—women can read letters from husbands working in other provinces, read newspapers, fill out applications for jobs, and, most important, fend for themselves and their children in many new ways (Reinhold 16). As a result, in several provinces they have initiated programs of shared child care—including early childhood education of female and male preschoolers alike—that frees school-age daughters to attend school (Leonard and Landers).

As part of the grassroots dynamic of this and many similar projects, women are sharing the stories of their lives, hardships, and aspirations with each other. What they are doing in these communities is what the writing community, at its best and most vulnerable, is also doing. In looking at how post-colonial women writers are dealing with the son preference and educational prejudices they grew up with, as well as their often painful experiences with colonial educational systems and the speculative freedoms that fiction offers them, we find that in novels many of these issues take on nuanced, tragic, and comic dimensions. Most important, in their compelling articulation of race, class, and gender bias and the modes of resistance it invites, female writers are proving the inescapable point that education is not only good for women, it is risky business for patriarchy.

Although issues relating to the education of girls, women (and sons) appear in the works of many writers, the two novels chosen for this chapter, because they seem to provide the most provocative accounts, are by African writers. They were written in English and reflect, for the most part, the perspective of a privileged middle class, but rather than erasing issues of difference, this perspective highlights the pluralistic nature of privilege and sheds a harsh interrogative light on educational outcomes.

## Exploring Son Preference:
## Tsitsi Dangarembga's *Nervous Conditions*

In her set of essays entitled *Writing and Being* (1995), Nadine Gordimer discusses the writer's imagination as a "looter among other people's lives" (1). It climbs into the attic or descends into the cellar to root around among chests of old papers (memories), old clothes (costumes)—artifacts from the whole variety of lives that make up a single life, which in its more tidy, unified appearance, is itself a gallant fiction. The mature writer loves differences, allowing them to *be* differences, without losing faith in contiguous voice and articulatable, if complex, identity. That means giving herself the freedom to explore human events, even historical events, from a variety of angles.

Using Primo Levi's idea of the *metamir*, a metaphysical mirror that "does not obey the law of optics but reproduces your image as it is seen by the person who stands before you," Gordimer further defines the speculative freedom that fiction allows. Standing before historical and personal events and personages, the writer observes (receives? creates?) "a set of intimations the individual does not present to the ordinary mirror of the world" (5). It is in entertaining these intimations that the writer enters the hidden dynamics of the place and the time she was born to. It is in stitching them together that she transforms history and experience.

In that Gordimer, a White South African, lived and wrote during and after the period of apartheid in South Africa, the act of imagining takes on both a personal and political significance for her. That she is a feminist further intensifies the venture. As she describes her life's work, "It was with my stories and novels, my offering of what I was learning about the life within me and around me, that I entered the commonality of my country" (132).

A desire to enter the commonality of gender politics, as well as national politics, may explain why Gordimer chose to explore son preference in a novel entitled *My Son's Story* (1990), by appropriating the narrative voice of an adolescent male. Crossing race, gender, and age lines to do this, Gordimer offers us a chance to explore what son preference and educational privilege look like to a son caught up in his own adolescent struggles. Moreover, she shows how a young male might become critically conscious of the many effects of his socialization. The narrator is a budding writer producing his first "novel," which falters between autobiography and fiction, moves ahead by fits and starts, but in the end, reflects a maturing consciousness that exceeds what he would have been able to know at the time of the narrated events. He is thinking beyond the events that make up his "published" account. Thus, we are led to believe that whatever his naive sense of privilege, the narrator is becoming increasingly complicated and self-editing with age and experience, especially in terms of gender. Adolescent views mix with postadolescent interpretations, arrogance with fear and epiphany.

In *Nervous Conditions* (1989), Tsitsi Dangarembga, a Black African writer from Zimbabwe, explores son preference through the adolescent experience of a young woman who is also "writing" from beyond the events she describes, but who has known, if not fully understood, the painful effects of gender difference from the very beginning of her life. Tambudzai introduces her story with the blunt statement, "I was not sorry when my brother died" (1), and she spends the next two hundred pages of her narrative explaining how such a statement can be possible.

As we find out, it is possible because her older brother unthinkingly assumed every privilege that came his way as first-born male—including the privilege of a first-rate education—and did all that he could to widen the gap between his way of life and that of his sisters and family. If he had been acting alone, out of selfish myopia, he might actually have been less frightening. But in that "he was doing no more than behave, perhaps extremely, in the expected manner" (12), as did Gordimer's male narrator, he represents a threat to an entire population of bright but thwarted "sisters." After all, in his exploitative attitude toward his sisters—making them carry his luggage from the bus stop when he returns from school, taunting them with the indisputable fact that he is the "natural" one to be educated, freely stealing Tambu's crop that she is saving for her own school fees—he is only reflecting the attitude of the world around him. He is, as Tambu must admit, "sincere in his bigotry" (49).

Her father too taunts her with her desire to learn. "'Can you cook books and feed them to your husband?'" (15), he asks, constantly reminding her what "women's work" is. The combined weight of her gender socialization(s) leads the reader to believe that Tambu's triumph over guilt is a hard and well-won release from misogynist and racist "general laws" (38, 115–16).

Tsitsi Dangarembga had her own troubled journey toward release. Leaving Rhodesia during the independence movement, she pursued a medical career in Britain, but recognizing that her homesickness was counterproductive, she returned to her homeland, soon to become Zimbabwe, to study psychology. There she wrote *Nervous Conditions*. But it had no title until she read Jean Paul Sartre's introduction to Frantz Fanon's *The Wretched of the Earth* and found the line: "The status of 'native' is a nervous condition introduced and maintained by the settler among colonized people with their consent" (17). In this book, Fanon, himself a psychiatrist, describes the physical symptoms of colonial distress and resistance, including anorexia and muscular dysfunctions. Like Dangarembga, he saw that the personal was deeply political, and in choosing this title, she has reinforced her own attempt to describe "a point of contact between individual psychology and colonial politics" (Sugnet 35).

But Dangarembga goes beyond Fanon in demonstrating that "woman," as well as "native" is not a natural category but a constructed one, and having been constructed and hierarchicalized, can be reconstructed. Therefore, her narrative style, like that of Nadine Gordimer in *My Son's Story*, revolves around an adolescent subject-in-process, in this case a rural African girl who has suffered multiple subordinations and has had to build her defenses slowly and haltingly out of "fragmentary realizations" (intimations) of her true worth and agency in the world (Sugnet 34). We watch her do this. In the end, when she has left her rural village, passed through mission school, and "graduated" to convent school, we hear her pronouncements on the future as ideas that have resulted from "a long and painful process . . . whose events [have] stretched over many years" (204). We are called to recognize that the text is not hermetic, process continues, and Tambu's interpretive reflections are ones that could only have taken shape after the events that seem to contain them. Dangarembga has created Tambu as the metaphysical mirror to her own life and the lives of many young women coming to personal-political consciousness during transitional times.

The novel, set in the 1960s in Rhodesia some 20 years before independence, focuses on two related families, one living in the rural area, keeping the family farm, and one living in town, headed by the family patriarch Babamukuru who, as an industrious first-born son, was given the privilege of a good education, including study in England from which he returned a prince in the eyes of the family. Babamukuru is head master of the mission school where Tambudzai's brother Nhamo is selected to attend. It is only when Nhamo dies of a fever at school that Tambu is allowed her chance. In an odd twist of fate, she becomes a surrogate "first born" and is given her brother's educational privilege, including the privilege of leaving the farm with all of its domestic and subsistence workload—a clear advantage for her, but a move that leaves her mother doubly burdened.

Another irony in Tambu's move toward liberation is that she is so grateful to her uncle for taking her to his school that she cannot see that his ways are as offensive and entrapping as those of the rural patriarchs. Babamukuru is forced to be the colonial "good boy," pleasing his White supporters, which also means ensuring his children behave with European manners and that his household presents European ideals of propriety, cleanliness, and hygiene. In this highly constructed world, women are secondary citizens, which means that Tambu lives in her aunt and uncle's home for several years before finding out that her baby-talking aunt has an earned master's degree.

This is not a tidy plot, and the nervous conditions of these assorted natives are many. Babamukuru's place in the colonial "chain of being" requires him to be groveling and pleasing to one group of persons and domineering to another. When his daughter, Nyasha, talks back, he has to control her, even if he respects her position: "'How can you go about disgracing me: Me! Like that! No, you cannot do it. I am respected at this mission'" (114). One power relationship requires another, meaning that his schizophrenia is endless. Babamukuru's wife, Maiguru, hides her resentment and boredom with acquiescent babble and cloying nurturance of children and husband. Tambu vacillates between wanting to go home to relive elements of her traditional childhood and dreading the return both because of how the farm is disintegrating and the incessant reminders she receives there of her mother's lack of options (she does not yet see that her aunt also lacks options). But perhaps the most notable nervous condition in the book is Babamukuru's daughter Nyasha's escalating anorexia.

Having been educated as a young child in England, Nyasha has lost most of the Shona language and a sense of African style. When she first appears in the family midst, she is wearing a ridiculously short Western dress and cannot speak their language. As this dividedness continues to shape her sense of homelessness, she talks and eats less and less. Finally, she is locked in her room, studying around the clock, vomiting after every meal, and becoming thinner and thinner. She cannot love and obey her Anglicized father, nor can she wholeheartedly embrace the rural traditions that ground most of her relatives (no matter how neurotic) in community.

But hers is not the only "eating disorder." Tambu's mother stops eating as a protest against her daughter leaving the farm for the same school where her son became sick and died (56–57) and, later on, as a protest against Tambu's further "removal" to convent school (184). At the family gathering during the Christmas holidays, special food is prepared for the patriarchs, whereas the others (mostly women and children) eat rotten meat. At the mission school, everyone is expected to eat with knife and fork as a sign of social achievement, rendering Tambu almost paralyzed with embarrassment at first (82).

But for all of this misery, the novel is more about modes of resistance than it is about diagnosis of illness. In the very beginning of her narration, Tambu tells us that her story will be about escape (her own and Aunt Lucia's), entrapment (her mother's and Maiguru's), and rebellion (Nyasha's). Some acts of resistance in the novel are active and physical. When Tambu finds that her brother is selling the mealies she has been growing to raise school fees, she physically attacks him at Sunday School (22). When Nyasha's father calls her a whore (after a minor flirtation) and tries to beat her, she fights back until the two of them are rolling on the floor (115). When Lucia is accused of whoring, she twists her sex-partner's ear in front of the whole family council and both physically and socially debases him (144). Even Maiguru runs away from home for a week and makes Babamukuru come after her (172–73).

Other forms of resistance are far more subtle. Lucia's escape from what is sure to be an abusive marriage and her return to school are as much matters of pragmatic planning as of her robust physical nature (Uwakheh 8). As for Nyasha, it seems reasonable to conjecture that her anorexia is as much a form of resistance to cultural pressure as it is self-destructive internalization of inferiority and smallness, especially because Tambu labels Nyasha the rebel. Nyasha is making it clear that she will swallow no more of Babamukuru's "borrowed" colonial rhetoric, no more of his self-righteous sermonizing. She will not eat what he places before her, expecting undying gratitude. In a mad frenzy she speaks fragmented truths about the colonial context of family agony: "Their history. Fucking liars. Their bloody lies. . . . They've trapped us" (201). And she forces the intensity of her disturbance on her parents until she is taken to an African psychiatrist and given appropriate care.

When Charles Sugnet speaks of the fact that both Tambu and Nyasha frame their resistance within a "third space" that avoids binary choices (obey or join the outlaws), he echoes Julia Kristeva's idea of the *chora*, the undifferentiated creative space within each person where language and reality are anticipated (annunciated). Nyasha is going back to the bare bones of her existence with her refusal to speak and her eating disorder; but will she be able to rise phoenix-like as a newly constructed African woman? Tambu seems to inhabit the *chora* space more gainfully, for the very narrative she produces is her construction of self.

In this process, she recognizes a world far more heteroglossic than one made up merely of Shona and English. It is a world where characters move back and forth between indigenous and colonial language (Nhamo will often answer in English if spoken to in Shona), but where Babamukuru's pretentious rhetoric, Maiguru's baby-talk, Nyasha's flippancy, and Tambu's father's groveling speech and eager imitation of the phrases of his family superiors are equally determinant of the world Tambudzai has to navigate.

The fact that she is reflecting on her navigations from a future vantage point adds a further linguistic tension to the novel, one between mature and immediate articulation. Speaking early on of how intensely she dislikes her brother, she admits that she "felt guilty about it" then, because a brother "ought to be liked." She judges herself in the moment as one who "must dislike him very much indeed!"(11)—an intensity for which she has fully forgiven herself by the time she writes the first sentence of the story. Chiding herself for her young admiration of all things belonging to Babamukura, in this case his home, she says, "had I been writing these things at the time that they happened, there would have been many references to 'palace' and 'mansion' and 'castle' in this section" (62). In writing about the White missionaries, she makes clear that, at the time of her attendance at the mission school, she totally bought the "official story" of their largesse, and, desiring "to admire and defer to all the superior people" she found at the mission, she liked the missionaries (103). Yet in a parallel passage, reflecting a far more complex point of view, Tambu informs us that she has subsequently been told "whether you are called an expatriate or a missionary depends on how and by whom you were recruited" (103).

The use of the familiar "you" in this passage echoes other places where Tambudzai directly taps into the reader's consciousness: "Nor am I apologizing for my callousness, as you may define it" (1); "You have met Anna" (85); "If you remember when I was at home" (110); "You will say again that I was callous" (195). But in the reference to "expatriates" and "missionaries," "you" has special power to arrest the eavesdropping first-world reader by reminding all outsiders (the been-to Dangarembga as well?) that one enters culture by invitation and that invitations are inevitably tainted by intention. When, in her ultimate "beyond the text" passage, Tambudzai reminds those of us who have just observed the embarrassingly private scene where Babamukuru engages in a fist fight with Nyasha (because she will not reinforce his sense of his power by mindlessly obeying him) that victimization is always political, is always related in some way to gender inequity, and exists every bit as much in our world as hers, the "you" is especially convicting:

> You had to admit that Nyasha had no tact. You had to admit she was altogether too volatile and strong-willed. You couldn't ignore the fact that she had no respect for Babamukuru when she ought to have had lots of it. But what I didn't like was the way all the conflicts came back to this question of femaleness. Femaleness as opposed and inferior to maleness. (116)

This outcry, drawing the reader into solidarity with the complexity of the issues described, leads the mature narrator into yet another examination of her early complicity with the sources of power. She admits that in the middle of this fierce quarrel between Nyasha and Babamukuru, she "took refuge in the image of the grateful poor female relative" (116), hardly a resistant role. Although she confesses that even at the time she was embarrassed by her "acquired insipidity," she remembers that she nonetheless satisfied herself with the belief that she was conserving her energy for greater battles while Nyasha was simply "burning herself out" (116).

But Tambudzai's construction and reconstruction of reality is as much a matter of retrieval, of going back into the past to look for clues of significance/signification as it is judgment of her previous mis-readings of experience (a process that will be endless). For example, in a beautifully lyrical passage, she recalls how she worked side by side with her grandmother in the garden during a period when she was earnestly trying to raise a small crop to bring in money for her school fees. Here, she is taking in family history—"the episodes of [her] grandmother's own portion of history strung together from beginning to end" (18)—along with the art of storytelling, which will make her own story possible (Phillips 102). It is her grandmother who refers to the colonial powers as "wizards" (18) and who opens up the idea for Tambu that all power has a kind of wizardry about it, drawing subjects in without their consent.

Tambudzai retrieves the painful pieces of her mother's life and of their relationship. Recognizing that in leaving home for the mission school (in taking the place of the privileged son), she is increasing the burden of "women's work" for her mother and sisters, Tambu nonetheless concludes that the "clean, well-groomed, genteel self" she wants to become could never have "survived, on the homestead" (58–59). Fearing the entrapment that has been her mother's lot, she turns her back on traditional life and becomes deeply embarrassed by the defense mechanisms her mother has assumed—her use of illness and self-starvation to get attention; her acceptance of gifts from Baba and Maiguru while cursing the wealth of the givers; most shameful to Tambu, her willingness to go through with a sham wedding to her husband of many years in order to bring "respectability" to the family.

Yet what Tambudzai eventually comes to see is that her own separation from family and home is not all that different from Nhamo's; that Maiguru's status is built on unctuous service to her husband/god and is no less entrapping than Tambu's mother's; and that for all of her fears of what these women represent, she loves them. At the end of her story, which is only the beginning after all, she can declare her love without retracting a single complicating factor.

Probably the most important retrieval Tambudzai undertakes in her narrative, however, is picking up the pieces of her friendship with Nyasha, trying desperately to understand their differences, without judgment (although, of course, that is impossible because she finds herself evaluating Nyasha at every turn in the road). Here, Dangarembga's method seems most to echo the belief of Helene Cixous that "writing is precisely working (in) the in-between, inspecting the process of the same and of the other without which nothing can live," and doing so by "an incessant process of exchange from one subject to another" ("The Laugh of the Medusa" 739).

Tambu remembers how disgusted she was by Nayasha's loss of voice, which appears to have happened to her while she was living in England: "I missed the bold, ebullient companion I had had who had gone to England but not returned from there" (51). She records how she could not understand why it was so hard for Nyasha to be grateful to Babamukuru and Maiguru for the privileges she received from them: "Nyasha had everything, should have been placid and content. My cousin was perplexing. She was not something you could dissect with reason" (96).

Yet mostly she remembers how a deep and abiding friendship grew up between the two of them in the palaverous "girl talk" that drew them into a place shared by no one else, a place somewhere between Nyasha's rebellion against the compromised world of the mission and Tambu's complicitous cooperation with what that world could do for her: "Looking back, I see that that is how our friendship began" (78). Their talk is long and involved, "full of guileless openings up and intricate lettings out and lettings in" (78). This relationship seems to a mature Tambudzai to have been her first love affair, one where she freely submitted to the more complex mind of her cousin. Nyasha could "pluck out the heart of the problem with her multi-dimensional mind and present it to me in ways that made sense" (151). Nyasha's intricate thinking was not the kind of intellectual puffery assumed by Tambu's brother Nhoma, but mind play that met story with story, that knew how to extend the search for solutions, that entered into a dialogic imagining.

For all of these reasons, their differences, described in the very first paragraph of the novel as those between rebellion and escape, are essential to Tambudzai's mature attempts to understand what went wrong. Despite Nyasha's wisdom, her rebellion seems to Tambu to have been tragically self-destructive. Nyasha's world became smaller and smaller—ultimately her room and her books—while she became fleshless and disembodied, until, wound tight, she erupted in rage, the ultimate bulimic purgation. Declaiming colonial power and its ability to make groveling fools out of her whole family, she ranted:

> "Why do they do it, Tambu," she hissed bitterly, her face contorting with rage, "to me and to you and to him [Babamukuru]? Do you see what they've done? They've taken us away. Lucia. Takesure. All of us. They've deprived you of you, him of him, ourselves of each other. We're groveling. Lucia for a job. Jeremiah for money. Daddy grovels to them [the English]. We grovel to him. . . . I won't grovel. O no, I won't. I'm not a good girl. I'm evil. I'm not a good girl." (200)

Protesting, "'I won't grovel, I won't die,'" she crouched "like a cat ready to spring."

Her rage is a distinctly anti-colonial rage; ironically then, a (White) psychiatrist says that she cannot really be ill, for Africans do not suffer in that way; she is merely "making a scene" (201). It is at this point that Tambudzai begins to understand the danger of her own complicity: "I was beginning to have a suspicion, no more than the seed of a suspicion, that I had been too eager to leave the homestead and embrace the 'Englishness' of the mission; and after that the more concentrated 'Englishness' of Sacred Heart" (203).

This suspicion that an "acquired insipidity" allowed her to preserve her energy and move ahead through the scholastic ranks, while Nyasha was consuming herself, has ultimately become Tambudzai's impulse to write, to explore, to enter the wilderness of a desire to understand and speak a language more inclusive, more complex, more compassionate than the borrowed phrases of parents, teachers, and been-to relatives. This language, seeded by Nyasha's babbling anguish, passionate in its rhythm

(Nyasha rocks as she speaks) and its fragmentary incantations, has become Tambudzai's "springboard for subversive thoughts," her anticipation of "a transformation of social and cultural structures" (Cixous, "Laugh" 736).

She ends her story where she began, in a particular "present." She has reached a station on the road to honest self-reflection and free speech; it has been a "long and painful process," yet there is far more to tell. This narrative is only a part; all articulation is only a part. But as Tambu has worked to shape this particular account of what she has seen and heard, her real power has come not so much from unmasking forms of domination that have circumscribed her life and the lives of women she loves, but even more from her increasing ability to interpret the ongoing effects of these systems of power and to discern the openings for change that exist within them. She has truly become the "mature writer" that Nadine Gordimer describes, one who loves differences, allowing them to be differences, without losing faith in contiguous voice and articulatable, if complex, identity. That Dangarembga has Tambu end her narrative by saying "this story is how it all began" (204) is our best clue that the process of liberation is unfolding before her.

## Son Preference and Been-to Privilege: Ama Ata Aidoo

If inequities in educational opportunity account for much of the stunting (physical and mental) of the girl child, and yet education remains the key to her liberation, it is worth looking at how the colonial venture, with its lure to Europe as well as its missionary schools, has complicated all of this. A number of novels deal with these phenomena: the importation of Western notions of the feminine, the exportation of native talent to Western universities and job markets. *Our Sister Killjoy* (1977) by Ghanaian novelist Ama Ata Aidoo is one of these. In this work, son preference is an analog for those who assume power and privilege, taking the son out of family per se, and seeing the destructive impact of "favorite sons" on their struggling compatriots and sisters.

*Our Sister Killjoy* has been called a dilemma tale, for it faces head-on the question of how an African woman can receive the best education possible without succumbing to either African male or Western notions of success. Acceptance of either has been called a "dangerous social habit" by critic Chimalum Nwankwo; for her, Africans who "accept an inferior status as a result of colonialism" and women who accept a passive status in the post-independence period are equally problematic (151). It is no surprise then that Ama Ata Aidoo should want to explore this particular dilemma, having been the minister of education in Ghana from 1981 to 1982 and believing that education is "the key to *everything*" (James 11). Yet, as her fiction indicates, using that key can be particularly tricky for women.

In an introduction to Ayi Kwei Armah's *The Beautiful Ones Are Not Yet Born* (1969), Aidoo has said that "in [Ghanaian] society, women themselves believe that only two types of their species suffer: the sterile—that is, those incapable of producing children—and the foolish. And by the foolish they refer to the type of woman who depends solely on her husband for subsistence" (Odamtten 9). Women have to be resourceful, wise, and strong to survive; Ghanaian tradition validates this strength. In an interview with Adeola James, Aidoo simply states, "If I write about strong women, it means I see them around" (12). So it is a painful irony for her to say in another breath that educated females in Ghana are some of the most insecure women in the country, insecure because having been exposed to Western-based education that presents images of womanhood "at variance with indigenous models," their identity has become confused (Odamtten 9–10). It is this confusion that she explores through Sissie, the blunt, opinionated protagonist of *Our Sister Killjoy: Or Reflections of a Black-Eyed Squint*, so named because Sissie's railing against the pretensions of her expatriate African "siblings," her insistence on looking at the world through a critical squint, makes her distinctly unpopular among the African crowd in London.

To write this "novel" (Aidoo would prefer to call it a fiction in four episodes), Aidoo has chosen "a defiant artistic form" (Nwankwo 155). It defies the distinction between poetry and prose, interspersing cryptic verse bits of the "hidden transcript" of Sissie's emerging political consciousness with prose narration of the "official" events in her life, and eventually adopts the letter format. It defies unified voice by mixing first- and third-person narration, in both the poetic and prose sections.

Sissie, a university student in Ghana, has been given the honor of participating in a summer volunteer program, gathering students from all over the world to engage in environmental and development projects. Her assignment is in Europe, where she is the only, and therefore remarkable, Black on her team. She is wined and dined by dignitaries before leaving home—after all she is a youth ambassador, sent to prove that Africans are educated, economically viable, and therefore capable of charity to the world.

In Europe, she develops a divided consciousness; seeing many things for the first time and taking them in much like any naive tourist would, she is also African, also other, also beginning to see that the world is politically-racially-sexually very complex and well worth the exercise of critical thinking and ironic representation. Critical commentary accompanies narrated events in the novel through poetic "asides." These asides are sometimes memory, sometimes direct commentary, sometimes bits of overheard conversation, sometimes political counterpoint that goes beyond Sissie's present awareness, but is very much part of the intellectual world she is coming to inhabit. In their spontaneity, wit, and irony, these asides imply a voice (or voices) speaking against fixed versions of reality. If Julia Kristeva is correct in saying "poetic language puts the speaking subject in crisis" ("Revolution in Poetic Language" 25), we can also assert that crisis demands the "play" of poetic language.

Critic Vincent Odamtten suggests that Aidoo, very much in tune with oral aspects of story, may be reincarnating the Bird of the Wayside narrator from her stage play *The Dilemma of a Ghost* (1965), to deliver these lines (119). The Bird of the Wayside, a marginal figure, does not worry about being offensive; furthermore, she represents both the immediacy of told story, and the distance of third-person reflection. At times, this "trickster" commentator seems to be holding open a critical place for Sissie, until Sissie is ready to assume it on her own, as she does at the end of Part 3 where she engages African expatriates in open debate, unmasking their excuses for staying in Europe. The merging of the Bird's consciousness with Sissie's is completed in Part 4, where Sissie, flying home, composes a letter to the lover she has left in London, explaining why she prefers Africa to romantic relationship at the present time. But while the Bird of the Wayside narrator seems to prefigure Sissie's emerging sensibility, it would be a mistake not to entertain the possibility that she also *is* Sissie (an explicit subject-in-process) all along. In this, Aidoo practices what Elaine Showalter calls the "double-voiced" discourse of women's writing that always contains a "dominant" and a "muted" story ("Feminist Criticism in the Wilderness" 473). Aidoo seems to allow for several of each.

In writing about this novel, Sara Chetin finds the multiple voicings totally in keeping with Aidoo's chosen focus on female education:

> A product of a Western education, the modern African woman writer creates a fragmented voice that reflects the alienated experiences of an African woman who is in search of a new language, a new way of conceptualizing these experiences that ultimately aim to synthesize the fragmented consciousness of an uprooted people. (146)

And it is clearly uprootedness that Sissie comes to lament and resist. She sees that education extracts a big price. One does not want to go back to the "glorious" days when "Tubercular illiterates / Drag yams out of the earth with / Bleeding hands" (56–57). Nor does she (Sissie or Bird of the Wayside, or both) think it is worth singing and dancing "Because some Africans made it" (57): "EDUCATION HAS BECOME TOO / EXPENSIVE. THE COUNTRY CANNOT / AFFORD IT FOR EVERYBODY," she laments, and asks, "Dear Lord, / So what can we do about / Children not going to school" (57). Son preference here has been rewritten as class (and urban) preference; the results are the same. Those left behind because unprivileged become the malnourished beasts of burden. This is what fires Sissie's call to professional, privileged Africans, the "favorite sons" of family, tribe, and Western professors, to go home and work. To stay in Europe, after all, is to stay in a place where son preference, privileged patriarchy, brought on the Holocaust. When Sissie's German friend Marija admits that since her son Adolf(!) is going to be an only child, she is very happy he is a boy, the poetic aside reads/says:

> Any good woman
> In her sense
> With her choices
> Would say the
> Same . . .
>
> For
> Here under the sun,
> Being a woman
> Has not
> Is not
> Cannot
> Never will be a
> Child's game . . .
>
> Beside, my sister,
> The ranks of the wretched are
> Full,
> Are full . . .
>
> And there is always
> SOUTH AFRICA
>   and
> RHODESIA,
> you see. (51)[4]

It is our privileged position to eavesdrop on Sissie's ruminations; we are let in on the intimate process of a young woman coming into consciousness and voice. We observe all of the complex ways that the "hidden transcript" of her desire to speak a convoluted and silenced set of truths undercuts the "official story" of her life, the latter provided both by an enlightened government policy that sends the best specimens of Ghanaian youth as showpieces to Europe, and by factual narration.

If all language emerges out of separation and our attempt to rebuild connecting links to the world and each other, Aidoo's protagonist is at a profound stage of "coming into speech." She is leaving the motherland, entering the world of privilege usually accorded to promising "sons of Africa," and learning to articulate the alienation of that process in such a way that her reattachment to Africa is lyrically possible. She is coming into a language of her own, one that can express her dismay at the cold logic of the expatriates she meets, without emulating their style of argument. She is a subject-in-process that takes us with her on the journey no less than Dangarembga's first-person narrator did.

Part 1, "Into a Bad Dream" is a sort of preface that sets up the "going," and in the spirit of a preface, written following the conclusion so that it might reflect the whole, appears to be narrated by the protagonist at a point far beyond the awareness she carried into the experience of exile. The narrator of this section seems not only to combine present and past experience, but to speak easily in both poetry and prose, and to reflect a collective consciousness—an internal–external consciousness—through the reiterated phrase "some of us." In this, it seems very like the short, intimate description of Sissie's return to Africa that makes up the postscript to Part 4.

Part 1 begins with a poetic invocation, that is also a kind of benediction: "Things are working out / toward their dazzling conclusions . . . / . . . so it is neither here nor there, / what ticky-tackies we have / saddled and surrounded ourselves with, / blocked our views, / cluttered our brain" (3–5). The first two lines appear on separate pages, suggesting there is no rush to fill space with words. In fact, there may be some fear associated with doing so, commitment to any telling (even retrospective) being inherently reductionist; thus a handful of words are surrounded by negative space, by, in Vincent Odamtten's terms, the "blank of whiteness" (120).

The rest of the novel will show us the ticky-tackies that this first section intimates, and the reader is warned that dangerous (male) moderates will try to silence the protagonist's emerging voice by informing her that "[her] problem is that [she is] too young. [She] must grow up" (6). Yes, but how? One suspects that no moderate would approve of the journey this particular young woman is about to take (has taken); he certainly would not approve of the nonlinear, multivoiced way that it is represented.

Sissie, called here by her nickname as well as "Our Sister" (sister to herself?) "enters" the narrative at a cocktail party given to send her off to Europe. She is the only "insignificant" guest. There is one other African, a man named Sammy, who laughs at all of the jokes; he is the quintessential "been-to" male who stayed abroad for a very long time and who makes "Our Sister" fidget in her chair. This is a restlessness she will feel many times in the course of her journey, because "time was to bring her many many Sammys" (9).

Leaving Africa in the "dead hours of the night" (10), she enters Europe feeling as if she is at the beginning of the world, an ameoba even, waiting to be. And for the first time, recoiling from both cat-calls of "Black girl" and the pig-pink of German coloring, she experiences the shock of racial difference. Yet we are also told that she is to feel the same sense of beginning years later in Kenya, and that for the rest of her life she will regret being "made to notice differences in human colouring" (13). We are led backward, as it were, into immediate events through three separately paged words, "Where, When, How" (14–16), at the end of Part 1.

In Part 2, "The Plums," the narration of events and the Bird of the Wayside poetic asides are in tension. The "double-voiced" discourse is exploratory here, immediate, naïve. We are taken into the first stage of Sissie's journey, where the dominant story is what she observes and the muted story is only beginning to take shape in her consciousness and language. The African "girl child" has here crossed over into the process of searching for a fully articulated self. Desire and meaning are at a generative crossroad; she is moving out of protected space (a cultural womb of sorts) and into a world of linguistic choice. For starters, she is a Ghanaian woman who speaks English in a country where German is the mother tongue!

The dissonance between dominant and muted stories begins at once. A young German woman, Marija, appears in the prose narrative, pushing her baby in a pram. She mistakes Sissie for an Indian, people with whom she has pleasant associations. But in a few short pages we are given a fierce set of poeticized commentaries that contradict this surface "niceness." We are reminded of the class and gender violence perpetuated by German feudal lords, living in picturesque castles (19), and we are called to sympathy for Indian "migrant birds" who, lacking sufficient "feathers," have dropped diaspora-like from the sky into alien territories:

> They
>     drop
> and
>     drop
> and
>     drop, over
> Many
> Seas and
> Lands,
> Until the
> Last wing
>     falls: and
> Skins bared to the
> Cold winds or
> Hot,
> Frozen or
> Scorched,
> We
> Die. (22–23)

Sissie thinks it quite abnormal that this young Hausfrau with a husband named Adolf, should like the Indians that work in her supermarket. But Sissie knows little of the history of Indian migration herself . . . yet. The set of asides here may well represent an emerging political consciousness that she is being driven to discover by the discomforting emotions she is experiencing; in the next section we find poetic musing on the associations between Indians, pre-Columbian South Americans, Eskimos, and other ethnic disparities. Her own experience of disparity and dislocation is causing Sissie to want to see a wider, more complicated picture. But she is only beginning to intuit its meaning. The Bird of the Wayside is prefiguring the shape that her mind and authentic speech will take.

    Meanwhile, Sissie speaks in the moment. She explains to Marija that "Sister" is a love name, used by people who like you very much, but that her being called "Sissie" is a result of being in school with many boys, all of whom treated her like a sister—not a totally positive remembrance. Thus, Aidoo has her act out a role in the official story of the events of her life, even as the hidden transcript of her reactions—

the poetic asides—take shape. Out of all of this "palava stew" emerges the Sissie that will be and the language she will use to declare that emerging self.

Most important, we have in Part 2 the beginning of Sissie's fierce stand on brain-drain, on the "privilege" that keeps so many Africans—most of them male, most of them favorite "sons"—in Europe. Memories of an Indian doctor living in Germany, memories of images of dire need conveyed by those travelling in Calcutta (gathered before or after the present moment?) appear in Bird of the Wayside reflections, leading to the all-important question: "Why did you not go back?" (30). Woven into a fairly straight account of the events of Sissie's stay in Germany—of her escalating relationship with Marija, of the uselessness of the work performed by the foreign volunteers—are her ruminations on a number of cultural disturbances related to "been-toism." There is the issue of standards of beauty, imposed from the West:

> If you want to believe the
> Brothers
> Telling
> You
> How Fat they
> Like their
> Women,
> Think of the
> Shapes of the ones they
> Marry
>
> How
> Thin
>
> How
> Stringy
> Thin. (47)

She reflects on the past greatness of a Ghana that now feeds on the "offal of the industrial world" and forces her sons to desert her (53). Acknowledging that "EDUCATION HAS BECOME TOO / EXPENSIVE. THE COUNTRY CANNOT / AFFORD IT FOR EVERYBODY" (57), she is led to accept and lament simultaneously the urgency for "Foreign 'Varsities' where / Honorary doctorate degrees / Come with Afternoon teas" (58) and to face the all too prevalent notion at home that "there is ecstasy / In dying from the hands of a / Brother / Who / Made / It" (59)!

She leaves the German setting in an unsettled state of mind. She is described as more curious than compassionate in the face of Marija's lonely pleading for one more meal together, and adopts distancing male behavior: "Sissie felt like a bastard. Not a bitch. A bastard. . . . It hit her like a stone, the knowledge that there is pleasure in hurting . . . an exclusive masculine delight that is exhilarating beyond all measure" (75–76). But in that this reflection comes in the voice of the prose narrator, we have to wonder whether it is the whole story of Sissie's response, or a description of her instantaneous and immature "write off" of powerful emotion. For following this comes a long poetic rumination on the power of empire to destroy place in which the speaker wonders if Munich, the home of "The Original Adolf of the pub-brawls / and mobsters who were looking for / a / Fuhrer" (81), can be separated from those Germans who elected him. This presents a much more sophisticated sense both of Marija's desire to connect with the "oppressed" African woman and Sissie's refusal of that complicity, but her rejection in this case is not without pity: "Ach. Munchen, / Marija, / Munich- / It is a pity, Marija, / But / Humans / Not places, / Make memories. / Nein?" (81). Sissie, the subject-in-process, is finding her way into complicated thinking and syntax.

Part 3, "From Our Sister Killjoy," is an interesting station on the journey. The take-charge narrator is still in place, telling what events look like in the moment, but she now speaks of "Our poor sister. So, fresh. So touchingly naïve then" (89), adopting a more intimate tone. The Bird of the Wayside commentator is also in place, recording an internal world of memory, emotional reaction, and thoughts-in-the making. The new development here is that the internal voice is less fragmented and focuses on issues surrounding a particular "privileged son" named Kunle. In addition, the epistolary form begins to take shape. Part 4 will be a single letter, but the title of Part 3 suggests that it too is focused communication. Moreover, Part 3 contains an imagined letter home from an anonymous first-person been-to:

> My dear brother,
> I have been to a cold strange land where dogs and cats eat better than many many children. . . .
> Where women who say they have no time to bear children and spoil their lives would sit for many hours and feed baby dogs delicate food with spoons, and make coats to cover the hairy animals from the same cloth they wear, as sister and

brother and friends in our village would do on festive occasions. (99)

It also contains an imagined letter from Kunle's mother, written in first person, but using both prose and poetic form, reflecting both external and internal consciousness, and containing both present and timeless reality (105–6). This is the letter that truly stings, the one with convicting power, one of "THOSE LETTERS FROM HOME! / Letters / For which we died expecting and / Which / Buried us when they came . . ." (104). In this letter, the mother tells her expatriate son the sad story of his small sister, who has just had her first menstruation and is already impregnated, and pleads with him that there are many jobs to be done at home. The mix of voices and pronouns is more than mere chaos here, it represents the anguished chaos of the mother's position and the creative chaos out of which Sissie's authentic voice will arise/is arising. When the narrator says that "Kunle, like so many of us, wished he had had the courage to be a coward enough to stay forever in England" (107), we have commentary that sounds very much like it emerged from the prefatory (concluding) part.

Sissie has tested her voice against the voices of her London-based compatriots, those enamored of the doctor in South Africa who performed the first heart transplant—putting the heart of a young Black man into a White chest—and she has become angry at their naiveté, at their worship of science at all cost. That anger, on behalf of "Little / Village / Girls" who cannot even dream of such miracles, makes her want to tell Kunle "that our hearts and other parts are more suitable for surgical experiments in aid of . . . health and longevity" (100). When Kunle dies in a car accident, his heart stays in his chest, "Stopping only when / The flames had / Swallowed it up" (107), and the British insurance policy he had purchased with such self-assurance brings in nothing. Sissie's coming to awareness and articulation of the complicated truth has its painful price—an obsession with irony—as well as its pleasure.

In Part 4, "A Love Letter," when Sissie has achieved a unified first-person voice (one of many she may eventually possess), she uses it to address all of her expatriate "brothers" through the one she loved and trusted the most. That this is called a love letter is not ironic. She argues carefully and well against African professionals burning out their "brawn and brains trying to prove" their worth and to earn a flicker "of recognition from those cold blue eyes" (130). At the same time, she admits that the man she writes to almost met her half way, has years of complex socialization to overcome, and at least wanted to call her by her proper name in place of the diminutive Sissie.

The narrator of events and Bird of the Wayside commentator would appear to have merged in Part 4, but the struggle with language is hardly over. In addressing "My Precious Something," Sissie laments that she must use a language that has enslaved her, necessitating that her words always come "shackled" (112). But it is hard to pin down the source of her distress. Is it speaking in English? Is it speaking in any grammatical system (always the fear that signification strangles primary emotion)? Is it fear of the sophisticated speech expected from any well-educated person? It may be all three; it is certainly the latter. She laments that she and the recipient of the letter do not share a private world; therefore they must speak in a public tongue, risking the listening presence of many others (including, of course, the eavesdropping reader of her story). Furthermore, the recipient has taken on enough Western notions and idiomatic ways for her to be unsure what he, and other African males educated abroad, are really asking of her: "it seems as if so much of the softness and meekness you and all the brothers expect of me and all the sisters is that which is really western. Some kind of hashed-up Victorian notions, hm?" (117).

Yet, for all of her distress, she writes herself out in a letter that could be sent or not, could become public or not. She rehearses all of the excuses given by her African brothers for staying in Europe, and ends with a simple plea for them to eschew an empty idea of privilege for one that endures: "So please come home, My Brother, Come to our people. They are the only ones who need to know how much we are worth" (130). In coming to this realization she has clearly found her own worth as one who has refused to pretend: "I should have been a different me. Then I could have pretended that the differences were not so terrible" (127). But they are. Recognition of difference is the only possible starting point for a cross-cultural, cross-gendered awareness, but, again, it has its pain as well as its pleasure.

Sissie's need to communicate satiated, a third-person narrator tells us that she settles back to watch that "crazy old continent" Africa come into view. For the moment she is at peace, the narrative voices are integrated, and even if the world waits outside "hungry as a tiger," she is better prepared to meet it than before.

## An Indian Postscript: Meena Alexander's *Nampally Road*

Meena Alexander's slim novel *Nampally Road* (1991) tells the follow-up story of an expatriate who has come home. Having gone to England to study in order to avoid arranged marriage, the all but universal fate of a young woman in India (30–31), Mira has studied Wordsworth, become a writer, and come back to Kerala to teach at a time of civil unrest. One of the first crises she faces is the realization that Wordsworth may have no relevance at all in the politically turbulent world she has entered. It's one thing to say that education is the key to everything, but only if the curriculum teaches students about their own lives and struggles. She is challenged by her students, by her leftist lover who has refused to leave India for education, by Rosamma, a female activist who has become as hard as any of her male counterparts, but mostly by Rameeza, a woman gang-raped by the police for no reason other than the fact that she was out late at night with her husband. (Her husband is killed to facilitate the rape.) Razeema has no political credentials, even though her abuse makes her a political icon, but she is a real human being who has suffered simply for being female.

If anyone helps Mira re-enter the post-colonial environment, it is Razeema. Her experience contains the ubiquity of undeserved suffering at the hands of gratuitous power. She cannot be abstracted. She has a name and a history, and perhaps a future. One suspects that Mira, the escapee from arranged marriage, the expert on Wordsworth, the lover who thinks more about her lover's safety than his politics, the writer with nothing to write about, has found her subject. Perhaps in remembering (retrieving) Razeema's story, she will find a way to shape a version of the future that frees women (and others) from dependency and constant fear. If she does so it will be her act of "pen-and-paper" resistance, her act of reconstructive nationalism.[5] If done well, it will, like all of the stories cited in this chapter, clear a space in reality for the telling of secrets about women's and girls' complex intelligence, voices, and value.

## Other Novels to Consult for the Themes of Son Preference and Education of the Girl Child

Son preference and stinting on the education of daughters appear as themes in Buchi Emecheta's "self-documentary" novel *Second Class Citizen* (1974), in which Adah's early struggle to get an education in the face of family deference to her younger brother is later transferred to expectations that she will serve her husband's educational and personal needs before her own or those of her children. Assumed privilege is also a theme in *The Joys of Motherhood* (1979), where Nnu Ego's bragging on and devotion to her sons, to the detriment of her daughters' education, is a blind hope that they will care for her in old age. Amaka's deliberate education of her daughters for economic independence is a refreshing counterpoint. In *Double Yoke* (1983), Emecheta uses a college-age male narrator to explore son preference "from the inside," much as Gordimer does in *My Son's Story*, while J. Nozipo Maraire from Zimbabwe depicts the problem of been-toism in *Zenzele: A Letter for My Daughter* (1996), in which a mother tries to warn her daughter about the blind side of educational privilege. Simi Bedford's *Yoruba Girl Dancing* (1991) also deals with an African girl trained in first-world schools, but with very little parental guidance, for her father has never gotten over his disappointment that his first child was not a son. In Flora Nwapa's novels of rural mothering, *Efuru* (1966) and *Idu* (1970), it is clear that although being childless is a terrible social stigma, being the mother of only daughters is a distinct problem as well, for both economic and social status reasons. Kamala Markandaya's *Nectar in a Sieve* (1954) likewise develops the theme of sons as hoped for economic security. But, once again, sons leave home to find success and the daughter proves faithful. Rosario Castellanos' *The Nine Guardians* (1957) takes as one of its central themes the death of the protagonist's brother, which is doubly mourned by the mother because he was the only son. The daughter is left to deal with her lack of guilt over her brother's death. *Eva Luna* (1987), by Isabel Allende, tells the story of a young orphan girl whose godmother reminds her that if only she were a boy she could go to school. But she is not. Therefore, she is put into service and must scratch out a life and an education for herself. She does so brilliantly!

## Notes

1. A chart on page 3 of *The World's Women 1995* gives comparative statistics for girls born per one hundred boys in selected Asian countries between 1982 and 1989. A similar chart on page 86 of *The World's Women 2000* indicates no change in 1993.

2. A chart on page 35 of the *Human Development Report 1995* gives comparative statistics on early death for boys and girls in selected countries from 1984 to 1990.

3. A chart on page 119 of *The World's Women 1995* gives comparative statistics on time use of children in rural areas in India and Nepal in 1990 and 1989, respectively.

4. One of the ways that gender conflict enters *Our Sister Killjoy* is through heterosexist bias that privileges male control over assumed female passivity. When Sissie realizes the full weight of the psychosexual element in her relationship with Marija, she has memories of a European missionary "destroyed" by nocturnal findings in a girls' dormitory and immedi-

ately wishes that "she was a boy. A man" (67). Then she might take control, and all would be well.

5. In *Women Writing in India* (1993), editors Susie Tharu and K. Lalita articulate the need for such reconstructive acts when they say:

> In distinct contrast to other critical efforts to define an ancient and timeless "Indian sensibility" to locate the "authentic Indian," our attempt here is to understand the nation and nationality not as an essence, but as a *historically constituted terrain,* changing and contested, and its citizen-subjects as subjects-in-struggle, and therefore also always "in process." (53)

# Chapter 7
▼▼▼▼▼▼▼▼▼

# *Feminization of Poverty: Economic Justice and Issues of Power*

> Who am I, a poor Chicanita from the sticks, to think I could write? How dared I even consider becoming a writer as I stooped over the tomato fields bending, bending under the hot sun, hands broadened and calloused, not fit to hold the quill, numbed into an animal stupor by the heat.
> —Gloria Anzaldua, "Speaking in Tongues"

In *Eva Luna*, Isabel Allende tells an old, old story. A poor peasant child, taken in and raised by missionaries, fails to respond to the call of the religious life and is put into domestic service. She has an illegitimate child, dies a bizarre death from a bone lodged in her throat, and so launches another poor girl child into the world. The appointed godmother, herself a house servant, takes a fatalistic approach to Eva's plight—"*If you were a boy,* you could go to school"—and sends her out to work for a cruel and parsimonious mistress. Fleeing abuse, Eva takes to the streets, finds work for a brief time in a brothel, and after a police raid on the red light district, turns into "a filthy urchin who rambled aimlessly by day, scavenging food, and by night took refuge in dark corners to wait out the curfew" (136). A friend later sums up her early life: "You were born a bastard with blood of every color in your veins, you never had a family, no one sent you to school or had you vaccinated or gave you vitamins" (266).

How many children are forced to live like this because their mothers are poor, without institutional protection, and of mixed or unacceptable race?

## The Platform for Action and Issues of Poverty

Section A: "Women and Poverty" of the *Platform for Action* tells us that more than one billion people worldwide live in "unacceptable conditions of poverty" (paragraph 47). Most of these persons live in developing countries; most of them are women and their dependent children. The *Platform* goes on to define *poverty* as a condition of life wherein lack of income and resources for a sustainable livelihood result in "hunger and malnutrition; ill health; limited or lack of access to education and other basic services; increasing morbidity and mortality from illness; homelessness and inadequate housing; unsafe environments; and social discrimination and exclusion" (paragraph 47). In addition to these immediate material manifestations, poverty is often accompanied by lack of participation in decision making, therefore subjecting the poor to formal and informal forms of servitude.

Paragraphs 48 and 50 of section A tell us that the number of women living in poverty has "increased disproportionately to the number of men" and that where whole households fall below the poverty line, women bear a disproportionate burden in that they must manage increasingly scarce household resources. Rural women fare the worst of all.

Causes for the "feminization of poverty" are listed as disparities in economic power-sharing, migration of labor that puts extra burdens on family structures, macroeconomic policies (including structural adjustment policies), and failure of development personnel to engage in gender analysis (paragraph 47). Paragraph 48 reminds us that countries undergoing economic transition often experience an increase in gender-based poverty, and that rigid or confused social structures contribute to women's poverty, no less than rigid or confused economic structures (paragraph 48). Finally, women's poverty is related to lack of economic opportunities for women—including lack of access to credit, land, and skills education—and to the failure of social welfare systems in more developed nations to respond to the specific needs of women (paragraphs 51, 52).

Calling for the democratic participation of women in economic decisionmaking at the micro- and macrolevels, section F: "Women and the Economy" outlines specific avenues of redress for the impoverishment of women. Women as "preferred workers" in many forms of factory-based production need to be encouraged to organize and bargain for fair wages and safe working conditions (paragraphs 151, 158). As women work more hours in income-producing work, they need to be relieved of some aspects of domestic and subsistence labor (paragraph 153). Gender analysis needs to accompany the reformation of financial and labor markets as well as structural adjustment policies (paragraphs 155, 160).[1] The workplace needs to become more family-friendly, including provisions for child care and flexible working hours (paragraph 161). And, last but far from least, women need to be hired for and promoted into managerial positions where they can contribute to and oversee the design of policies like the ones just listed (paragraph 162). Above all, the *Platform* acknowledges that participation of women (and other oppressed groups) in the articulation of their needs and in the design of policies to supply these needs is the bottom line for social reform.

To return to the story of Eva Luna, it is her articulation of multiple versions of reality, as well as myths of success and retribution, that gives Eva an edge in life. From her early days on the streets, she is recognized as a gifted storyteller, weaving together the causes of human suffering with plotted resistance. She amazes the prostitutes with her ability to reinvent the world. She amazes the Asian storekeeper who takes her in, the armed guerrilla who falls in love with her, the theater people who employ her, and even the general who tries not to be amazed. The silencing of her mother has become Eva's license to speak and to participate in the magic realism that provides both her escape from poverty and her participation in reform. Like Allende, she is a triumphant Scheherazade in the Latin context and makes us wonder what other "tellings" can teach us about the convoluted relationships of personal and economic worlds.

## An Expanded View of the Feminization of Poverty

If chapter 4 was about the naming of the mother and motherhood; if chapters 5 and 6 were about fighting the fearfulness and dependency demanded of women; this chapter is about naming the causes of women's/mothers' poverty and about resisting the dependency and fear it creates. Martha Chen leads off the discussion in *A Commitment to the World's Women* (1995), with a wonderfully compact and clear essay on "The Feminization of Poverty." As background, she reminds us that when the international women's movement was launched with the first global women's conference in Mexico City in 1975, participants generally shared the belief that continued economic growth in many parts of the world would lead to the betterment of women's conditions. By 1985, international recession had dispelled that optimistic notion and had demonstrated that issues of international debt, trade, and environmental degradation had particular consequences for women. In addition, changes within the family—"the migration of working spouses and companions, and high rates of desertion and divorce worldwide" (23)—were burdening women in whole new ways.

So although life expectancy, literacy rates, and political participation for women were on the increase, the absolute number of women living in poverty was increasing as well (23).

Thus, the UNDP *Human Development Report* for 1995 reveals that of the estimated 1.3 billion persons living in poverty, more than 70 percent are female, and that the number of rural women living in absolute poverty has increased by over 50 percent since 1975 (36). Furthermore, the writers report that the so-called developed world is hardly immune to these trends. Although approximately 40 percent of the poor in the United States were women in 1940, 60 percent were women in 1980 (36).[2]

**Female-Headed Households**

Clearly, these figures are linked to the increase in female-headed households. As Chen informs us, "Households headed by women alone have a higher risk of poverty than households headed by men and women together because they have fewer resident working members, more dependents, smaller landholdings, and inferior access to extension services, information, credit, and labour markets" (26). In *Half the World, Half a Chance* (1993), Julia Mosse reports that female-headed households make up 20 to 30 percent of households in the Caribbean and Central America, 27 percent in sub-Saharan Africa, 16 percent in North America, 11.7 percent in India, and can go as high as 90 percent in refugee populations (45).

The reasons given for this alarming increase include the migration of husbands (sometimes wives) looking for work; separation and divorce, which Judith Bruce in "The Economics of Motherhood" reports to be on the increase almost everywhere; separation as a result of natural and military disasters; and widowhood, which may also be connected to military conflict. Bruce reminds us that in some places in the world, widows are both social and economic pariahs. She cites the case of India where, in some areas, "a widow is seen as being the 'cause' of her husband's death and is treated as a 'stranger' by her deceased husband's family" (44). She also says that in cultures where polygamous marriages and multiple unions are allowed, much of the men's excess fertility occurs after they are 45, thus increasing the risk of fathers dying before the children in their second and third marriages have achieved maturity (45). Finally, she reports on how "nonconsensual sex" plays a role in the increase of female-headed households. In a study of adolescent single mothers in Seattle, Washington, it turned out that more than two-thirds had been sexually abused at some point in their lives; 44 percent had experienced forced intercourse. In

# Feminization of Poverty

another study in Kenya, nearly half of the girls who admitted to being sexually active reported "that their first intercourse was forced or that they were 'tricked' into it" (46).

As part of her analysis of changing family structures and women's poverty, Martha Chen concludes that "women are losing the few protections offered by traditional systems without gaining significant privileges and freedoms in the modern, capitalist structures that are supplanting them" (27). Responsible for their children and, in many cases, for providing food for the family at large, many women are forced into doing just about any work for cash—petty trading, repetitive factory work, domestic service, road construction, prostitution and "many other low-paid occupations in the 'informal' sector" (Mosse 38). As a result of working in temporary or part-time unskilled labor, women's wages in the nonagricultural sector are, on the average, only 75 percent of men's wages, and women are more vulnerable to layoffs and unemployment (UNDP *Report* 4, Neft and Levine 71).

### The Marginalization of Women's Work

Working at the margins of the market and of major development programs and projects, women often do not participate in assets such as "land, credit, seeds, livestock, technology and infrastructure" (UNDP *Report* 39). Where development initiatives allocate land ownership to men, rural women are particularly marginalized, especially if they are responsible for growing most of the family's food. The same lack of gender sensitivity applies to technology transfer. Mosse reports:

> [In Nepal] where women provide between two-thirds and all of the labour in many agricultural activities, and make many of the decisions about planting, use of fertilisers and so on, it was found that of all the agricultural advisors trained to work with villagers, only one was a woman, and she had been trained in home economics. (128)

Mosse further reports that in some places in Africa, where cash crops have been introduced to the male population, women find their labor appropriated to their husband's fields and are neither compensated for their labor nor given sufficient time to produce a surplus of subsistence crops to sell for their own and their children's needs (131).

When structural adjustment policies (SAPs) are put into place by international lending bodies, governments are often forced to reduce social spending (i.e., food subsidies, infrastructure, water supplies, education, safety-net programs) that increases the reproductive work of women— queuing for water, gathering fuel, procuring sufficient food, community organizing and health care, care for the aging (Mosse 121, UNDP *Report* 40). Not only is this reproductive work uncompensated, it often does not enter official systems of accounting, meaning that much of women's work is invisible to standard economic instruments used to measure growth and efficiency.

In a now classic article on the effect of structural adjustment policies on the deregulation and feminization of labor in free market zones ("Global Feminization through Flexible Labor"), Guy Standing points out that SAPs cause less social spending and an increase in privatization of manufacturing and export-led production. Although loss of social programs forces more laborers from the family into the labor market, privatization, and export-led production encourage an infusion of multinational corporations (seeking unskilled workers with good manual dexterity) into developing countries. Because women need income, are (because of domestic responsibilities) transient or temporary and therefore willing to accept low wages and poor conditions, and are unlikely to unionize, they become the "preferred workers" in many textile and electronics industries. These jobs are welcome in poor countries, but often present unhealthy work conditions, offer little skills education, and do not pay a living wage.

### Avenues for Change

Gender discrimination in the workplace prevails through lower wages for women, often a result of questionable segregation of skilled and unskilled labor; lack of job training and advancement for women; outright seclusion from certain fields (in Egypt women cannot serve in the judiciary, the police force, or the army); inadequate child-care facilities and flexible hours for working mothers; and lack of benefits that accompanies deregularization of labor and "preferred worker" status (Neft and Levine 54–68). What would it take to reverse such discrimination? Martha Chen suggests several things: a fair assessment of women's contribution to economic growth, taking stock of their paid and unpaid labor;[3] promotion of redistribution of wealth schemes such as gender-equal land reform, price and wage policies, subsidies, public investment in education and health care; and finally an expansion of economic opportunities for women in the formal sector and a loosening of credit markets for women's businesses. What might success in some of these initiatives look like?

## Micro-Credit

In terms of the expansion of credit, who has not heard of the Grameen Bank? *The World's Women 1995* reports that "many of the world's poor women are self-employed in micro-enterprises and small businesses" (118)—the kinds of enterprises that give them the flexibility they need. Using comparative analysis, *The World's Women 2000* reports that although one in ten economically active women in the developed world is self-employed, numbers rise to two in ten in Southern Asia and three in ten in sub-Saharan Africa (116). Often, such women have been at the mercy of informal moneylenders who give them funds to buy supplies on the short term and charge them exorbitant interest. In 1976, Dr. Muhammad Yunus, professor of economics at Chittagong University in Bangladesh began to investigate the needs of the poor surrounding his university and found that what they needed most was fair, reliable small loans. He began to supply them with such loans, distributed by his graduate students (Bornstein 44). Trying unsuccessfully to interest a local bank in the venture, he and his students founded the Grameen Bank in 1978 and soon moved toward a policy of lending primarily to poor women: "Women borrowers proved to be more disciplined and resourceful—their payments came in more regularly and the profits they earned benefited the entire family" (Counts xiv). *The World's Women 1995* verifies his findings that women direct more of their resources to children than do men, citing a representative case study in Côte d'Ivoire that revealed that "additional income under women's control led to increases in expenditures for food and large decreases in expenditures for alcohol" (129).

The Grameen philosophy demands that women borrow in a group and assume responsibility for one another's loans, thus seeking a middle ground between cooperative and individual enterprise (xii). Other micro-credit programs in other places in the world find group accountability culturally inappropriate, but the Grameen methodology has worked well in Bangladesh and, interestingly enough, in Chicago (Counts). Oxfam America reports success using the Grameen approach in a project in Bangladesh entitled Uttaran, which fosters gender equity at the village level along with economic growth. Lending money to both women's and men's groups, local directors of Uttaran encourage men and women to discuss their projects and problems openly in a village setting and to share domestic chores by way of giving both men and women time for their income-generating projects. Women have started a rice mill and a roof tile business, while tackling the freedom and rights of widows and outcast Hindus by including them in the organization of the work ("Community").

### Organization and Public Pressure

International news coverage of multinational "sweat shops" that employ thousands of young women in developing countries has brought the need for international regulation and organization of labor to the forefront, encouraging the partnering of labor unions in developed and developing countries and calling on the International Labor Organization to be proactive. A small but significant victory involves Asian textile factories in El Salvador, supplying the Gap and other U.S. merchant chain stores. Labor organizers brought an outspoken textile worker to a prominent Gap store in the New York area during the Christmas rush in 1995. Bob Herbert, an African American editorial writer from *The New York Times* laid the groundwork with op-ed pieces in October that gave Maria Julia Hernandez, head of Tutela Legal, a human rights organization in El Salvador, an opportunity to share her office's findings of abuse. Gap heard, and agreed to allow international monitors into all of its Central American subsidiaries. Gap compliance was a small victory, to be sure, but one demonstrating what can happen when justice issues cross national, racial, and gender lines and when personal story infuses the public-consumer consciousness.

Another U.S. writer-activist working for public consciousness is Kathryn Edin, sociology professor at the University of Pennsylvania, who has set out to reform our notions of the welfare mother specifically, and single mothers in general. In a book written with Laura Lein, *Making Ends Meet* (1997), Edin documents the difficulty of any single mother getting off the welfare rolls when the only jobs available to her do not pay a living wage and when she risks losing rent and transportation subsidies, as well as child-care and health care benefits. The system "requires" women to cheat, Edin argues, to accept under-the-table pay from unreported work and unregistered "gifts" from fathers, boyfriends, and family members. But cheating can also be a form of resistance, she argues, the "hidden transcript" of poor mothers' determination to "make ends meet."

Denying the "culture of poverty" explanation for why so many single mothers fall into the welfare trap, Edin claims that poor neighborhoods with poor single mothers often breed efficiency and survival through the exchange of money-saving techniques that "equip [mothers] to make do with less and avoid serious material hardship" (210), as well as allowing them more time to be with their children.[4] This kind of resistance fights discrimination by fighting stereotypes about poverty and single mothers. Collecting some 300 portraits of poor mothers has allowed Edin and Lein to put a human face on statistics and to illustrate that statistics alone have a dangerous reductionist effect. Their work is a wonderful complement and companion to what certain novelists have been doing all along.

## Buchi Emecheta: Exile in the City

In her powerful autobiography *Head Above Water*, published in 1986 after most of her novels, Buchi Emecheta shares her personal experience of being a single mother on welfare. Journeying from Lagos to London at age eighteen with two small children in tow to join her husband Sylvester, Emecheta is shocked by the gray dreariness of her place of debarkation, Liverpool. Her internal dreariness does not dissipate for some time, for she has three more children in close succession (five all told before the age of 22!) and realizes simultaneously that Sylvester is neither going to get a serious job nor become a serious student. She begins to write to "save" herself, both materially and psychologically. But when her husband burns the draft of her first novel, *The Bride Price*, out of seemingly deep discomfort with her ability to articulate the vulnerability and cultural confinement of Nigerian women of marriageable age, she knows she has to separate from him, in resistance to these very conventions.

When friends try to reunite them at a family wedding, arguing that Sylvester has been no more lazy and violent than other Nigerian men, she is kind, but refuses. Meanwhile, she writes her "self-documenting" novels *In the Ditch* (1972), and *Second-Class Citizen* (1974), which boldly expose the patriarchal legacy of Nigerian marriage and of the British Welfare State simultaneously. She has no desire to resume the protected role preserved for her in traditional culture nor to fall into the state-dependent status of the single mother, trying to survive in the colonial "motherland." Yet mother she is—to her five children, the young people she encounters in her role as social worker, fellow graduate students at the university, and characters in her books that have a multiplicity of problems with the prescribed reproductive role for women.

### *In the Ditch*

Chronologically, *In the Ditch*, Emecheta's first published novel, deals with events that succeed *Second-Class Citizen*, but provides a more pointed study of urban poverty. The protagonist Adah, a young Nigerian woman with five children, is on her own in London. When we first meet her, she is facing off against a large rat in substandard housing and having to deal with a Nigerian landlord who, to get her and her children out of his house, has switched off their electricity and resorted to practicing a bizarre form of "juju," while their Irish neighbor looks on amazed. Adah, in anger and wry humor, contemplates the uselessness of his gesture: "No, the juju trick would not work in England, it was out of place, on alien ground. God dammit, juju, in England you're surrounded by walls of unbelief!" (4). In a few short pages, the reader is plunged into a world where gender, ethnic, and class differences provide a rich palaverous discourse.

This is a world of poverty and forced dependence, where identities, both personal and political, keep shifting according to fragile circumstances, and differences are filtered through desperate need. It is a world of "outlaws," of persons who live on the edge of subsistence, who live below the amenities of London culture, who occupy the wild zone where witchery is not unthinkable. It is the world of desperate women: single mothers and women trying to hold onto partners while they run the gauntlet of welfare services in a depersonalized urban setting.

Helene Cixous describes such an arena as that of the "unorganizable feminine," where reality is named with the "loving precision of poetic naming" rather than the "repressive censorship of philosophical nomination/conceptualization" ("Castration or Decapitation?" 488). Emecheta taps into the energy of this world by articulating the convoluted experiences of Adah and the women she comes to befriend, as they seek to keep a complex self-hood in the face of bureaucratic reductionism and are forced to face the multiple differences that exist between them. Thus, Emecheta becomes an authorial outlaw practicing "vitalization of the other, of otherness in its entirety" (487). And she does this with the fierceness of the protective mother, the insight of the dark outsider, and the power of the political resistor.

Shortly after the juju incident, Adah gets word that the City Council has found her a new apartment at the infamous "Pussy Cat Mansions," where welfare mothers go to contend with each other, halls smelling of garbage and urine, and incessant green mold that grows on the kitchen cabinets.[5] Most of the other tenants are on the dole; Adah fights such dependency, even though she is receiving no support from her children's father who has soundly renounced them all in court. But she is eventually forced to succumb. When she is told that she is endangering her children by leaving them alone in the "school sheds" because she has to deliver them early in order to get to her job, she realizes that she must swallow her pride and accept help. So she, too, enters the labyrinthine world of social case workers, inadequate stipends, racial prejudice against her "type," paraffin heaters that are cheap to run but start fires, angry neighbors as humiliated as herself, and, eventually, partnerships (risky solidarities) that take shape among the inhabitants, in spite of themselves.

Adah describes herself as one who has fallen "in the ditch" of poverty and state charity, a place where one has to look poor to get services, realize that ends will not meet without strategic cheating, and admit that the neighbors she wants to avoid may be her best support. The many points of view contained within this third-person narration are beautifully contradictory. Adah is clearly the center of consciousness, but sometimes she is naive and untutored about the workings of British bureaucracy; sometimes she is strategically savvy. Sometimes she appears saintly: "Carol sensed she was dealing with a woman who would give everything for her children" (28). Sometimes she comes across as offensively touchy: "People in Adah's position are usually on the defensive all the time. Even when shown kindness or politeness, they usually don't know what to do with it. Instead they grow suspicious and remote" (25). As the novel makes clear, Adah is navigating a whole new world for herself—culturally, racially, economically, relationally—and we enter her multiple reactions to this world (even as she remains a discrete "she").

One of the early examples of this shifting consciousness occurs when Adah's "Family Adviser" (caseworker) pays her first visit. Adah is getting dinner for her five children and, assuming the visitor is a Jehovah's Witness, grumbles her way to the door, only to meet a cooing White woman, "large, fleshy and hippy, like a rich African mammy after a session in fattening room" (24). Before anything can be said, class, race, and bureaucratic tensions are in the room.

Adah doesn't know whether to nod or shake hands, and her mind races to the inevitable: *"She's come to tell me something nasty"* (24). But the woman is politely professional, if condescending—in Adah's mind "one of a race of women whom one was never sure whether to treat as friends or as members of the social police" (25). She repeats the complaint that Adah's children make too much noise and should not be left alone so often; after all, London is not Africa where doors are left open and children can be watched from the kitchen. But before the woman gets to this "business," she urges Adah to call her "Carol" in the same breath that she says "'I see you are a Ghanaian'" (25). Adah snaps her rebuttal, "I am not Ghanaian," and the narrative point of view shifts abruptly to the defensiveness described above. No consciousness remains singular in this scene, not that of the characters, or the narrator, or the reader. We all enter into the multiple ways that difference is negotiated. When Carol tries to correct her mistake by telling how much she loved visiting Lagos, Adah inwardly recoils at how many outsiders claim to know all about Lagos and, of course, all about her before she's confided anything!

Adah's defensiveness continues past Carol's offer of help in the evenings so that she can continue to go to school, not because she does not welcome help but because of the inevitable compromise involved: "Adah would have to swallow her pride as a woman, her dignity as a mother, and let Carol help her" (28). When help arrives—young students serving with a social task force—Adah is deeply grateful but uneasy in their presence. She nearly weeps at how they have cleaned the apartment and cared for the children, but wonders why their efficiency should intimidate her in the confines of her own house and scolds them for not taking the tea she has left for them. Emecheta creates a "feminine textual body" that spares none of the ambiguities of the Nigerian mother living on the edge of a state to which she must feel grateful but where she will never feel fully welcome.

For Adah, it is almost impossible to separate welfare from a patronizing colonialism. The cloying parental attitude of the most well meaning of caseworkers is ominously reminiscent of a sanctimonious British acceptance of the "White man's burden." So for all of her newness to the welfare system, it isn't really new at all. Near the end of the novel, she finds a way to think about the connection, and thereby recognizes her need to separate from her caseworker's care in a strategic fashion:

> But she would still like to be on friendly terms with Carol. She had been spoonfed for so long that she could not cut off from Carol and the Children's Department just like that. The position she was in reminded her of young nations seeking independence. When they got their independence, they found that it was a dangerous toy. She would eat her cake and have it. She would support the move, but must be friendly with "them." (95)

In the course of this novel, Adah experiences all of the disorientation of the cultural and economic exile. She wants to tell her co-tenants that she went to a colonial school with standards equal to the best British girls' schools (21), but is ultimately too self-doubting to make such a move: "She was always frightened that her real self was not good enough for the public. She would gladly play any role expected of her for the sake of peace" (75–76). Being on the dole makes her doubt everything about who she is and what she is worth. But, gradually she begins to realize that the women who live in Pussy Cat Mansions have developed a communal way of life that is much more like her own Nigerian traditions than the individualistic lifestyle of the British culture at large. And she revels in that familiarity: "As a sort of community had worked itself into being, everybody knew the business of everybody else. That sort of life suited her. There was always a friend to run to in time of trouble" (88). But ultimately there are no easy resting places for Adah. Communal poverty is, in ways, as much a prison as the paternal welfare system. As Chikwenye Ogunyemi describes the dilemma: "What helps Adah survive the prison-camp atmosphere of Pussy Cat Mansions is female bonding, which unfortunately also binds and prevents her from moving on" (236).

She is afraid to move beyond the familiar, and is one of the last inhabitants to accept a resettlement when the termination of Pussy Cat Mansions as Council housing is announced. In the process of coming to grips with that fear, she learns a great deal about identity politics (what is a "problem family" after all?) and learns to fight back against her own lethargy: "The world had a habit of accepting the way you rated yourself. The last place in which she was going to incarcerate herself was in the ditch" (127). Ironically, a good part of this resistance comes out of Adah's complicated relationship with her social advisor, Carol.

When the residents of Pussy Cat Mansions act out their own separation anxiety by holding a meeting where they castigate Carol for her encouragement of their dependency while lumping them all together as "problem families," Adah, who is studying sociology, and who has enjoyed several professional conversations with Carol, sets them straight. Knowing full well the danger of reductive labels, she gives them the "classical" (inclusive) definition of problem families; but rather than finding this clarifying, the crowd turns on Adah for her learning and her racial difference (98–99). Having now been identified as one of Carol's favorites, Adah must face the fact that she has done Carol, as well as herself, a great disservice by this inappropriate outburst of "learning," and she must admit that her scapegoating has come as much from her assumed superiority as from her race. No distinctions are easily made; all are problematized by personal and political factors.

So Adah learns how to articulate herself by means of a wildly heteroglossic set of inner and outer voices, requiring an almost exhausting honesty. When an old woman dies alone in one of the Mansion apartments, Adah silently prays, "*O, God, let me die in my country when my time comes. At least there'll be people to hold my hand*" (117). Almost immediately she remembers people who died terrified and running in Nigeria during the

Biafran War: "There was no safety anywhere, really. One never knew" (117).

In "The Laugh of the Medusa," Cixous describes the kind of thinking and writing that creates such a character as undoing "the unifying, regulating history that homogenizes and channels forces, herding contradictions into a single battlefield" (738). This "undoing" takes a certain kind of linguistic shenanigans, a certain kind of "signifying" at the edges of laws and institutions—a spending of energy to unpack hidden stores of personal and cultural pride. When Adah pretends not to know English, "shaking her head like a toothless baby," in order to avoid the tedious futility of explaining to the Housing Department clerk why she doesn't want a particular apartment, we laugh at and admire her trickster tactics.

In writing this second manuscript (the first having been burned by her husband), Emecheta has learned to wield the linguistic audacity that would make her a novelist, writing her way out of obscurity and exilic loneliness. Poverty and fear of dependency seem to have taught both her and her protagonist how to talk back, how to avoid the place "reserved for the guilty (guilty of everything, guilty at every turn: for having desires, for not having any . . . for being too motherly and not enough; for having children and for not having any)" (Cixous 737).

Ogunyemi refers this signifying power back to the original palaver, that between colonial officialdom and the Black subjects they were trying to manipulate and diminish. A Black woman like Adah learning to navigate through and "speak to" the social bureaucracy in London, a Black writer like Emecheta learning to navigate through and "speak to" the publishing industry in England—these are major reversals, major renunciations and affirmations, all stemming from a refusal to accept racial and gender inferiority: "[They demonstrate] that, with the will to power, a black woman can escape the deadly claws of white bureaucracy" (234). Thus, they escape the worst ravages of their poverty. Kathryn Edin's welfare mothers, beset by debilitating, guilt-producing stereotypes would do well to read this one.

### Bessie Head: Writing Between the Lines

Bessie Head's three novels *When Rain Clouds Gather* (1967), *Maru* (1971), and *A Question of Power* (1973), explore the social causes of poverty and engage in visionary consciousness about what might reverse the downward spiral into rural poverty (even into the poverty of madness). Her tragically short life was lived *between the lines* of comfortable categories of identification. She was born in South Africa to a well-to-do White woman, marginalized by mental disorder, and an unknown Black man. Even Head's maternal grandmother did not know the child's race, put "White" on her birth certificate, and sent her out to be fostered in a White home. When the "mistake" was detected (South Africans seem to be especially good at detecting signs of racial difference), she was sent to a colored family, and spent the rest of her life under the onus of being a half-breed. Educated in a mission school and mentored by an English missionary named Margaret Cadmore, she nevertheless gravitated toward Hinduism out of respect for the work of Mahatma Gandhi. In the midst of a troubled marriage and a troubling relationship with the Pan African Conference, Head left South Africa for Botswana where she was denied citizenship for fifteen years and remained virtually stateless during that period. An inspired writer, she had bouts of madness and lived in the exilic world between lucidity and hallucination.

Through experience, Bessie Head learned that poverty results, in part, from persons falling through the cracks—racially, politically, educationally, and personally. Using Head's own words, her biographer Gillian Stead Eilersen says that "she observed with distress the way in which many coloured people, who might be semi-literate or illiterate, had become 'trapped in a round of misery, poverty and week-end drunkenness'" (57). Living in rural Botswana, she observed that the same dynamic was true for many refugees and despised tribals such as the Masarwa (or Bushmen). Her novels reflect, in part, these ruminations on causality. The first, *When Rain Clouds Gather*, speaks of the hardships engendered by exile; *Maru* looks at racial politics; and *A Question of Power* combines issues of madness and the complex nature of political and personal evil. As Head herself identifies these works, they deal with "refugeeism," "racialism," and "patterns of evil" ("Social and Political Pressures" 12). In short, no less than the "city" novels of Emecheta, they deal with outlaws, with those who live on the fringes, see life as a labyrinthine set of overlapping systems demanding one's loyalty, and risk telling the whole complicated (sometimes contradictory or unbelievable) truth. By exploring cracks in the systems of oppression, this kind of writing raises the possibility of change.

In addition to diagnosing social ills, Bessie Head participated in visions for the alleviation of poverty and racism. Working with both the Bamangwato Development Association south of Serowe and with the gardening initiative of Boiteko, a self-help project in Serowe, Head cooperated with development personnel from all over the world and came to believe that grassroots efforts to alleviate poverty made more sense than grand national projects. At the same time, she was writing her major works where, despite stark descriptions of rural life, she allows her narrators and characters to dream about new ways of living and relating. One might say that, in the cracks and undefined spaces of external reality and internal consciousness, she not only found causes for oppression, but room for rewriting outcomes.

Head's connections with feminist thought reflect the life she lived outside of mainstream categories and in the company of the poor and disenfranchised. In a conversation with Alice Walker, she once said, "When you are truly alone and umpampered . . . the question of women's lib does not even arise. You just do everything for your self and every now and then a male buddy knocks in a nail you can't reach" (Eilersen 237). But in a later interview with a development volunteer, she explains that she writes a great deal about women because "they accept a much larger share than men of the responsibility for the species, they draw attention to their situation" (268). For Head it would seem that if women suffer the most under poverty, they may also be the greatest resource for the alleviation of poverty. It is this kind of practical sensibility that drives her writing about women and that circumscribes her love of the poor. As Eilersen comments, Head lived close to poverty all of her life; it was familiar, oddly hopeful, and suited her indifference toward material possessions (275).

Head's work, "a systematic study of women's roles and handicaps in society" (Ola 46), involves looking at how women have been kept in their place by traditional rituals but also observing how newly literate women, existing in a kind of historical limbo, seem uncertain about their sense of place. Dorothy Driver speculates that Head does not want to revive the past as much as to "cut another route, taking the past as a point of reference" (164). Her novels are all about this reconstructive, enriching act, one which Linda Beard refers to as "a conscious, although devastatingly subtle, act of reclamation" (582).

### *When Rain Clouds Gather*

In Bessie Head's first novel, all of the major characters are exiles. Makhaya is fleeing political arrest in South Africa. Paulina, the women's organizer, is fleeing the shame and economic ramifications of a husband who committed suicide. The elders, Dinorego and Mma-Millipede, are economic and emotional refugees from the northern part of Botswana. The agronomist Gilbert and the police Inspector George Appleby-Smith are voluntary exiles from England (to a country that was never officially colonized). There are several very strong women in this entourage. Paulina is the ultimate survivor, even if her behavior is occasionally frighteningly bold. Mma-Millipede advises the entire community on spiritual and practical matters. Dinorego's daughter Maria is mysteriously and powerfully withholding of her opinions. Yet it is Makhaya, the political refugee, to whom Head claims to feel closest. Thus, as author, she has made a womanist move, a declaration of gender inclusiveness, from the very start, and might agree with Elaine Showalter that the "wild zone" that makes up women's discourse always overlaps with and, to some extent, speaks through dominant language systems ("Feminist Criticism in the Wilderness" 474).

These characters are gathered in Golema Mmidi, an experimental agricultural community, where nature seems to reign supreme and can cause a terrifying downward escalation of loss:

> Almost six weeks of the rainy season had to pass by before the oxen, fed on the fresh green growth, were strong enough to plough. In the meanwhile, all the good rain needed by the crops might fall in those six weeks. This created anxiety, and often a man would harness his plough team too soon, only to have them topple over from weakness created by the long walks in search of the scant grazing during the dry season. (40)

Part of the problem the community faces is their loyalty to fixed ideas of how crop and cattle farming should relate—fixed ideas that are destructive of family relations and have little connection to true community values. The men take their cattle outside the village to grazing fields that stretch farther and farther away with their decimation, whereas the women grow crops at home. Cattle speculators, middle-men, are getting very rich through brokering poor men's livestock (26), and women, who do the major portion of the farming, have been excluded from education in new farming techniques (34):

> The women were the backbone of agriculture while the men on the whole were cattle drovers. But when it came to programmes for improved techniques in agriculture, soil conservation, the use of pesticides and fertilizers, and the production of cash crops, the lecture rooms were open to men only. Why give training to a section of the population who may never use it but continue to leave it to their wives to erode the soil by unsound agricultural practices? Why start talking about development and food production without taking into account who is really producing the food? (34)

Head's careful research into development history makes possible an illuminating case of gender blindness in this novel.

Gilbert, the outside expert, suggests that villagers try combining cattle and crop production by letting the cattle feed on crop residue and grain surplus close to home, thus freeing men to help with subsistence agriculture and freeing both women and men to do more with cash crops. But such a plan requires fencing the land to keep cattle out of current crop-growing areas. When conservatives protest that tribal land cannot be individually owned, therefore fenced, Gilbert argues that to combine grazing and farming activities will utilize a form of cooperative farming that satisfies the very deepest community values in their social history. He argues here for a flexible and creative interpretation of tribal injunctions, a use of the past to build the future. Along the way he points out that dangerous tribalism has kept farmers in Botswana from growing millet—healthy for both land and persons—because "inferior" tribes consume it.

This all sounds very good. But why does Head, an African woman, introduce salvific ideas through the White male outsider? Is she simply reflecting a reality she observed in Botswana? Is she lashing back at the injustice both she and her son suffered, as coloreds, from Black Africans? Is she offering a powerful statement about the exilic condition itself—that *all* are outsiders in some form or other and it is perhaps those that wear their "statelessness" most openly who have learned how to negotiate the future most creatively? Writing about this novel, Huma Ibrahim speculates that "an exile is especially equipped to see the past and present more clearly simply because she occupies the displaced zones that people 'at home' cannot perceive" (52). Head well knows the exile state and here allows that consciousness free play in a variety of male and female characters.

It is interesting that Matenge, the corrupt tribal patriarch, argues most vociferously against accepting ideas from outsiders: "I'll tell you something about Gilbert. He knows nothing about Botswana agriculture. He ought to be in England where he received his training in agriculture. The only man who knows how to do things here is a Batswana man" (65). God forbid they trust an anti-capitalist outsider (or an enterprising woman like Paulina)!

The refugee Makhaya, Gilbert's right-hand man, is a fine weaver of points of view here because he is African, but not at home in Botswana, a Zulu, but suspicious of ingrown tribalism, a man, but one who forwent his patriarchal privilege the minute his father died and he as oldest son could assume it. Explaining to his mother why he wanted his sisters

# Feminization of Poverty

to "address him by his first name and associate with him as equals and friends," he says, "Why should men be brought up with a false sense of superiority over women? People can respect me if they wish, but only if I earn it" (16). Yet his radical reversal of gender tradition, although admirable, is often confusing, and even insulting to the very women he wants to liberate.

Is part of Makhaya's complication that he tries to be a feminist in masculine terms? When Paulina makes overtures to him in the only manner she understands, by sending her daughter out to greet him in the mother's name, he answers almost cruelly, "Go and tell your mother I don't know her" (78). But Paulina is "a passionate and impetuous woman with a warm heart" (77) and does not insult easily. She "talks back" with her very decisive way of walking and being in the world. When Makhaya is eventually falling in love with Paulina, he insists on making his own tea, claiming, "It's time you learned that men live on this earth too. If I want to make tea, I'll make it, and if I want to sweep the floor, I'll sweep it!" (139). He manages to make a liberating move seem very much like prideful assertion, and overlooks the fact that Paulina has a specific way of making tea that is efficient and elegant and that she would like to preserve in her own home.

The most complicating evidence of his divided sensibility surfaces when Makhaya tries to protect Paulina from the horrifying reality of her son's death from malnutrition and tuberculosis in his cattle-grazing outpost. The young boy has been dead for several weeks. The insects have eaten his flesh, and his bones lie in a fetal position, the fingers curled in on the palms of his hands. He is the very portrait of malnutrition and poverty made worse by sustained drought (166). Paulina is no stranger to rural life's adversity, yet Makhaya assumes a patriarchal stance and will not let her view the body:

> "I must see the body," she said, but with dry taut lips.
> "I must see the body because it is our custom."
> "You see," he said, in a deliberately harsh voice.
> "All these rotten customs are killing us. Can't you see
> I'm here to bear all your burdens? Come on." (162)

He sends her home with Gilbert and cremates the boy's remains without consulting her. Then he gathers up the little wood carvings that Isaac, in his lonely hours at the grazing outpost, had made for his mother, never questioning whether she herself should have had the closure of retrieving them.

Burial customs are complicated, Makhaya is not from the same place as Paulina, and he unwittingly (perhaps unconsciously) alienates Paulina from her son's death. As Ibrahim comments on these acts, "His refusal to let Paulina see the remains of her child is a phallocratic one: he threatens to withdraw affection if she does not do what he wants her to do and she complies, though with a little hesitation" (83). Paulina's hesitation, no small thing, for she is deeply in love and vulnerable with grief and guilt over her son's death, may well be the kind of crevice in social habit that Head finds hopeful; it's a refusal of mindless obedience that stands to reform Makhaya every bit as much as Paulina, because he has already renounced traditional patriarchal privilege over his sisters, and wants to change.

In his work with Gilbert and the villagers, no less than his relationship with Paulina, Makhaya "does and does not try to obliterate 'the continual play of history, culture and power' represented by his apartheid South African past in favor of his peaceful present" (Ibrahim 54). This totally believable ambivalence circumscribes his participation, as trainer, in the women's tobacco-growing project. He takes a reserved and circumspect stance with the women he is directing, but is never austere, and pauses from his labors long enough to make tiny trees for Paulina's daughter's model village. Building any utopia, one made of tobacco sheds or miniature mud huts, requires the abdication of habits of privilege, and it is quite beautiful to see him lose himself in both endeavors. But the reader is left wondering if Makhaya knows just how much his success depends on Paulina's leadership of the women.

Paulina appears to be the only woman with sufficient charisma to organize the women into work groups. The women of Golema Mmidi both respect and fear Paulina. She's from the north of Botswana, a single mother, and sees the world in bolder terms than they, upsetting the gender hierarchy they are used to and have accepted:

> Things went along smoothly as long as all the women pretended to be inferior to this spineless species. The women had been lying to themselves for so long in their sexual frustration that they would not admit the real reason why Paulina dominated them all was because she was the kind of woman who could not lie to men. They followed the leadership of Paulina because she was so daring and different. It would have upset their world to have Paulina find a man she could get along with. (93)

Yet when Paulina does fall in love with Makhaya, she does so boldly, welcoming his affections without losing her authority. Paulina is a version of the "new" economically successful African woman who feels no need to overthrow older self-affirming practices.

Perhaps she represents too comfortable an integration. When Paulina gathers the women, they act out the historical ideal of hard-working, enterprising Botswana women: "No men ever worked harder than Botswana women, for the whole burden of providing food for big families rested with them" (104). Yet the alacrity with which they drop their other labor to pick up this very new crop is perhaps a stretch.

Has Head fallen into a wish fulfillment with her women? It is hard to believe that such a question would present much of a problem for her. She knows that women have to be both passionate and careful to survive. She knows that southern African women are experienced in marketing, and she is willing to extend their hands-on knowledge into enthusiasm for a new project in order to create its very possibility. The ordinary and the visionary are never mutually exclusive for Head. And she is willing to imagine that out of the bricolage of a woman's life— "babies, gossip, pots, food, fires, cups, and plates" (152)—could come a new way of taking responsibility, not just for domestic life, but for the community as a whole.

Nowhere does she tread this divide between the possible and the longed for more radically than in the last scenes of the novel. The corrupt tribal ruler Matenge, seeking revenge against Makhaya, has Paulina arrested for failure to report her son's death. When Paulina makes her way to court, the villagers decide to accompany her on the way to her "arraignment": "They were even excited in a silent way as though they had known this day would arrive when they would all face their persecutor of many years" (175). As they sit outside and wait for him to take action, Matenge knows that his protest against the revisionist economics being promoted and practiced in the village is effete and hangs himself:

> They weren't going to tolerate a man like him any longer because he would not give way nor understand that they needed co-operation from the man at the top to whom everyone had to go for permission to progress. . . . The end of it was that Matenge had to barricade himself up, not because the villagers were about to rise up and tear him to shreds, but because he was an evil pervert and knew it. (177)

When the narrator comments that this quiet communal support of a woman illegally arrested is part of a larger revolution, one is tempted once again to accuse Head of wishful thinking. But as Huma Ibrahim asks: "Why not credit the just expression of authorial desire instead?" (55–58).

An authorial desire that connects the African past with the present and future, a desire that critiques colonial influence but accepts voluntary exiles from Europe, a desire that is fully cognizant of the multiple causes of poverty but cares about the details of economic development as well, and one that gives women a prominent place in social integration (haven't they always been the keepers of community?) is a desire that holds promise of possibility. The fact that this promise is conceived within a small impoverished village, far from the colonial centers as well as the centers of apartheid, is proof that Head is willing to work her heartfelt vision from the ground up. Even God becomes a matter of bottom–up desire as Mma-Millipede "realizes" that two destinies face the people of Africa—one preached by the followers of Solomon in all his material splendor and one preached by those who follow the God with no shoes (185). And she is sure that it was the God with no shoes "with his queer, inverted reasoning" who brought Makhaya, the radical (if backsliding) reformer, face to face with the hanged body of Matenge, in the context of Paulina's and the community's defiant courage.

The fact that Head's authorial desire is born out of exilic palava—out of a gathering in of many points of view previously silenced: the refugee, the British outcast, the widow, the mystic, the poor—lends credence to her argument. How else is she to speak in hope, if not to say, "We the precocious, we the repressed of culture, our lovely mouths gagged with pollen, our wind knocked out of us, we the labyrinths, the ladders, the trampled spaces, the bevies—we are black and we are beautiful" (Cixous, "Laugh" 735)?

### Maru and A Question of Power

Bessie Head's next two novels deal less directly with issues of economic development, but in that they explore causes of oppression and contain surprises arising from authorial desire for social change, they are well worth brief mention in a chapter on poverty and the will to power. *Maru* is a tale of racism, illustrating the total superiority assumed by most tribes in Botswana toward the conquered and enslaved Masarwa (or Bushmen). It is also the tale of a poor woman, a Masarwa, who because she is disenfranchised, becomes the plaything of two village strongmen. Moleka and Maru, both contenders for the role of Paramount Chief in Dilepe, fall in love with this woman, the new Masarwa school teacher named after her missionary godmother Margaret Cadmore and able but unwilling to pass for colored. Their competition with each other and with their own emerging sense of racial justice cause them to do rash things. Moleka invites his Masarwa slaves to eat at his table. Maru gives up his political aspirations to marry Margaret and so enters a form of voluntary social exile. Margaret is the unwitting pawn of such "generosity." By combining issues of gender and race, Head illustrates how purveyors of the structures of power, even those seeking enlightenment, work to oppress the poor and excluded.

Leaving the omniscient narrator behind in her third novel, *A Question of Power*, Bessie Head enters into stylistic cacophony, taking her protagonist Elizabeth into the depths of madness where multiple voices jeer at her, and two, in particular, tyrannize over her. If the madwoman Elizabeth is the ultimate embodiment of the disenfranchised underclass, the poorest of the poor, combining slave, exile, half-breed, and rape victim, her solicitors—Sello the corrupt monk and Dan the corrupt politician—are incarnations of the misuse of power.

The ending offers Elizabeth freedom. Having reached a state of comfortable, even hopeful lucidity, Elizabeth demonstrates that what we have read is, at least, two narrations—Elizabeth recording her horrors for posterity and Elizabeth repeating the voices of hell *as she hears them* (Tucker 171). What has intervened in Elizabeth's life and consciousness and brought her to coherence is the beauty of the ordinary—her responsibility for her son Shorty, her work in a community garden project with her Botswana friend Kenosi and her American friend Tom. What has intervened is her *will to creativity and agency*. As Margaret Tucker puts it, "*A Question of Power* is about finding freedom from and amidst oppression; by exposing hierarchies of power and, in particular, the objectification of women as the foundation of patriarchy" (181). It is appropriate then that Head openly and generously recognizes her readers' interpretive freedom in their approach to this strange novel. Speaking to a researcher she says:

> I hardly recognized my novel in your symbolic interpretation of it, but you are excused. *A Question of Power* is a novel readers take fierce possession of. The canvas on which the tale is drawn is BIG, the tale drawn on the canvas, small, sketchy and uncertain. . . . This very attitude of uncertainty is an open invitation to the reader to move in and re-write and reinterpret the novel in his/her own way. (cited in Eilersen 252)

Authorial control gives way to readerly desire here in a deliberate and demonstrative move.

Bessie Head, writing out of a very specific personal and political context, nonetheless illustrates the truth of the border-crossing refugee—that all fixed identities and articulations are (and should be) subject to reevaluation. Erratic, blunt, sometimes mad, Head makes dis-ease, as well as utopian vision (and palpable hope), the center of her writing life. Both are necessary to an honest encounter with poverty—and so much more.

## Perceptions of Poverty: Clarice Lispector's *The Hour of the Star*

Clarice Lispector's final novel, *The Hour of the Star* (1977), written as she was dying of cancer, is a stark portrayal not so much of what it means to be poor as of what it means to be *perceived* as poor. Born in Ukraine in the 1920s, Lispector emigrated to Brazil with her parents when she was several months old. Giovanni Pontiero comments that "as a child, the sight of human deprivation and injustice in the impoverished Northeast caused her to tremble with rage" ("Clarice Lispector: Dreams of Language" 286). As a young adult, she studied law to fight injustice in the penal system and demonstrated with politicized university students. Pontiero observes that in her 50s, when she was seriously ill, Lispector became "almost obsessively" nostalgic about the area where she had spent her childhood and made a journey to Recife to renew her contact with the people there ("Afterword" 89). Out of that remembrance and reconnection she invented the protagonist of *The Hour of the Star*, Macabea, who is "barely literate, ugly and undernourished . . . superfluous and vulnerable in an aggressive metropolis" (Pontiero, "Dreams" 85).

Orphaned, Macabea is raised by a forbidding aunt, and makes her way to Rio de Janeiro where she gets a job as a typist and lives with four nondescript roommates (all named Maria) in the red-light district. "Gauche and rachitic, Macabea has poverty and ill-health written all over her: a creature conditioned from birth and already singled out as one of the world's inevitable losers" (Pontiero, "Afterword" 90). Life doesn't get much worse than this!

As the novella opens, Macabea is about to lose her job because, although she has learned to type, she has never learned to spell. One should not pity her and question her life. But the reader has little time for pity, because he or she has to contend with a surprising and difficult narrator—one who is cold and tedious and exploits all of the notions about the poor held by middle-class boors. Lispector has played quite a trick here; instead of encountering an empathy-producing other, the reader must face an exaggerated reflection of his or her own prejudices and accompany a narrator struggling (unsuccessfully and in all the wrong ways) to convince himself he can connect with his subject. As Helene Cixous describes the reader's/narrator's/writer's perplexing co-journey: "In the dedication, we are on the side of someone who has lost his poverty. The movement of the story is going to be the attempt . . . to find by way of meditating on a poor being, a little bit of lost poverty" (*Reading with Clarice Lispector* 150). Is the narrator's quest a painfully ironic reflection of Lispector's return to her roots prefatory to dying? Is Lispector, by foregrounding the voice of the distant male, revealing her own inevitable, if undesired, distancing from the poor? Is Lispector, like the reader, trying to get past the narrator to Macabea? Is the narrator's statement that a man must tell this story because a woman would "weep her heart out" (14) a judgment on him, on Lispector, or on both? "As soon as one opens the book, one is suspended," claims Cixous, beginning with the takeover of Lispector's voice in the dedication (the narrator claims to *be* author) and a multiplicity of possible titles.

Rather than waiting until he has something coherent to say, the narrator plunges us into the chaos of his precompositional ruminations by referring to a set of musicians (all European) who have made him explode into himself. He is now so full of himself that he can declare to be the reader as well, "this me that is you," "and you too," "you perhaps" (8). Distinctions are blurred rather than played off against one another, and before the "author's" dedication is even finished, the reader feels sucked into an alliance he or she is not sure is desirable.

Instead of waiting until he finds a title he likes, the narrator asks us to pick among many, each one providing a different hermeneutic. Is this seemingly premature move a clever offering of difference or only the appearance of play that masks tyrannical control, not only of subject matter, but of the reader's time and ingress into the story as well? We will only enter when he is ready for us to enter and through the portal he chooses. The story is called *The Hour of the Star* (in actuality, the moment of death), which was not even at the top of the proffered list.

The narrator, Rodrigo S. M. (he even signs his name in a pretentious fashion), admits that he is cold. As he says, "I want my story to be cold and impartial. Unlike the reader, I reserve the right to be devastatingly cold, for this is not simply a narrative, but above all primary life" (13). What does he mean by primary life? Is it the commonality (lowest common denominator) he contrives for his protagonist? He calls Macabea's experiences unremarkable; she's "a harmless virgin nobody needs" (14), an accident of nature like thousands of others (36).

So much of his attention is absorbed into how he is going to set up the telling of such a "primal" tale, that the reader wonders if he will ever get to the telling. One pretentious authorial affectation follows another, until the reader recognizes that the narrator is actually afraid of encountering someone like Macabea. She forces him "to seek a truth that transcends [him]" (20). Yet for all of his authorial deliberation, he does not escape repetition of the most obvious stereotypes about poverty (Olimpico proudly displays his good tooth; Gloria wears cheap perfume; Macabea's idea of modernity is drinking Coca-Cola), nor does he escape the blatant arrogance of believing he can be the voice for the voiceless: "my mandate is simply to reveal her presence so that you may recognize her on the street" (19). All is meanness and reduction, masculinized nomination, not the genteel inclusivity he promises.

In writing about Rodrigo's relationship to his subject, Marta Peixote notes that Macabea "possesses a peculiar power as a site for the narrator's investments. Providing his guilt, forcing him to live in her skin, she drags him through the misfortunes he invents for her" (93). This is an agonizing place for him to be, so he distances himself imagistically. She is a "vagrant bitch" (18), convinced that she "doesn't deserve a dog's affection" (28) and simple-mindedly smiling at people on the street without realizing that "they don't even notice her" (16). So instead of our finding out what complex wisdom and endurance a woman like Macabea might possess, we find out what little courage and imagination he, who once "caught a glimpse of perdition on the face of a girl from the North-east," actually possesses. While he believes she is his subject, his fear of what she represents controls the narrative.

What an odd reversal of roles we find here, reminding the reader of nothing so much as the "trick" that the prostitute Liza plays on Dostoevsky's narrator of *Notes from Underground* (1864). Like the obsessive man from underground, Lispector's bourgeois narrator preaches incessantly, enjoys his own supposed pain, pontificates about the nature of culture and poverty to an audience of "gentlemen"—all the while exploiting, and inventing, a patient female victim. Like the underground man he fears the "Hell of human freedom" (36), and knows that his castigation of the girl comes from the fact that she "embodies a truth [he] is anxious to avoid" (39). (He even shares a toothache with the man from underground [23].) But unlike Dostoevsky's Liza, who refuses to accept the underground man's payment for services rendered, Macabea remains totally unaware of (or indifferent to) the narrator's brooding concern, survives the betrayal of her worthless boyfriend, and insists on dying in hope, unaware once again that Rodrigo S. M. has had a hand in whether or not she should die at the end of his piece. Has she had a life all along that even the narrator cannot reduce to embarrassing commonalties?

The narrator appears to embody, in part, the blunt tyrannical side of the authorial will that Lispector manifests more ironically. He is the ever present reminder that narrative, the naming of the other, can be violent and abusive. If he ever finds the poverty he claims to seek, it will be within himself, within his need to mock Macabea's "foolish" belief in happiness (12), and her struggle for dignity in her job: "She was a typist at last, even though she appeared to have some difficulty in stringing two consonants together" (15). The "question of power" is written all over *The Hour of the Star*.

What does it mean, then, that the narrator says at one point that "poverty is ugly and promiscuous"? Does he really believe that material poverty has forced herself on him (29), demanding his narrative skills (and his love)? If so, he, anxious to be rid of the behest, turns this seduction on the reader and claims to be merely mediating a simple but ancient story:

> If the reader is financially secure and enjoys the comforts of life, he must step out of himself and see how others live. If he is poor, he will not be reading this story because what I have to say is superfluous for anyone who often feels the pangs of hunger. Here I am acting as a safety-valve for you and the tedious bourgeoisie. I know that it is very frightening to step out of oneself, but then everything which is unfamiliar can be frightening. (30)

The irony, of course, is that we do need to step outside of ourselves—what he, our guide, is having such a hard time doing.

The fortune teller Macabea consults near the end of her life gives her a future, the rest of us (author, narrator, reader) appear to give her morbid curiosity and judgment (especially of her acquiescence—why does she not resist?). By making readers complicit with the text, by making them intimate with the narrator's defenses, Lispector seduces us into a confrontation, not so much with the otherness of the poor as with our own disdain for things we cannot easily fix.

This is a rough realization. It makes us uneasy. We want Macabea to be less mousy, more feisty, angry when betrayed, aware that being run over by a yellow Mercedes is not an encounter with luxury. We want her to rise from the pavement and scorn the narrator's tacky benediction on her death. In short, we want her to be more like us who know our rights and assert them with confidence. We want her to be an outlaw with a mission statement, not one who speaks a palaverous discourse full of unanswered questions, like the ones she keeps asking her boyfriend Olimpico. But Macabea is not the kind of person who would easily have found her way onto a delegation on their way to the global debates on women's poverty at Beijing. Lispector reminds us of this with consummate skill. And unless we look for ways to hear and value the complications of a life such as Macabea's, without oily charity, our efforts at justice or at writing about justice will be meager. Resistance to the misuse of power needs to be in the observer as well as the direct victim, to be vigilantly self-editing, wildly seeking, and always respectful.

Taking on the voice of masculine obsession with definition, Lispector has driven our desire for libidinal wholeness underground, where it continues to haunt the text. That the narrator claims to have died at the moment he wrote Macabea's death indicates that even he seeks more than he could set forth. Our discomfort with this discrepancy is the gift that the dying Lispector offers us. It is a gift like that of the whole company of writers discussed in this chapter who refuse to submit to or entertain a simplistic codification of the means of suffering.

## Other Novels to Consult for the Theme of Feminization of Poverty

Other novels written by women explore the complications of poverty in women's lives. A classic study of rural poverty is Kamala Markandaya's *Nectar in a Sieve* (1954), in which human relationships are all confined within economic forces and irascible nature, but honest love somehow survives. A devastating portrait of the vulnerability of the poor woman is given in Rosario Castellanos' story "Modesta Gomez," that appears in her collection *City of Kings* (1960). A poor rural girl in domestic service is impregnated by the son of the household, marries an abusive husband, and then, to survive, becomes an abuser (ambusher) of poor Indian market women. The same poor-on-poor violence occurs in Castellanos' *The Book of Lamentations* (1962), in which one of the often ambushed market women is brutally raped by a *patron*, then, upon manifesting signs of pregnancy, is married off to a retarded man and forced to give up her child, her only possession, to the Indian woman who took her in. Echoing the theme that poverty makes women vulnerable is Isabel Allende's *House of the Spirits* (1982), in which scores of peasant women are subject to the sexual whims of Esteban Trueba but can claim nothing from him in the

Feminization of Poverty                                                     179

name of their children. Forced sex is closely allied to survival sex, often the refuge of poor women. Mahasweta Devi's story "Douloti the Bountiful," found in *Imaginary Maps* (1995), examines sexual slavery as a result of poor tribal women's commodification at the hands of their families as well as their clients. Nawal el Saadwi's *Woman at Point Zero* (1973) and *God Dies by the Nile* (1974) both deal with issues of sex as survival for poor women—in the first work through prostitution, in the second through both prostitution and rape. Buchi Emecheta's *The Joys of Motherhood* (1979) studies the dynamics of prostitution as a way out of poverty for Adaku, and poverty as a trap for the poor women in polygamous marriage through Nnu Ego. In *Joys*, the erratic nature of the informal market (especially devastating for women) is clearly demonstrated, as it is in the first part of Tsitsi Dangarembga's *Nervous Conditions* (1989).

**Notes**

1. The *Non-Governmental Organisation (NGO) Beijing Declaration* is even more direct than the *Platform for Action* in its attack on the global market and structural adjustment programs as a cause of poverty, especially for women:

> The global economy, governed by international financial institutions, the World Trade Organization and trans-national corporations, impose Structural Adjustment Programs on countries in the South and economic restructuring in countries in the North in the name of fiscal health. The result is increasing poverty, debt and unemployment. The resulting reductions in social programs and services in the areas of health, education and housing harm the very people they purport to assist.

2. Even more alarming are statistics reported in *The World's Women 1995* indicating that the highest ratios of poor women to poor men—130:100—are to be found in Australia and the United States (129). Granted, these ratios are based on relative rather than absolute poverty, but the high level of gender-weighting remains alarming.

3. Efforts to expand the instruments by which improvements in human welfare can be assessed have been under way at the UN for some time. Several measures alternative to the traditional measures of economic growth (GNP [gross national product] and GDP [gross domestic product]) are the HDI (human development index), which measures average achievement of basic human capabilities (i.e., the ability to live a long and healthy life with adequate education and health care); GDI (gender-related development index), which takes note of disparities in achievement between men and women; and GEM (gender empowerment index), which measures the comparative ability

of men and women to participate in economic and political planning (UNDP *Report* 73).

4. Also arguing against the "culture of poverty" theory, Muhammad Yunus has said in an interview that he believes poor women make good credit risks because, for one thing, they have had to be good domestic managers with few resources. Their very poverty has made them responsible ("Beyond Beijing: Women and Economic Justice").

5. Expanding on the significance of the name "Pussy Cat Mansions," Ogunyemi says:

> Its name also signifies [the tenants'] weakness and sexuality as women. Built on a cemetery, its tenants are the living dead, buried in the societal ditch. In its grim, fairy-tale atmosphere, they wait for a Prince Charming, in the form of the disinterested state, to wake them from the unwholesome tomb where they live in an almost vegetative state. (235)

# Chapter 8

▼▼▼▼▼▼▼▼▼

# *Imaging Women:*
# *Fighting Stereotypes and Building Agency*

> The expression in art of what really exists beneath the surface is part of the transformation of a society. What is written, painted, sung, cannot remain ignored.
> —Nadine Gordimer, *Writing and Being*

In *The Story of Zahra* (1995), Lebanese novelist Hanan al-Shaykh tells us about a young woman forced to live out the stereotype[1] of the passive female, in spite of, or perhaps because of, her mother's transgression and her father's violent response to that revolt. When the father discovers that his wife takes Zahra with her on her sexual trysts, he beats his daughter to extract information, plunging her into the dark confusion of not knowing where her loyalties lie or what to do with her own female body. When her older brother Ahmed gets the best morsels of food, the best education, she accepts the difference. When her cousin—or uncle—"pesters" her, she remains silent. When her brother's friend Samir wants to marry her, she knows it is "because I am docile, because he has never seen my teeth, because I do not rival his own self-importance" (29–30). When Malek, a "friend of the family," a married man with children, seduces her, she acquiesces without passion, even to the docile acceptance of two clumsy abortions. When she finally does marry, it is out of fear that someone might surmise her sexual liaison and its negation of the image that she (taking in everyone's expectations) has so carefully created for herself:

> the image of which I had run off hundreds of copies for distribution to all who had known me since childhood. Here is Zahra, the

mature girl who says little, Zahra the princess, as my grandfather dubbed me; Zahra the stay-at-home, who blushes for any or for no reason; Zahra the hard-working student—quite the reverse of her brother, Ahmed; Zahra, in whose mouth butter would not melt, who has never smiled at any man, not even at her brother's friends. This is Zahra—a woman who sprawls naked day after day on a bed in a stinking garage, unable to protest at anything. Who lies on the old doctor's table. (40)

Living out the stereotypes of the acquiescent daughter/sister/girlfriend has pushed Zahra into their very violation. How is she (or any woman) to escape this kind of double jeopardy?

### Addressing Perceptions of Women: The *Platform for Action*

Recognizing that perceptions of women are intimately connected with women's presence (or lack of same) in positions of influence and public stature, section G: "Women in Power and Decision-Making" of the *Platform for Action* laments that although the *Universal Declaration of Human Rights* grants everyone the right to take part in the government of his or her country,

> women are largely underrepresented at most levels of government, especially in ministerial and other executive bodies, and have made little progress in attaining political power in legislative bodies or in achieving the target endorsed by the Economic and Social Council of having 30% women in positions at decision-making levels by 1995. (paragraph 182)

*The World's Women 1995* reports that by 1995, only 24 women had ever been elected heads of state or government; only 23 countries had more than 15 percent women at the subministerial level; and although women's membership in parliaments had increased slightly in Africa and Latin America, it had declined in eastern and western Asia (151–52). *The World's Women 2000* warns that although there has been a very slight increase in women's representation in Asia between 1995 and 2000, "women are under-represented in national parliaments everywhere" (164). What may be even more disturbing is the fact that female delegates to the UN General Assembly had only increased from 4 percent to 20 percent in the years between 1949 and 1994, and that although women presently make up 30 percent of all employees at the

UN, they only fill 15 percent of upper management positions (Neft and Levine 18).

Section G of the *Platform* asserts that two of the reasons why women are underrepresented in political decisionmaking positions are that gender stereotyping "reinforces the tendency for political decision-making to remain the domain of men" (paragraph 183) and that "unequal division of labour and responsibilities within households . . . limits women's potential to find the time and develop the skills required for participation in decision-making in wider public forums" (paragraph 185). Section J: "Women and the Media" suggests that lack of gender sensitivity in the media is a major cause of the perpetuation of traditional stereotypes of women and that, in addition to media failure to present "a balanced picture of women's diverse lives and contributions to society in a changing world," pornographic media products negatively affect women's abilities to participate in high level social discourse (paragraphs 235, 236).

What avenues for redress does the *Platform* offer? Section G: "Women in Power and Decision-Making" suggests that governments (and other actors, such as the UN) set specific targets for women's participation in administrative positions, that they encourage women's participation in political parties, develop communication strategies to promote debate on new roles for men and women, and encourage women's NGOs to participate in development debate and planning (paragraph 190). This section, as well as section H: "Institutional Mechanisms for the Advancement of Women," suggests that gender analysis become part of all planning for social policy and program, so that the impact of new initiatives on the lives of men and women can be part of decisionmaking (paragraphs 189, 200). Section J: "Women and the Media" calls for governments (and other actors) to encourage the media: to refrain from "presenting women as inferior beings and exploiting them as sexual objects and commodities;" to begin presenting women as creative human beings and key actors; to utilize indigenous and other ethnic forms of storytelling, poetry and song; and to depict in programming the equal sharing of family responsibilities (paragraphs 242, 243, 245). All of this would require gender balance in the appointment of programmers and advisors to media-monitoring bodies, in addition to the recognition of women's media networks (paragraph 239).

The suggestion that storytelling be part of the dismantling of restrictive stereotypes is, of course, quite pertinent to this study of the political impact of women's novels. Returning to the story of Zahra, the reader can see that although she adopts certain defiant defense mechanisms against fixed ideas of who and what she should be, these defenses are chiefly unconscious and self-destructive, meaning that the real transgression is al-Shaykh's—the way she presents these mechanisms—and the reader's—the way he or she receives them.

What are Zahra's acts of revolt? One might say that her continuous scratching at her facial acne is a way of refusing to be attractive to men. One might say that her periods of madness are ways of avoiding coercive relationships. One might say that the letters she writes to her uncle in Africa, suggesting that she come to visit him, are a way of escaping Lebanon and father/brother/lover/abortionist. One might say that her final sexual liaison—this time experiencing physical pleasure—with a sniper during the civil war in Lebanon is a way of using violent interruption of culture to interrupt her own passive trajectory. But the fact that she becomes pregnant (again) and is shot on the street—most likely by her sniper lover—keeps the reader from feeling that Zahra has ever really broken free from either material bondage or "the image."

In writing the novel, however, al-Shaykh *has* broken free. She has exposed the terrible entrapment of women like Zahra; she has risked social censure by writing such a story in Arabic; and she has risked cultural misunderstanding by allowing it to be translated and disseminated cross-culturally. In such a novel, the personal becomes political and the political becomes personal, while political ideology (mostly in the voice of Ahmed) remains in the background. This kind of contextualized story can open up many levels of private and public debate—if the reader is ready for them.

### Fighting Stereotypes/Building Agency

What is discussed in this chapter is not a new topic; our whole study of the complementarity of development discourse and post-colonial women's novels has focused on the violent side of identity politics and the need for women's agency to emerge out of honest encounter with difference—internal, communal, cross-cultural. As the UNDP *Human Development Report 1995* asserts, gender equality

> requires an entirely new way of thinking—in which the stereotyping of women and men no longer limits their choices, but gives way to a new philosophy that regards all people as essential agents of change and that views development as a process of enlarging the choices of both sexes, not just one. (99)

Most of the theories that have shaped *Aeroplane Mirrors* reflect the struggle to bring agency out of encounter with diversity—theories that arise from anthropology, from feminist politics, from study of the novel, from linguistics, and from observations of how systems of power actually work. In all of the issues addressed so far—mothering, violence against women, son preference, the feminization of poverty—the foundational issue has been how to change and complicate perceptions of women so that women have more freedom to act and to create.

Global economist Amartya Sen helps define that foundational issue in an essay entitled "Agency and Well-Being." In order to make a distinction between welfare and agency approaches to women's development, he turns to the medieval distinction between "agent" and "patient," saying that although a patient is a person whose well-being requires the interest and help of others, an agent takes an active rule in pursuing his or her well-being. In Sen's view, a viable agenda for women must transcend notions of women as "patient solicitors of social equity" and promote them as "active agents of major social change" (104). This agenda would require (and continue to cause) expansion of the perceptions and definitions of women's roles.

For example, he argues, women's working outside of the home improves their social standing because their contributions to their families become more visible, their voices in family decisionmaking become more audible (less dependent, more informed), and they become part of the public dialogue, even if in very subtle ways (105). Ironically, he continues, this increase in self-esteem and agency for women improves child survival (as well as fertility control)—issues often considered to be based in the domestic realm. Whereas conservative thinkers would argue that working mothers endanger child welfare, Sen argues that, globally, "higher levels of female literacy and labour force participation [are] strongly associated with lower levels of relative female disadvantage in child survival" (107). In Sen's thinking, women's self-esteem, women's agency, and family well-being are inextricably linked, although such a linkage is not necessary to justify the enhancement of women's influence.[2]

In an essay entitled "Development as a Moral Concept," Elizabeth Reid warns, however, that gender analysis itself may be flawed in that it reduces social analysis to the "undifferentiated universals" of men and women. Gender analysis, even when carefully conducted, cannot fully account for "choice, capabilities, freedom, moral commitment, doubt, failure, and transformation," she argues, and, therefore, forces commentators into "exceptionalism" (i.e., My male friends are different from the point I just made!). Furthermore, she fears that fixed gender ideas—even when they promote an understanding of "violation, neglect, indifference"—are too easily internalized into "a disabling condition of the surrounding culture" (115). (*The Story of Zahra* beautifully illustrates the power of internalized perceptions.)

What Reid would like to see is a restructuring of concepts that would allow development thinkers to differentiate among women as well as between women and men (117) and to improve women's (and men's) well-being through improving the quality of human interaction (123). Of interest to *Aeroplane Mirrors* is the fact that she locates women's stories as one place where this kind of reconceptualizing and interaction is taking place:

> Women's stories, insights, and life histories [are] being used to question classical canons of objectivity and subjectivity, to dismantle accepted options of the public and the private, and to develop new analytical concepts to assist in understanding and elaborating issues around the quality and purpose of women's lives. (119)

But before turning to a discussion of specific women's novels in this chapter, it is only fair to look at ways in which development thinkers are themselves calling for conceptual and structural change.

### The Dynamics of Critical Mass

In an essay entitled "Strategic Locations," Kathleen Staudt argues that although research is scanty, it indicates that increased numbers of women in leadership positions not only opens doors of opportunity for women, but provides more gender-balance in decisionmaking. She examines the dynamics of underrepresentation—how being a token woman (in government, business, or any institution) can affect performance—and how critical mass might be achieved. Tokenism is clearly connected with identity politics. The token is often expected to speak for all members of her group, assigned to stereotyped tasks, and forced to overcome "boundary-heightening behavior" on the part of the dominant (male) group. In response, she may feel that she must outperform her colleagues, remain invisible, and conform to stereotyped behavioral expectations, leading, at times, to "excessively feminine or maternal behavior" (130). However, once a critical mass of nondominants (women) is achieved, they tend to participate more openly in decisionmaking and to exhibit diverse behaviors.

In looking at ways that critical mass might be achieved, Staudt considers "Human Capital" frameworks, ones where the education and training of women are utilized to increase the pool of female managerial talent; "Group-Structural Perspectives" frameworks, where "old boy" networks for recruitment are diversified and integrated into merit-based hiring; and "Gendered Organizational Culture" frameworks, which work on changing the values and ideologies that prize male presence and thinking in leadership positions (137). Sharing the concerns of the *Platform for Action,* Staudt argues that the first two will not work without the latter and speculates that cultural changes may come about through "subcultures for change inside institutions" (such as active equal employment offices) and through crisis of the kind that demands ideological and structural change (138).

### Women-Centered NGOs

In "Women-Oriented NGOs in Latin America," Ken Kusterer argues that women-centered development organizations function very much like the "subcultures for change" that Staudt discusses. He argues that such organizations serve immediate needs, serve as mutual support groups, and make political interventions based on first-hand experience with problems (185). He does not claim that traditional NGOs do not perform these functions, but says they are less likely to perform them simultaneously and with such a strong experiential base. Furthermore, he argues that women's NGOs lead to democratization through extensions of these roles—through personalized discussions of issues, through mobilizing persons leery of win–lose politics, through delinking political organizations from political parties, through creating competition between political parties for independent constituencies, and through stressing grassroots action (even to the point of creating tension with government programs) (188-89).

An example of the evolution and effectiveness of women's NGOs is the "community kitchens" of Peru. Women living in squatter settlements have discovered that if they pool their resources and buy and cook in bulk, they can provide one basic meal a day for their families. Because of their efficiency, their targeting of the poorest of the poor, and their lack of corruption, they have become the perfect vehicle for local distribution of national and international food aid (Kusterer 187). An example of a women's NGO functioning on an international scale would be the World Women's Watch (WWW), called for by the UNDP *Report,* which would study gender disparities, compile reasonable targets for national governments or international organizations, organize literacy training, and so on.

An example of women's organizations working at both the local and international levels comes from Reena Bernards' report on the November 1991 conference on "Women and International Conflict," organized by the Association for Women in Development (AWID). Bringing together pairs of women from opposing sides of the conflicts in South Africa, Northern Ireland, Israel and the West Bank, Cyprus, and Sri Lanka, they created a safe place for discussion of grassroots cooperative peace actions. Israeli and Palestinian women, active in Women in Black, a group that stands vigil on Friday afternoons to protest Israeli occupation of the West Bank and Gaza, so impressed Catholic and Protestant women of Northern Ireland that they talked about jointly and publicly attending funerals of "all victims of 'random assassination'" (202). Through such activities—including Black and White women of South Africa sitting together in the homes of families that had been fire-bombed—powerless women reported feeling more powerful in both their private and public lives. Of interest to this chapter, they seem to have achieved empowerment through utilizing and transforming, rather than dismissing, prevailing stereotypes. As Bernards comments, "As soon as women sit down with each other they are able to experience their commonalities as mothers, as women who are second-class citizens in their own societies" (201). A statement such as this is clearly an overstatement, moving uncomfortably toward essentialism, but taken in context, it seems appropriately descriptive of this particular gathering and allows for strategic indirection to be part of social change.

### *Co-madres*: From Hidden Transcript to Public Power

Nowhere is the utilization and reconceptualization (even the disturbance) of a familiar gender role more obvious than in women's organizations arising during periods of dictatorial rule in Latin America; no where has agency been more carefully constructed from available "materials." In speaking of the formation of *co-madres* groups—groups of women that lobby for information about and release of political prisoners in countries such as Argentina, Chile, and El Salvador—the UNDP *Report* says that it was women's traditional public invisibility in Latin America that allowed them to become actors in the peace movement (101). Part of the weaponry used by these women is the traditional (partly *machismo*, partly Catholic) veneration of women's roles as wives and mothers.

In tracing the history of the *Agrupacion de los Familiares de Detendio-Desapracidos* (Association of the Relatives of the Detained and Disappeared), the official name of the *co-madres* organization in Chile, Patricia

Chuchryk explains that in the early 1970s, under the dictatorship of General Pinochet, the same women kept running into each other outside of prisons and hospitals, all of them looking for information about missing sons, daughters, and husbands. They soon decided that they could get more accomplished and present a more forceful front if they acted collectively. After attempting to work (largely unsuccessfully) through the judicial system—utilizing *habeas corpus* and court depositions—they came to adopt more unconventional methods "such as hunger strikes and chaining themselves to the gates of the government palace and the Supreme Court" (135). In this process, "mothers," traditionally confined to the private sphere, became "political subjects." As one participant, Maryse Navarro, explains the logic of their transformation: "[as women we participate in the *Agrupacion* because] we are the women and mothers of this land, of the workers, of the professionals, of the students, and of future generations" (Chuchryk 140). They have succeeded because their politicization was both unexpected and unnoticed, granting them freedom of movement and the ability to congregate without suspicion, and because traditional values honoring the mother would not allow them to be publicly insulted and slaughtered (not, of course, that individual members have not been harassed and tortured).[3] Their lives would never be the same:

> many of the women had acquired a new sense of themselves as political beings. They [saw] themselves as occupying a public political space that they had not occupied previously. For them, their participation has also involved the process of becoming politically educated. (141–42)

One suspects their daughters' lives will never be the same either!

### Beginning in Childhood

Many theorists argue that the best way to change social perceptions is to change the way children are socialized. The *co-madres* are important to such a change because they mix private and public worlds, familiar roles and new uses of these roles. Daughters raised in households with politically educated and actualized mothers have a good chance of becoming change agents in their own right. As Elizabeth Debold, Marie Wilson, and Idelisse Malave say in an article entitled "A Mother Daughter Revolution": "By reclaiming our connections with each other, as women, we transform mothering from an act of selfless nurturance confined to private life to a political act of solidarity through which we create a community of women for our daughters to join" (238). Obviously, an unmarried or childless woman could feel quite at home in such a solidarity move, for what is really being talked about here is a redefinition of power such that "power with" replaces "power over" and the "power to (re)name" remains front and center.

Indian theorist Kamla Bhasin argues that men from the leisured class (and castes) have always controlled knowledge, thereby controlling definitions and names. Male psychologists, for the most part, name women's neuroses; male physicians name their ailments; male historians write (or erase) their histories; and male economists define (or dismiss) the value of their work (235). Power means talking back, writing back. For this, the education of girls is crucial.

As discussed in chapter 6, the gender gap in education needs to be closed, curriculum materials need to be related to life experience, the value and intelligence of girls need to be publicly discussed and celebrated, and gender stereotyping that presents girls and women as economic and social liabilities needs to be resisted. In *The Burden of Girlhood* (1995), Neera Sohoni describes a prize-winning poster from India bearing the slogan: "Your Daughter Will Never Be as Good as a Son, Unless You Give Her a Chance." Part of the poster's text reads: "In the context of the twentieth century, and an India poised for the future, do your bit to emancipate the Indian woman, and give her the opportunity to gain knowledge and the freedom to use it. Start with your daughter" (194). Great advice!

### Tackling the Media

The *Platform for Action* and many other sources suggest that fighting stereotypes and building agency for women has to involve the media, as the poster contest in India just cited so nicely illustrates. This raises almost endless questions about control, however. If there are more women than men as students in communications departments (Neft and Levine 158), why are there so few female executives and programmers? At what point would critical mass be achieved in the media industry? In a case such as the one Chikwenye Ogunyemi cites (see chapter 4) about the book jackets of African women's books so often picturing women with children tied on their backs, who picks the images and why? One way to approach questions about (and transformation of) media images is through the exercise of "lucidity," "critical thinking," and "rewriting."

### Lucidity

What would it mean to be lucid about the misogynist effect of media stereotypes and pornographic media images? Alicia Ortiz, an Argentinean writer, discusses the fact that identity is based on how we, as human beings, are read from the outside and reflected back to ourselves. Thus, she insinuates that stereotypes are born out of desire; in the case of stereotypes of women—more often conceived as recipients of desire than as desirers—they are born out of the desire of the male for what a female can be for and to him. This desire defines how he looks at her and thus how she sees herself. Putting it in context, Ortiz says:

> From the age of twelve, the Buenos Aires woman learns to be seen, and thus, to exist. The gaze of the Other constructs her. ... Without this mirror which structures her identity, she would live—of course—but her life would be clouded, dulled, without brilliance. (116)

Given the glorification and commodification of the male gaze through advertisements, fashion displays, films, and so on (increasingly a global phenomenon), a woman can find (or lose) herself in a veritable hall of mirrors.

In North American culture, Susan Bordo and Naomi Wolf are infamous for applying the idea of the commodified gaze to how women see and treat their bodies. Bordo calls it going from the old metaphor of the body politic to the new metaphor of the politics of the body (21). Because her focus is often on body "weight," it is interesting that Bordo situates the changeover (in European culture) from weight control for the sake of spiritual value (i.e., the women mystics) to weight control for the sake of aesthetic value within the late nineteenth century, when colonial empires were at their height. One is driven to think once again about the colonization of women's bodies (see discussion of Jamaica Kincaid in chapter 4 and the discussion of Tsitsi Dangarembga in chapter 6) and to understand why Frantz Fanon included eating disorders in his discussion of the "nervous condition" of colonized persons.

Naomi Wolf includes weight control within the larger Western beauty industry and analyzes its danger in terms of prescribed behavior more than prescribed appearance: "The qualities that a given period calls beautiful in women are merely symbols of the female behavior that that period considers desirable: *The beauty myth is always actually prescribing behavior and not appearance*" (13). The kinds of behaviors she refers to in Western culture include competition between women (diminishing the possibility of solidarity), worship of youth (therefore of experiential and sexual ignorance), and disdain of aging (thus erasing the power of experienced, postmenopausal women). What she is saying here moves across borders, however, both because of her foundational analysis—aesthetic values always include behavioral imperatives—and because, with so much of Western aesthetics and consumerism being projected (through television, film, and advertising) into developing cultures, some of the behaviors she describes are on the brink of becoming global.[4] Lucidity means being aware of how the media-embodied gaze controls behavior.

### Critical Thinking

An extension of lucidity is critical thinking—analyzing where particular images and stereotypes come from, whom they serve, whom they omit—and making these questions part of the public discourse. No one has done this better, perhaps, than African American writer-critic bell hooks. As a university professor in Harlem, New York, she seeks to help her students learn how to interact critically with media images—how to "read" the complicated intersections of race, class, and (always) gender that occur there. Only by thinking critically, she argues, can they escape being controlled, often demeaned, by what they see and consume from popular culture. Recognizing that her students learn more about race, sex, and class from films than from all the theoretical literature that she assigns, she says: "I wanted to talk about what these discourses were saying and to whom." Furthermore, she wants to create "a space for *critical intervention* in mainstream cinema" (italics added, *Reel to Real* 3). It is intelligent, self-preserving intervention that she seeks and that she produces in essays, op-ed pieces, and film reviews. Ultimately, what hooks calls for, and what this study hopes to celebrate, is the "decolonized imagination," that which "critically intervenes and challenges dominant/hegemonic narratives by compelling audiences to actually transform the way they read and think" ("Conference Presentation," 57).[5]

### Rewriting

As an outgrowth of critical thinking, bell hooks calls for the rewriting of "master narratives" produced by systems of power to shape the behavior of their constituents. This call inevitably creates a dilemma for anyone trying to discern the place in culture of "subversive fictions." In that novels reflect culture as well as speak against culture, in that they are critiques as well as objects of critique, they function on all sides of the critical agenda. The novels included in this study invariably embody aspects of master narratives and deconstruct them. They both perpetuate aspects of the status quo (including grammar and syntax) and reconstruct reality (through the very act of fictionalizing). By nature, they are multifaceted and heteroglossic, whereas the voices of individual characters and narrators may be conservative and linear. Thus, all the writers of these works are critics, all their readers must be critics, but all the readings they produce will be, to some degree, misreadings.

That being said, one can still chart changes within the development of women's novels that validate the assertion that progress in critical thinking and rewriting is possible. Rachel DuPlessis writes about one of these changes in her book *Writing Beyond the Ending* (1995). She notes that in Western novels about women (some written by women) in the nineteenth century, romance plots and quest plots could co-exist only until the ending when romance absorbed quest and the heroine either married or committed suicide—melodramatically (Flaubert's Emma Bovary, Tolstoy's Anna Karenina, and Kate Chopin's Edna Pontellier are nearly perfect examples). But, she argues, it is the project of twentieth-century women writers to write *beyond* the common endings and to invent open narratives that allow for new options—transgressive imaginings—of the future. Here, DuPlessis' analysis seems to extend to the whole range of bold narratives produced by post-colonial women who, although they have their own cultural master narratives to contend with, are only minimally controlled by the Western romantic myth, and have fluid oral traditions to inspire them.

Although the content of fiction, of course, matters—while hopeful endings like those produced by Bessie Head, and transformed, feisty characters like Ama Ata Aidoo's Sister Killjoy and Meena Alexander's Draupadi, give the reader hope and energy—the real rewriting is more a matter of stylistics than of plot or character. It is a matter of stylistics as politics. We have looked at a number of "tricks" and significations that open up fictional narrative: the subject-in-process protagonist/narrator; the self-addressed letter; the flamboyant mixing of poetry and prose, of oral performance and writing; the embracing of palaverous discourse; the unification of surprise ending and bold authorial desire; heteroglossia itself, including ironic uses of colonial languages and unapologetic inclusion of "foreign" words; the "outlaw" language of women "talking back" to fathers/sons/lovers. The novels discussed in this chapter will focus on the interface of stereotype and diversity of experience/thought/speech, but the discussion builds on all that has gone before, the beauty being that novels (even didactic ones) are always and by their very nature more experiential and speculative than prescriptive and institutional.

## The Tragedy of Stereotype: Claribel Alegria's *Ashes of Izalco*

The novel that Nicaraguan-born, Salvadorian writer Claribel Alegria wrote in collaboration with her husband and translator Darwin Flakoll, *Ashes of Izalco* (1989), begins with a chaotic mix of voices. Carmen, a middle-aged Salvadorian woman married to a North American businessman, is in Santa Ana, El Salvador, for her mother's funeral. The whole family has gathered, including the pseudo-Marxist uncle, the ne'er do well alcoholic brother, the liberal-thinking but patriarchal father, selected family servants, cousins, assorted aunts and town matrons, the ghost of a dead brother, and, for sure, the ghost of recently dead Dona Isabel. A surprising voice that intervenes (much like North America has always intervened in Central American events) is that of Dona Isabel's one-time North American lover Frank Wolff. He intervenes into the family palaver through the pages of his diary, which he left with Isabel when he returned to North America and which she has eventually bequeathed to Carmen.

At first, the reader feels as if he or she has entered a labyrinth of seemingly disconnected memories, immediate reflections, political obsessions, and personal addictions. That seems to be quite fitting, however, for the events remembered in the narrative—events surrounding the mother's early life—occurred during one of the most disturbingly complex periods of Salvadorian history, *La Matanza* (The Slaughter), a peasant uprising in the 1930s that resulted in the extermination of 30,000 farmers, urban workers, and students and all but wiped out the indigenous population of the country. At the end, General Maximiliano Hernandez Martinez, himself of Indian lineage, set up a brutal dictatorship that quelled all dissent. ("And he seemed like such a quiet little Indian" [76], Carmen's father comments ruefully.)

Alegria is far from neutral about Salvadorian politics and history. Although committed to nonviolence in her own life, she was in direct sympathy with the revolutionary Sandinista National Liberation Front (FSLN) that took control in Nicaragua in 1979, and supported the Farabundo Marti Liberation Front (FMLN) that campaigned against the rightist government of El Salvador all during the 1980s. Recognizing the sacrificial role of women in the liberation struggle in El Salvador, she wrote the biography of rebel leader Ana Maria Castillo Rivas, appropriately calling it *They Won't Take Me Alive* (1983). In an introduction to Alegria's collection of poems, *Flowers from the Volcano* (1982), (referring both to political upheaval and the active volcano Izalco outside of San Salvador), Carolyn Forche, revolutionary poet from the United States, describes Alegria as a poet-novelist

> who has called herself a cemetery, willing to provide herself as a resting place for those whose bodies have never been recovered, the friends whose flesh has been mutilated beyond recognition. They are the dead who have become "too many to bury" who do not cease to exist but seem to besiege surviving poets with pleas to witness on their behalf, to add their names to a litany and, in so doing, illuminate the senseless brutality. (xi)

For all of her revolutionary sentiments, however, Alegria is a defender of "pure art," and rarely produces what would qualify as propaganda. *Ashes of Izalco* is less about political ideology than about the tragedy of an intelligent middle-class woman who, despite the political and social turmoil swirling about her, cannot revolt, cannot break out of the rituals and expectations that her class, race, and gender have superimposed on her. The political context reminds the reader of what the middle-class finds so hard to do or to allow. In leaving Frank Wolff's diary for her daughter, however, Isabel seems to be trying to warn Carmen about the dangerous enclosures of such a life.

There are many complex pairings in the novel, not the least of which is that between the writer and the bereaved reader of this diary. The North American lover, Frank Wolff, has described her mother in terms that surprise and disturb Carmen: "The picture he paints of Mother is so different, so strange . . ." (34). She has her own ideas of who the mother was: "'Home' for me was to watch her coming along the corridor, pausing now and then, keys jingling, to straighten a chair or arrange a flower vase" (38). Together, Frank and Carmen seem to dance over the mother's grave as competitors for her memory. His diary and her recollections compose the book—the "I" switching back and forth with tense reciprocity. Yet the differences with which they compose the narrative account are remarkable.

Carmen is a collector of data and memories. The sections she "narrates" are often third person. She speaks (using personal names for family members), is spoken to, entertains flashbacks, and lets the conversation meander, gathering in statements from anyone who seems to be passing through the room. In one of "her" scenes, she listens as family members recall and misread the mother. Alfredo says "she was always happy, always so good-humored." Dad contradicts him with "Your mother was a quiet woman—serious and quiet." While Eduardo remembers that the older she got "the more she turned to the left." Carmen, taking all of this in, even as she sits hoping that her mother never knew about an abortion she endured at her husband's behest, comments on how everyone, including Frank, saw the mother differently, like the six blind men trying to read an elephant (133).

Frank's diary, however, is strictly first person and analytical. He describes and interprets each "player" according to how he or she has entered the drama of Frank Wolff's life—his intermittent dissipations and attempts at rehabilitation. When he falls in love with Isabel, his romantic quest becomes the centering reality, and all persons are depicted according to their abilities to further or frustrate his cause, including Isabel herself. The script unfolds according to his desires, his association with second-rate philosophical fiction, and his need to control others when self-control fails. Any ambiguity in the text of the diary is there to serve shifts in his personal "story" line.

This pairing of linear self-serving plot with eclectic narrative gatherings places Frank and Carmen in time (his life is lost, hers is at a significant turning point) and in gender stereotypes (he is the conqueror, she the tentative seeker). In other pairings, the mother Isabel, identifying with and longing to visit Paris, is coupled with a physician husband who identifies with Nicaragua and the politics of Sandino, but who practices medicine in the political backwash of Santa Ana, El Salvador. Carmen is married to a North American "organization man" who does everything (including making love) according to a clearly delineated schedule and who could *never* understand his mother-in-law's affair with a recovering alcoholic from his own country. (He is, of course, completely unaware of how his desire to control Carmen corresponds with Frank's "creation" of Isabel.) Her husband accuses Carmen of being too emotional, treats her like "some kind of doll," and pretends to know her reactions in advance. Playing off the *Ladies Home Journal* series "Can this marriage be saved?", Carmen, the pretend-American wife, wonders if there is anything left to save (73).

In the face of the dull plateau of her marriage, Carmen cannot resist facing the questions her mother's life asks. She wonders what kept her mother in Santa Ana and what would have been her lot had she, Carmen, stayed there and had something concrete to blame for her ennui. Oddly enough, Carmen has had to recognize that although her mother was isolated, although she was detached from the world of overt politics, Isabel possessed an unusual measure of innate political realism. She once asked her Marxist brother Eduardo if he had ever imagined what a revolution was really like. "Those people are filled with hatred," she asserted about the Russian Revolution, "they wouldn't stop chopping off heads until the country was running with blood" (41). The irony (and the tragedy) is that Isabel has no idea at the time that she is describing her own country.

For all of her insight, however, Isabel is no citizen of the world; provincial Santa Ana is her home, no matter how strange she sometimes feels there (52). Facing the inevitability of her psychological exile with "pliant resignation," she only dreams of Paris. Like other well-to-do matrons, she passes her days complaining about servants (70), tolerating her husband's infidelities, listening "to women talking interminably about dresses and babies and parties," listening to men talk about "next year's coffee prices" (89)—entering into a "small, dull round of activities that repeats and repeats and repeats itself day after day" (89). She is a living stereotype of respectable, middle-class, provincial Salvadorian womanhood.

Until Frank Wolff shows up, that is—needing her husband's medical care and regaling her with tales about Europe and with the desperate compliments of a man who has lost his way. She sleeps with him once, contemplates running away with him, but is reminded amidst the mounting anxiety of social and personal unrest of how much her family means to her and ultimately of how cowardly and insular her life has made her. She sends him away.

Ultimately, Isabel seems to know that life with Frank would be as role-defined as life in Santa Ana. She would be a character in his latest novel, reflecting his fantasy of the moment. When he first meets her, Frank "reads" Isabel as desperate: "She seems to have resigned herself to living out the rest of her life in Santa Ana, to acting out the limited roles of doctor's wife, exemplary mother and devout Christian" (108). There is a ring of truth in what he observes, but in that this reading so clearly serves his own need to see himself in the role of hero, it unjustly reduces Isabel to the role of languishing romantic heroine. Finally, Frank must admit that, in Isabel's rejection of him, she has seen through his need to create her as the "small town doctor's wife," vulnerable to his erotic initiatives, and is therefore quite right in refusing a future that will accord her no more freedom of selfhood than life in the provinces. Yet he is so self-pitying in his final admission that it is hard to grant him an honest epiphany. Frank remains trapped in his own script. Having watched his friend Virgil die in an act of heroic solidarity with the peasant revolution, Frank, knowing himself incapable of such selflessness or courage, pens a line about raising "a candle to glimpse the face of truth" and leaves town (172).

His is a fairly predictable story. Why then does Isabel leave the diary for Carmen? Does she fail to recognize the "familiarity" of her own meager affair? Or is it because, for all the other embarrassing, histrionic passages it contains, the diary records her lament to Frank that Carmen's life is repeating the sleepy ritual of her own life: "I watch Carmen growing up here, and I feel real anguish to see her heading straight into the trap, the same net of insipid, conventional behavior that snared me" (112). And, indeed, by her own admission, Carmen has been snared, even though she has left Santa Ana and lives in Washington, DC. As she herself describes her life: "Apart from trips to El Salvador and to California to visit Paul's parents, we've never traveled. When we go on vacation or do anything outside our normal routine, Paul plans it like a military operation" (27). Through reading the diary, Carmen is forced to go from seeing her mother as the placid mirror of her own lowered expectations to suspecting that Isabel's final "gift" is "a slap in the face from the other side of the grave" (121).

The ending is inconclusive. The mother is buried. The diary has been read. Carmen is about to return to her life as wife and mother. Or is she? What she has come to realize in interacting with family in Santa Ana and in reading the private thoughts of her mother's lover, is that her mother's life was circumscribed not only by geography, not only by the traditional expectations for a middle-class woman in Central American society, but by the self-centered perceptions of each of her significant "others" as well. Frank's perceptions may have appeared the most coercive because he wrote his down. But husband, brother, son, all had their agendas for and definitions of Isabel. What Carmen pieces together is a new, problematized version of the mother, one that recognizes and even celebrates cracks in the facade. She is helped to do this by Eugenia, her aunt by marriage, who has stayed by Isabel's side through it all—through the death of a son, a husband's infidelity, years of smoldering desires (135). What Carmen will do with all of this remains to be seen, but no options are closed down. Alegria's willingness to project beyond the ending, to allow the reader to imagine beyond the ending, saves the work, an avid critique of gender roles, from enclosed tragedy (political as well as personal) and holds open the possibility that some new choices could be made.

### Stereotype Under Erasure: Anita Desai

A number of theorists, including cultural critic Chandra Mohanty and development philosopher Elizabeth Reid, call for a complication of the word "woman," even as it is used within a particular context (i.e., "third-world woman," "working woman," "woman writer"). To question such a term is to refuse essentialist thinking, to refuse predictable and confining cultural space, to resist simplistic notions of difference (male vs. female) in the search for equity and agency. The attempt by women activists, educators, development workers, and writers to deconstruct entrenched (and even faddish) stereotypes of women, is an attempt to honor the complexity and diversity of women's experiences and to use that difference to promote multiple notions of worth and success (as well as to comprehend and articulate the many ways that women have been compromised and exploited). Alegria's portrait of the tragic potential in cultural stereotypes, and the even more tragic complicity of women with cultural stereotypes, is one way that a novelist can expose the absurdity of generalization. The creation of female characters who share an intimacy, even a family origin, but who are radically different in thought and behavior (even from themselves) is another. Anita Desai's *Clear Light of Day* (1980) is a fine example of the latter methodology.

Desai embodies the post-colonial propensity for *mestiza* consciousness. Her father was a Bengali and her mother a German; she grew up speaking English with strains of German and Hindi woven in. Echoing the exilic consciousness of Bessie Head, she says, "I see India through my mother's eyes, as an outsider, but my feelings for India are my father's, of someone born here" (Robinson 80). She also says that the only place she can really call home is one where no one belongs, although she has lived in India until recently. The linguistic and geographic diversity that Desai has experienced is beautifully evident in her creation of multiplex characters.

### *Clear Light of Day*

Like Alegria's *Ashes of Izalco*, *Clear Light of Day* plays out a personal plot against political chaos, in this case the partition of Pakistan from India at the point of independence in 1949. Also like *Ashes*, it takes its characters from "present time" back into the turmoil of social upheaval and their own adolescence. As Andrea Robinson comments on this work, it weaves together "pre-Partition and post-Partition Delhi, childhood and adulthood, Hindu, Muslim and British cultures" (81).

The novel tells the story of four Hindu siblings in Delhi whose parents do little more than entertain and play bridge and who are subsequently raised by their eccentric "spinster" aunt. Most of the attention in this third-person narration is placed on the two sisters, Bim and Tara, Bim serving as the primary center of consciousness. Tara has married and moved away (her husband is an ambassador); Bim has stayed at home to care for the increasingly incapacitated alcoholic aunt and for a retarded younger brother who plays the same gramophone records over and over, every day. But although, at first read, Tara seems to fill the role of the dutifully married and submissive wife and mother, and although Bim seems to be an eccentric spinster-in-training, there are many ways that these sisters not only reverse roles, but in which their roles and character complications bleed into one another.

As the book opens, Tara has returned home for a family wedding (her older brother's son's) that Bim has no intention of attending. (Having once adored the older brother Raja, Bim cannot forgive him for marrying the daughter of their landlord and, upon the father-in-law's death, assuming the role of landlord himself, rather than simply bequeathing the house to her and Baba.) We meet Bim, a professor of history, in the act of demythologizing family history. "Bim was fierce," the omniscient narrator tells us. And she is, referring to the older brother Raja's poetic affectations as an incarnation of Lord Byron on his deathbed. His verse is terrible, she tells a still worshipful Tara, "Have you tried reading it recently? It's *nauseating*" (25). Nor, in her revisionism, does she spare Tara, and the sacred "joys of motherhood." Feeding her cat from a china saucer, Bim confronts Tara with "I know what you're thinking. . . . You're thinking how old spinsters go ga-ga over their pets because they haven't children. Children are the *real* thing, you think." When Tara admits she has been thinking of her daughters in that moment, Bim counters with, "Exactly. That's what I said. You think animals take the place of babies for us love-starved spinsters. . . . But you're wrong. . . . You can't possibly feel for them what I do about these wretched animals of mine" (6–7). Fulfilling and mocking the stereotype of the self-enclosed single woman simultaneously, Bim throws Tara (and us) off the track.

Tara has her own contradictions. Although she has lived out the role of traditional wife—submissive, placating, allowing her husband to describe her as "hopeless" before their marriage (17) and to attempt to "train her" and turn her into an "organized woman" (i.e., as close to his idea of the ideal man as he can get) after marriage—it is Tara who ultimately reminds Bim that, despite "that neat, sanitary, disinfected land in which she live[s] with Bakul" (28), it is she who left childhood and went out into the world, not Bim, the radical realist and student of the world.

The second and third parts of the novel take the reader back into the time of Partition and the adolescence of Bim, Tara, and Raja. (Their retarded brother Baba never leaves childhood, as his name suggests.) Here, in the past, both their complications and their typecasting of themselves and each other take shape, even as the complications of individual Hindu and Muslim lives are being forced into absurd and deadly antitheses. Whereas Bim loves study, Tara is terrified of the raucous world of school. Whereas Bim and Raja engage in wild, imaginative play—if he sees himself as Lord Byron, she can easily imagine herself as Florence Nightingale, or some other heroine—Tara allows herself to slip into the easier world of wanting to be a mother. In late adolescence, while Bim is taking on family responsibilities (following her parents' deaths and during Raja's prolonged bout with tuberculosis) and seems to be navigating somewhere between male and female cultural roles, Tara becomes absorbed into the social world of female neighbors. Yet in one marvelously liberating scene, Bim leads Tara into Raja's room where they put on his clothing and experience the liberating world of trousers and pockets. Tara marries these symbols of freedom; Bim puts them on psychologically.

In the final section, a surprise occurs. Bim's seemingly simple, realistic life explodes into a volcano of pent up anger and passionate loves. Having turned her back on Raja's romanticism, having eschewed the sentimentality of romantic marriage and motherhood, having learned to control history (both familial and cultural), she discovers that she is resentful and bitter, that she has "lived in too extreme a fashion, has become too much of the socially responsible one" (Afzal-Khan 82). But she also discovers that no one's reading of her "sacrifice" can suffice to make it make sense. She will have to live, as she has lived so far, as something of a stranger to herself, but a stranger who knows that much of her oddity comes from the wild and inarticulate affections she holds for her strange siblings. Meanwhile Tara, finally entering the family history with something like complex understanding, "crie[s] desperately, turning towards the house now, and Bakul, as if against her will 'but it's never over. Nothing's *over* ever'" (174). Does this final cry mean that her life and her subjectivity are also not finished, that more could come, more could be discovered, more could be constructed?

The tenor of the novel would seem to say so, for none of the usual stereotypes hold up in its pages. The female neighbors who "socialize" Tara into the marriage game eventually divorce their husbands (having first been rejected by them) and survive by running a dance school at home. Bakul, the ambassador-husband, who wants to control his wife's thoughts and movements, nevertheless admits that had the sardonic, scholarly Bim been more physically attractive, she would have been the sister he would have chosen (18–19). Raja, the romantic adolescent, still writes poetry, but has become a successful business man, has married a Muslim woman across religious–political lines, and has fathered five children of his own.

Aunt Mira, the eccentric aunt, turns out to have been a virgin widow, we find out, not a spinster, and acts out exotic and violent fantasies in her decline. All of the characters defy easy identification, a characteristic of any good piece of fiction, but particularly important to this study in that the story focuses primarily on the otherness of women's lives. The reader has entered a world where the attempt (even if reluctant) to understand the "hidden transcript" of another person's life, as well as the recognition that such a thing is ultimately impossible, becomes an impetus for *self-respect*—out of which all agency evolves.

Nowhere is this dynamic more obvious than in Desai's willingness, through Bim, to face and articulate the complex reality of a weird sister like Aunt Mira. Mira appears to have lived on the dark fringes of her society from an early age. Widowed at fifteen, the marriage unconsummated, she became the family "maid of all work, growing shabbier and skinnier and seedier with the years" (104). Bim and Tara's family take her in like "a discarded house-hold appliance" (105), ostensibly with the idea that she will care for the backward Baba. But she becomes a lively playmate to all the children, an other mother to replace their distant, diabetic, party-going biological mother. Thus, the "cracked pot, torn rag, picked bone"—the woman below culture—becomes a dramatic player, and in her odd state, socializes the children by telling them stories with strange "loops and turns." She never becomes "soft or scented or sensual"; she never takes on the "nature" of mother. She remains witchlike, "wrinkled and desiccated—like a stick, or an ancient tree" (111), and her speech and actions retain this outlaw quality.

It is no real surprise that Aunt Mira becomes alcoholic and infantile when the immediate need for her ministrations is over, thus returning to her own unmet desire for sustenance. She sucks at her brandy bottle with "little, little sips, with little, little juicy sounds, and it would be so sweet, so sweet again, just as when they were little babies, little babies for her to feed, herself a little baby sucking" (79). At this point, Desai, through Bim's empathy, enters into Mira's head, narrating the world as it appears to her—her hallucinations, sense of imprisonment, anxieties for the children she imagines to be still infants like herself (89–90). Such affectionate interest in the mad, meandering ruminations—the collapsed time—of a minor character indicates Desai's own alliance with the outcasts of the world she grew up in: the religious minorities caught on either side of the Partition of India and Pakistan, the forgotten female pariahs of a patriarchal system. That Aunt Mira haunts the lives of Bim and Tara after her death is to be expected. She is the "hidden transcript" of women's experience that lurks behind their class privileges and that claims kinship.

It is quite likely that it is their troubled joint memory of her (and of a broken India) that cracks both Bim and Tara open to the possibility of new options for their lives. The ground shifts under them no less than under their gnomic aunt, who became their doll/child in her death. She is the "other" who makes them other to their own habits and brings the fiercely controlled Bim to the point where, "although it was shadowy and dark," she could see by "the clear light of day" that she had nothing but love for her family, and if she had "gashes and wounds in her side," it was because she loved imperfectly and inarticulately. Giving up her hold on analytical language may be the greatest sacrifice and the greatest gift Bim can offer, the one thing that allows Tara's desperation and despair to be real *and* familiar to her (174).

Near the end, Bim is left, as is Desai, and the reader, reaching out for a book that could "draw the tattered shreds of her mind together and plait them into a composed and concentrated whole after a day of fraying and unravelling" (167). But a plait is more like a palimpsest than a syllogism, and therein may lie the power of Bim's admission of inarticulate loves. We leave her, and the always inarticulate Baba, listening to the songs of an aging singer whose voice is both childishly sweet and "inclined to break" with the "bitterness of his experiences" (182). His passion and pain take her, the historian, into a place of "secret darkness" where time is both destroyer and preserver and where the "deepest selves of her sister and brothers," and those who have shared time with them, join with her own in a richness of possibility, both political and personal.

## Reconfiguring the Roles of Women: Assia Djebar

The exposure and the disturbance of stereotyping as a form of cultural control are clearly part of the process of building agency—so is the projection of new roles for women. The last novel discussed in this chapter, Assia Djebar's *A Sister to Scheherazade* (1987), attempts that task. The work does not, and cannot, present a fully formed myth of success; but it embodies the challenges, disturbance, and promise actualized by any quest for full acceptance and value. And it projects new models of thinking and acting. One can only wonder what will happen when a critical mass of complex, self-valuing, and self-directing female characters—such as appear in this work—have made it into the literary canon.

Although Arabic was the "mother tongue" used in Assia Djebar's home, she was educated in French boarding school at the behest of her father, a French teacher. In that French was the language of business and public debate at the time of her pre-independence childhood, it was an unusual gesture for an Arab girl to be initiated into its world. This move, not incidentally, freed her from wearing the veil. Although Djebar admits to a deep gratitude for her father's gesture of freedom and encouragement, she also admits to feeling alienated from the rich exchange that goes on among traditional women in gatherings of matrons referred to as "the harem," and to maintaining a love–hate relationship with the French language. (Having studied Arabic, she still does not feel prepared to write it, and uses a *nom de plume* to veil her Algerian relatives from harm that might come their way as a result of her honesty about what transpires in the harem and women's steam bath.) One of the more ironic expressions of this divided loyalty can be found in her 1985 novel *Fantasia: An Algerian Cavalcade* where she includes—within the French text—transcripts of interviews she conducted in Arabic with female freedom fighters, thus forcing the colonial tongue to contain its antithesis.

It is perhaps her (discomforting and energizing) experience outside of the systems of exploitation of women that allows Djebar to "look in" with defiance and love, to create characters that not only accept responsibility for their forward-moving lives but stay connected to those still bound. Issues of class are inevitably involved in such a double gesture, for only participation in the cultural "elite" could have made it possible. Thus, although *A Sister to Scheherazade* contains traditional women, it focuses on the lives of the middle class (both traditional and modern). In speaking of a similar gesture on the part of Ghanaian novelist Ama Ata Aidoo, critic Vincent Odamtten argues that her choice of middle-class characters is not an abandonment of the "ranks of the wretched" but a respectful refusal to speak for them (161). This sentiment would appear to apply to Djebar and a number of other writers discussed in this study.

Another trait Djebar, Aidoo, and other post-colonial women novelists share is an obsession with marriage as prototype of the institutional containment of women's options. As Aidoo states:

> Throughout history and among all peoples, marriage has made it possible for women to be owned like property, abused and brutalized like serfs, privately corrected and, like children, publicly scolded, overworked, underpaid, and much more thoroughly exploited than the lowest male worker on any payroll. ("To Be a Woman" 263)

In Djebar's writing, there is the added burden of seclusion to define the married state. In an attempt to write women out of the cultural confinements that restrict their development, Aidoo, Djebar, and others often risk dangerous clarity about the hidden practices of marriage, but none of them has resorted to formulas for success. All of the complications of fully lived lives-in-process are present in the characters they construct and in their acts of writing.

### A Sister to Scheherazade

In this double narrative by Assia Djebar, a liberated woman not only tells her own story but imagines the life of the second wife that has replaced her in the home of her ex-husband and, for a time, in the life of her daughter Meriem. The narrator, Isma, is the shadow behind the new marriage, the one struggling to understand her relationship to the second wife, whom, in the tradition of polygamous marriages, she has herself chosen:

> Two women: two wives: Hajila and Isma. The scenario of my story features a strange duet; two women who are not sisters, not even rivals, although—as one of them knows, while the other is unaware—they are both the wives of the man—The Man—to echo words that are murmured in Arabic dialect in the bedroom. . . . This man does not come between them, but nevertheless does not turn them into accomplices. (1)

Isma begins to weave her tale by imagining the thoughts and actions of Hajila. Using the intimacy of the second-person pronoun—"This morning, Hajila, as you stand in the kitchen" (7)—Isma tells Hajila's life as if she is telling it *to* Hajila. As Helene Cixous describes such a gesture, Isma desires "to watch–think–speak the other in the other" ("The Laugh of the Medusa" 747). Yet, Hajila does not yet know Isma, except as a vague projection of "Meriem's mother," a woman Hajila only thinks about with "passive curiosity" (10).

Isma is, like Djebar herself, the fortunate "unveiled" daughter of a progressive father, who has made sure that she is fluent in French and can make her way in the wider world outside Algeria. Falling in love with an Algerian businessman who has international connections, she has taken up a life of travel, weaving European thought and experience with Arab/Muslim tradition. One of her "gifts," in addition to her freedom from the veil and language mobility, is that she has married for love, rather than custom or expediency, and experiences almost obsessive pleasure with her husband—"The Man."

Interestingly enough, one of the ways that Isma tries to possess The Man who possesses her body and soul is by identifying with his four sisters and speaking incessantly about them to him. She becomes a familial Scheherezade, spinning out their lives for his entertainment and to position herself: "So, in the solitude of our bedroom, I talk to my husband at length about his sisters. I conjure up their presence. Night after night, I piece together the body of the man I love, with eyes that speak for me and groping hands that take the place of sight. . . . I have to make an effort to drag myself out of this abyss of kinship" (50). It is this abyss of intimacy that ultimately comes to frighten Isma and to make her feel that she is not as free as she at first thought she might be.

It is no great surprise, then, that in the uncanny oscillation of chapters swinging from Isma's story of her own struggle with and against The Man to her imaginings of Hajila, we hear, soon after the passage describing Isma's use of The Man's sisters as source of intimate story, how The Man rapes Hajila (Isma's appropriated sister) in an act of frustrated desire. Does he fear that Isma has "taken" his sensuality so that he might be impotent with his new wife? Is he fearful for his honor? Does fear create violence? Is he angry that Hajila cannot be Isma? Or does Isma simply imagine all of this?

In the very next chapter of the narrative, which is anterior chronologically (linear sequence proves irrelevant in such an exploration), Isma tells us how she comes to realize that desire, even if freely expressed, can become a trap for women who are the inevitable objects of desire in a society of veiled and allusive bodies. Almost without premonition, she feels a need to resist the usual ritual of her lovemaking with The Man. And her resistance takes the form of rambling, obsessive, erratic speech, a "landslide of words," speech that follows the rhythm of the love act itself and that seems to come straight from her body's perplexed anguish: "The passage from arousal to pleasure follows a meandering course: I continue the assurances of my love, I deny him my lips so that I can go on talking, weaving a tale of passionate words. At last my lips find no more words, only hissed, muted, babbled accompaniment of orgasm . . . " (67). This is poetic language pushed to the point of collapse in its attempt to create viability.

Eventually, Isma resists sexual intimacy with The Man altogether, part of that resistance stemming from an expanded understanding of the meaning of veiling and disclosure. Living without the veil has set her free, but it has also stripped her of the intimacy of the harem and the anonymity of complete disguise, without freeing her from the social masking that accompanies any attire and the psychological veiling that she has experienced in relationship to her husband:

> I was to jeer at him, "Are men ever really naked? You are never free of fetters, you are bound fast by fears of the tribe, swathed in all the anxieties handed down to you by frustrated mothers, shackled by all your obsessions with some ill-defined elsewhere! . . . Show me one really naked man on this earth, and I will leave you for that man." (86)

Although she strips herself naked in body and soul every time they make love, he remains shrouded, and so she leaves him, not for some mythically unshrouded man, but for what she believes to be the naked truth of herself (86).

First, however, she fulfills the role of the responsible first wife and arranges for her "second," a girl from a poor family whose widowed mother, grateful for such a wealthy and worldly-wise son-in-law, is sure to be an accomplice in the arrangements. Having chosen to stay in Europe after the separation, Isma has been forced by custody law to let The Man take their daughter Meriem back to Algeria, and so she has chosen Hajila as much to be "other mother" as to care for The Man's household.

But no sooner is Hajila, a veiled, Arabic-speaking woman, in place in the apartment that Isma has also chosen, than Isma, missing her daughter and suspecting that she has enslaved an innocent victim (1), returns to Algeria and begins to imagine the young wife's lust for freedom. She constructs lengthy scenarios in which Hajila sneaks out of the apartment, at first veiled and happy for this disguise of unbleached wool. Later, Isma imagines an encounter between Hajila and an unveiled woman with hennaed hair (she could not then have been French) playing with her child out of doors, and she "watches" Hajila remove her veil in order to move about with dangerous freedom: "You tuck the *haik* under your arm; you walk on. You are surprised to find yourself walking so easily, at one fell swoop, out into the real world!" (31).

Isma revels in the empathetic freedom she creates for Hajila. She repeats the scenario over and over again with ever more daring. But is this authentic compassion or simply a exploitative narrative game she is playing? Can Hajila really be free as long as she is living with an unloved and unloving husband—a man still grieving the loss of his first wife, a man who takes her virginity violently and drinks to excess? Can she really be free as long as she must endure the silent disdain of her French-speaking stepdaughter?

Isma reclaims her daughter. Her imaginings are woven with Meriem's reports of life in the apartment. Hajila's afternoon escapes are discovered by the husband who (as Isma tells it) beats her unmercifully for leaving the apartment unaccompanied, but even more, for not being Isma. Meanwhile, reflecting on the long history of sister-wives sharing men's lives, Isma begins to weave her double narrative together with the story of Scheherazade, who, functioning as strategist as well as poet, brought her sister with her into the royal bed chamber to wake her one hour before dawn when the executioner was scheduled to arrive. Recognizing the reality of that executioner—the dangerous husband whom women in the harem casually refer to as *l'e'dou*, the enemy (*So Vast a Prison* 14)—Isma crosses the line from imagined to actual involvement in Hajila's (and her own) dilemma. By this time, Hajila is pregnant with an unwanted child who will make her daily wanderings impossible.

Isma interrupts the double (now triple) narrative with a series of vignettes about her early life, and about trapped, brutalized women—the kinds of stories that might be told in whispers in the gatherings of women in the harem. One is of a woman banished by the men in her family for merely exchanging a glance with a handsome childhood friend. Another is of a romantic young girl, forced into austere wedding rituals and brutalized by her bridegroom on the wedding night. Only one story stands out for the resistance of a female character, a young girl who cannot understand her mother's acquiescence to her father's nightly sexual demands, even as the family size far exceeds resources. Isma, the outsider, the raconteur, feels some resentment at the girl's anger: "What I could not accept was the girl's blazing outburst of stark hatred, expressed towards the too-submissive mother" (133). A woman's experience is far too complex to warrant easy blame; yet Isma too wonders why she is compelled to convey "this cascade of misery" (127), this digression into the underworld of women's pain and exploitation. Is this what she needs to move from "authorial" control—not so unlike The Man's control—to true vulnerability?

It is, perhaps, this exercise of empathetic storytelling, reminiscent of the empathetic accompaniment by which the sister to Scheherezade stayed the storyteller's execution, that propels Isma to recount how she arranged to meet Hajila, her rival and intimate, the sister to her storytelling, in the hammam, the steam bath, the one place where Arab women can be freely naked and vulnerable. They wash one another's shoulders and backs, exchange a ritual kiss; then Isma presses an extra key to the apartment into

Hajila's hand. Hajila is now as free as she can possibly afford to be, and it is a deft writer's hand that allows Hajila's final act—imagined or real? accident or chosen? desperate or bold?—to remain open to conjecture.

Isma returns with her daughter to her hometown to teach the Arabic mother tongue and to finish her journey where it began. When the storytelling ends, the roles have reversed, or rather intertwined. Hajila, having "awakened" Isma's compassion, now creates her own story, while Isma, the storyteller, becomes the sister who rouses Hajila—as well as her daughter Meriem—and recognizes a certain urgency in the task: "I fear lest we all find ourselves in chains again in 'this west in the Orient', this corner of the earth where day dawned so slowly for us that twilight is already closing in around us everywhere" (160).

So this wonderfully strange narrative ends with a poignant mix of ancient myth, and modern story. What Isma has done is audacious. It was audacious to live outside the harem. It was audacious to love with abandon. It was audacious to abandon that love when it became obsessive and self-negating. It was audacious to create another's fate through arranged marriage. It was audacious to create another's life through imaginings. It was audacious to give Hajila the means of escape. It was audacious to reveal the secrets of the harem and the hammam. It was also boldly loving and responsible.

Changing expectations for the lives of women—therefore changing the lives of women (or men, or children)—has never been easy and never will. But no one can be free from the past without imagining the future. And as long as writers like Djebar and Aidoo (and Alexander and Allende) continue to spin their tales of critique and celebration, as long as they insist that public discourse embrace literary "play," that the personal and the political remain complex lovers—as long as they continue to wake us one hour before dawn, morning will come . . . again, and again.

## Notes

1. The word *stereotype* is being used in this chapter to refer to fixed ideas about who persons are (and are expected to be) based on racial, ethnic, educational, political, or gender aggregates.

2. As a footnote on the issue of fertility control, Sen points out that the increasing problem of sex-selective abortion, as a result of government fertility control programs in China and places in India, contrasts sharply with practice in the progressive Indian province of Kerala, where empowerment of women has resulted in a "shift in family preference away from the rejection of female children" and therefore away from attack on the female foetus (109).

3. During the period of refugee repatriation in El Salvador (the late 1980s and early 1990s) the *co-madres* in El Salvador used their collective power to make sure that no more than one son was taken off the land by military recruitment. When second sons were "taken," they marched together to the barracks, appealed to the officers' affections and concern for their own mothers, and insisted on their sons' release. I personally witnessed their success in the province of Morazon.

4. See the narrator's/Sissie's comment on the kinds of girls African men marry in *Our Sister Killjoy* (47).

5. An interesting example of media control of images of women occurred recently during the women's World Cup soccer matches. *The New York Times* published a major review article by Larry Rohter, "Brazil Averts Its Eyes" (July 4, 1999), claiming that the Brazilian press had completely blocked out coverage of their championship team because soccer is considered to be "a masculine domain." The next week, on the day after the U.S. team won the tournament, *The New York Times* did not print a single picture of the U.S. team, but instead printed a large photo of a male recruit to a Miami team!

# Chapter 9

▼▼▼▼▼▼▼▼▼

## *Conclusion: Unexpected Gifts*

> One person is saluting another on the bare fact of the humanity they share: irreducible, fraught with danger, and for this moment, survived.
> —Kathleen Hill, *Still Waters in Niger*

> A gift is something which never appears as such and is never equal to gratitude, to commerce, to compensation, to reward.
> —Jacques Derrida, at Villanova University

Kathleen Hill's novel *Still Waters in Niger* (1999) both is and is about "the gift." The Irish-American narrator tells us that she spent the early years of her marriage teaching in Nigeria, and one year of her early motherhood in Niger, while her husband was researching his dissertation. As she comes to realize in the present, however, she was far too ingrown in those years, far too distracted by her personal life, and, perhaps, far too afraid of the austerity of the desert and the poverty around her to really engage with the life and languages of Africa. Some seventeen years later, she has come to visit her oldest daughter Zara, who practices medicine in Matameye, Niger, and who has made few of her mother's mistakes. Luckily, the mother has the humility to learn from her daughter's experience, to let her daughter teach her and (re)introduce her to Africa

But there is more than cultural alienation involved here. The novel is also about separation between mother and daughter, about misunderstanding between first world and third world, about desertification that results from (international) greed, about the lack of "seeing" that leads all of us into dangerously essentialistic thinking, and, ultimately, about the complex relationship between giving and receiving. These are all subjects involved in the discussions of *Aeroplane Mirrors*, and they are articulated, in the case of this recent novel, by a first-world woman, who, while politically savvy and feminist, is still very aware that she has more to learn than to teach, more to hear than to say—who is open to the unexpected gifts rendered to her by her daughter, the desert, African women, and the poor. In this she models for first-world readers what it means to build unexpected solidarities with women and texts from very different places. In this, she also expresses the gratitude felt by the writer of *Aeroplane Mirrors* for all that she continues to receive from the writings here discussed.

The narrator of *Still Waters in Niger* has come to Africa seeking connection. It is not long after her arrival that her daughter hints that something irreparably alienating, although, in some ways laughably trivial, occurred on her sixth birthday, during the family's time in Niger. Much later in the novel, Zara comes to trust her mother enough to tell her that "the rupture" entailed her coming home from school in anticipation of welcome and festive surprises, only to realize/remember that her mother was in bed with malaria, and, in fact, so dazed with fever that she could only stare right through the child. Hearing this, the mother is aware that although she could not help being sick, her veiled gaze was typical of her "preoccupation with shadows" in those days—an inattention to the life around her worthy to be mourned. "Is it, once and for all, too late?" she wonders. Part of her present anxiety is that, in addition to learning Hausa, the language the mother could never master, and community custom, Zara has been adopted by generous other mothers in Niger. ("Was another woman beginning to take my place? Perhaps Zara would make comparisons, prefer a woman who was wiser than myself" [64].) Loss of intimacy translates to cultural loss when the mother realizes that Zara has become comfortable in a world where she will always be something of a stranger because she did not become a familiar when she might have.

This is akin to the experience of many of us who have failed to learn that which might have made us better citizens of the world, better caretakers of each other and of ourselves. "Is it, once and for all, too late?" Remembering the singing of three blind old women at the city gate of Zinder, the narrator speculates on the cross-cultural complexity and neglect reflected in their song:

> It was then, too, that waking slowly at night, we heard a solitary, plucked music that seemed to speak of the terrible unknowability

of this place where Arab, European, and the old desert races had all mingled and strained to bring forth the blind child who extended a gaping bowl at noon, as oblivious of the past as of the future. Wounded city, wounded child, wearing its history like a bruise. (36)

But, it would be a dire mistake to read this novel as an endorsement of victim and guilt mentalities. For, despite spread of the desert, despite malnutrition, despite infant diarrhea and "simple" diseases that Zara tries (often unsuccessfully) to fight, despite early marriages and multiple pregnancies (Zara's best friend and age-mate has five children at twenty-three), the land is achingly beautiful, the people complexly loving, and their spirit indomitable, even joyful. When Zara's neighbor, El Gouni, speaks of her daughter who has lost seven babies and seems to be losing touch with reality, El Gouni says, "If I could not release Marianma from her pain, if the lost babies could not be restored, then I knew I must embrace Marianma as one who suffers. But as one, too, . . . who has received the gift of sight" (157). What kind of a gift is that?

In his recent writings, French philosopher Jacques Derrida exhibits almost an obsession with the idea of gifts and how they work. He argues that, in ordinary circumstances, when a gift is given it enters into a circular "economy." The gift entails debt and necessitates reciprocity—whole cultural systems are based on rituals of exchange. But he also says that as soon as giving occurs, the gift can no longer *be* a gift: "As soon as I say 'thank you' for a gift, I start canceling the gift, I start destroying the gift, by proposing an equivalence, that is, a circle which encircles the gift in a movement of reappropriation" (18). What this means for Derrida is not that the gift is irrelevant, rather that it must be acknowledged as that which comes unexpectedly, that which, at least for a moment, is surprisingly and totally other, that which interrupts and disrupts our closed systems of checks and balances.

If we apply this thinking to text (edition means "to give out," as in a new "release"), then meaning is a gift, not to be seized and appropriated by the familiar, but capable of showing us difference. In a book entitled *The Prayers and Tears of Jacques Derrida*, John Caputo interprets Derrida's thinking about literary texts:

> Literary gifts require a living author who by committing herself to words and text agrees to death, agrees to deal herself death, *donner la mort*, to give a gift without return and let her text go up in smoke, or turn to ash, that is to say, to disseminate without re-

turn, however fit she may feel when she signs her contract and checks the royalty clause. (175)

In playful style, Caputo accepts Derrida's notion that the impossibility of "pure" gift (we always feel some reserve) in no way negates the beauty and necessity of gifting. If there were no "free" gifts, if we all simply followed the "rules of the contract," novels would be linear and authors in charge, once and for all, of what we receive from them; marriages could only be passionless exactments and work uninspiring drudgery. Language would be limited to the denotative, patriarchy fixed, and change impossible.

So we all hope for giving (and for-giving) that is not reckless, but that goes beyond our ready reserves and disrupts our accounting—in relationship, in politics, in reading, and in writing. The conference in Beijing went beyond any global gathering for women in history and asked for impossible reconciliations. The novels discussed in this book push the boundaries of narrative, add wild new voices to literary discourse, and force the art world to recognize its multiple kinships with global women's despairs and desires. As readers outside of the primary audience for these writings, first-world women (and men) are forced into the role of eavesdroppers, hearing things they did not expect to hear (that they were, perhaps, not intended to hear) but which enlarge their sense of life itself. They (I) have been gifted beyond measure.

The narrator of *Still Waters in Niger* is gifted beyond measure as well—first, through being shown hospitality by the very girl child she first housed. Second, she is received into the lives of many of the African women she encounters; one old woman recognizes her face from seventeen years earlier, surmises that Zara is the small child she had with her at the time, and grabs their hands "lifting them together in the air as high as she can reach" (125). The narrator is gifted by the ritual joy that circumscribes people's lives in Niger, as they salute one another daily "on the bare fact of the humanity they share: irreducible, fraught with danger, and for this moment, survived" (97). Most surprising of all, she is gifted with a small coiled snail shell, "a relic from a time of waters" from the hand of a beggar boy who has befriended her. Reminiscent of life-giving waters, of beauty in the middle of want, of one who knows how to give what he does not have, of the spiraled meaning that all symbols and stories offer, the gift sends her home quite different from when she came.

Participants at Beijing went home quite different than they came; readers emerge from these women's novels quite different from when they

## Conclusion 215

"went in" (if they have, like Marianma, received the gift of sight). Our conversation ends with a French philosopher and a North American novelist because they represent the developed world's need—and, in this case, honest attempt, male and female alike—to hear, to see, and to expect the unexpected (from unexpected sources) if they would participate in the building of a habitable world. Ultimately it all turns on an outstretched palm.

# *Appendix A: Beijing Declaration, Fourth World Conference on Women*

**Beijing Declaration**

1. We, the Governments, participating in the Fourth World Conference on Women,

2. Gathered here in Beijing, in September 1995, the year of the fiftieth anniversary of the founding of the United Nations,

3. Determined to advance the goals of equality, development and peace for all women everywhere in the interest of all humanity,

4. Acknowledging the voices of all women everywhere and taking note of the diversity of women and their roles and circumstances, honouring the women who paved the way and inspired by the hope present in the world's youth,

5. Recognize that the status of women has advanced in some important respects in the past decade but that progress has been uneven, inequalities between women and men have persisted and major obstacles remain, with serious consequences for the well-being of all people,

6. Also recognize that this situation is exacerbated by the increasing poverty that is affecting the lives of the majority of the world's people, in particular women and children, with origins in both the national and international domains,

7. Dedicate ourselves unreservedly to addressing these constraints and obstacles and thus enhancing further the advancement and empowerment

of women all over the world, and agree that this requires urgent action in the spirit of determination, hope, cooperation and solidarity, now and to carry us forward into the next century.

**We reaffirm our commitment to:**

8. The equal rights and inherent human dignity of women and men and other purposes and principles enshrined in the Charter of the United Nations, to the Universal Declaration of Human Rights and other international human rights instruments, in particular the Convention on the Elimination of All Forms of Discrimination against Women and the Convention on the Rights of the Child, as well as the Declaration on the Elimination of Violence against Women and the Declaration on the Right to Development;

9. Ensure the full implementation of the human rights of women and of the girl child as an inalienable, integral and indivisible part of all human rights and fundamental freedoms;

10. Build on consensus and progress made at previous United Nations conferences and summits—on women in Nairobi in 1985, on children in New York in 1990, on environment and development in Rio de Janeiro in 1992, on human rights in Vienna in 1993, on population and development in Cairo in 1994 and on social development in Copenhagen in 1995 with the objectives of achieving equality, development and peace;

11. Achieve the full and effective implementation of the Nairobi Forward-looking Strategies for the Advancement of Women;

12. The empowerment and advancement of women, including the right to freedom of thought, conscience, religion and belief, thus contributing to the moral, ethical, spiritual and intellectual needs of women and men, individually or in community with others and thereby guaranteeing them the possibility of realizing their full potential in society and shaping their lives in accordance with their own aspirations.

**We are convinced that:**

13. Women's empowerment and their full participation on the basis of equality in all spheres of society, including participation in the decision-making process and access to power, are fundamental for the achievement of equality, development and peace;

14. Women's rights are human rights;

*Appendix A*

15. Equal rights, opportunities and access to resources, equal sharing of responsibilities for the family by men and women, and a harmonious partnership between them are critical to their well-being and that of their families as well as to the consolidation of democracy;

16. Eradication of poverty based on sustained economic growth, social development, environmental protection and social justice requires the involvement of women in economic and social development and equal opportunities and the full and equal participation of women and men as agents and beneficiaries of people-centred sustainable development;

17. The explicit recognition and reaffirmation of the right of all women to control all aspects of their health, in particular their own fertility, is basic to their empowerment;

18. Local, national, regional and global peace is attainable and is inextricably linked with the advancement of women, who are a fundamental force for leadership, conflict resolution and the promotion of lasting peace at all levels;

19. It is essential to design, implement and monitor, with the full participation of women, effective, efficient and mutually reinforcing gender-sensitive policies and programmes, including development policies and programmes, at all levels that will foster the empowerment and advancement of women;

20. The participation and contribution of all actors of civil society, particularly women's groups and networks and other non-governmental organizations and community-based organizations, with full respect for their autonomy, in cooperation with Governments, are important to the effective implementation and follow-up of the Platform for Action;

21. The implementation of the Platform for Action requires commitment from Governments and the international community. By making national and international commitments for action, including those made at the Conference, Governments and the international community recognize the need to take priority action for the empowerment and advancement of women.

**We are determined to:**

22. Intensify efforts and actions to achieve the goals of the Nairobi Forward-looking Strategies for the Advancement of Women by the end of this century;

23. Ensure the full enjoyment by women and the girl child of all human rights and fundamental freedoms, and take effective action against violations of these rights and freedoms;

24. Take all necessary measures to eliminate all forms of discrimination against women and the girl child and remove all obstacles to gender equality and the advancement and empowerment of women;

25. Encourage men to participate fully in all actions towards equality;

26. Promote women's economic independence, including employment, and eradicate the persistent and increasing burden of poverty on women by addressing the structural causes of poverty through changes in economic structures, ensuring equal access for all women, including those in rural areas, as vital development agents, to productive resources, opportunities and public services;

27. Promote people-centred sustainable development, including sustained economic growth through the provision of basic education, life-long education, literacy and training, and primary health care for girls and women;

28. Take positive steps to ensure peace for the advancement of women and, recognizing the leading role that women have played in the peace movement, work actively towards general and complete disarmament under strict and effective international control, and support negotiations on the conclusion, without delay, of a universal and multilaterally and effectively verifiable comprehensive nuclear-test-ban treaty which contributes to nuclear disarmament and the prevention of the proliferation of nuclear weapons in all its aspects;

29. Prevent and eliminate all forms of violence against women and girls;

30. Ensure equal access to and equal treatment of women and men in education and health care and enhance women's sexual and reproductive health as well as education;

31. Promote and protect all human rights of women and girls;

32. Intensify efforts to ensure equal enjoyment of all human rights and fundamental freedoms for all women and girls who face multiple barriers to their empowerment and advancement because of such factors as their race, age, language, ethnicity, culture, religion, or disability, or because they are indigenous people;

*Appendix A*

33. Ensure respect for international law, including humanitarian law, in order to protect women and girls in particular;

34. Develop the fullest potential of girls and women of all ages, ensure their full and equal participation in building a better world for all and enhance their role in the development process.

**We are determined to:**

35. Ensure women's equal access to economic resources including land, credit, science and technology, vocational training, information, communication and markets, as a means to further the advancement and empowerment of women and girls, including through the enhancement of their capacities to enjoy the benefits of equal access to these resources, inter alia, by means of international cooperation;

36. Ensure the success of the Platform for Action which will require a strong commitment on the part of Governments, international organizations and institutions at all levels. We are deeply convinced that economic development, social development and environmental protection are interdependent and mutually reinforcing components of sustainable development, which is the framework for our efforts to achieve a higher quality of life for all people. Equitable social development that recognizes empowering the poor, particularly women living in poverty, to utilize environmental resources sustainably is a necessary foundation for sustainable development. We also recognize that broad-based and sustained economic growth in the context of sustainable development is necessary to sustain social development and social justice. The success of the Platform for Action will also require adequate mobilization of resources at the national and international levels as well as new and additional resources to the developing countries from all available funding mechanisms, including multilateral, bilateral and private sources for the advancement of women; financial resources to strengthen the capacity of national, subregional, regional and international institutions; a commitment to equal rights, equal responsibilities and equal opportunities and to the equal participation of women and men in all national, regional and international bodies and policy-making processes; the establishment or strengthening of mechanisms at all levels for accountability to the world's women;

37. Ensure also the success of the Platform for Action in countries with economies in transition, which will require continued international cooperation and assistance;

38. We hereby adopt and commit ourselves as Governments to implement the following Platform for Action, ensuring that a gender perspective is reflected in all our policies and programmes. We urge the United Nations system, regional and international financial institutions, other relevant regional and international institutions and all women and men, as well as non-governmental organizations, with full respect for their autonomy, and all sectors of civil society, in cooperation with Governments, to fully commit themselves and contribute to the implementation of this Platform for Action.

# Appendix B: Non-Governmental Organisation (NGO) Beijing Declaration, September 15, 1995

A decade after the Nairobi Conference, the Forward Looking Strategies have not been fully implemented by any government. We live in a world marked by growing poverty, inequality, injustice, unemployment, environmentally destructive economic growth, war, sexism, racism, xenophobia, homophobia and other forms of discrimination and violence against women. Moreover, the intersection of gender, race and poverty create multiple burdens of discrimination for many women of colour.

We, NGO women of the world, rich in our diversity, have gathered along with governments in the largest global conference ever to address women's issues and the existing barriers to our achieving equality, development and peace. We believe that these goals can be realized by ending the oppression of women and girls, by women's full participation in national and international decision-making, and transforming the social, economic and political structures which underlie and perpetuate poverty, racism, inequality, injustice, unemployment, violence and war.

On the eve of the 50th anniversary of the United Nations, despite the many obligations undertaken by its member states, women's human rights are not yet respected, protected and promoted as inalienable, indivisible and universal.

Resources are being persistently squandered on the military with no gain in peace and common security. The dominant development model and global market economy generate great material wealth for a few, while impoverishing many; create homelessness and environmental racism and degradation; encourage overconsumption and arms proliferation; deplete our natural resources and forests; pollute our air, water and soil; contribute to violations of women's civil, economic, cultural and political rights. The current growth model fails to meet the fundamental material and spiritual needs of the peoples of the world.

Women are major contributors to every economy but much of our labour is unrecognized and undervalued. We do two thirds of the world's work yet earn only 5% of its income, our labour serving as an invisible subsidy to the world's wealth.

The globalization of the world's so-called "market economies" is a root cause of the increasing feminization of poverty everywhere. This violates human rights and dignity, the integrity of our eco-systems and the environment, and poses serious threats to our health. The global economy, governed by international financial institutions, the World Trade Organization and trans-national corporations, impose Structural Adjustment Programs on countries in the South and economic restructuring in countries in the North in the name of fiscal health. The result is increasing poverty, debt and unemployment. The resulting reductions in social programs and services in the areas of health, education and housing harm the very people they purport to assist. The media, controlled by transnational corporations, acts as an instrument of social control, denying women's right to free communication.

Supported by the wisdom of our elders, inspired by indigenous peoples, energized by youth, and sustained by our sisterhood, we call for an end to these conditions and refuse to accept them as inevitable for the future of humanity. WOMEN'S RIGHTS ARE HUMAN RIGHTS.

WE CALL ON ALL GOVERNMENTS:

1. TO recognize and ensure women's equal rights to a decent standard of living, health, clean water and air, adequate food, clothing, and sanitation, safe and accessible housing, adequate social security and social insurance, education and legal aid as agreed in the International Covenant of Economic, Social and Cultural Rights.

2. TO take prompt action on the cancellation of multilateral debt; to enforce the accountability of international financial institutions and to ensure that all trade agreements are subject to human rights legislation, environmental and internationally recognised labour standards. Economic rights are human rights.

3. TO end the transboundary movement, dumping and stockpiling of hazardous, toxic and radioactive wastes.

4. TO promote and use science and technology for peaceful purposes and people-centered, sustainable and ecologically sound development.

5. TO encourage, not hinder, the free expression, full participation and full access for women with disabilities in non-governmental and governmental organisations locally, nationally and internationally.

6. TO recognise and implement initiatives taken by poor and grassroots women, including them, as full participants in the planning and distribution of resources.

7. Not to misinterpret or impose religious beliefs or traditional practices on women in ways that deny their inalienable human rights. We also call for an end to all laws and customary practices which deny girls and women their equal rights, and deny their equal access to succession and inheritance.

8. TO amend their intellectual property laws so as to make indigenous women the primary beneficiaries of the commercial use of their knowledge.

9. TO reject militarism in all its forms and create a culture of peace and human rights. They must redirect the $800 billion annual global military spending to peaceful purposes and convert military production to socially useful purposes. Governments must abolish weapons of mass destruction by banning testing, sales and stockpiling of nuclear, chemical, biological, and all other weapons. The production, trade and use of all landmines must be banned. We demand that our governments work together to solve conflicts without using violence, and that they fully include women in peacemaking and conflict resolution initiatives.

10. TO implement their commitments to measure and value women's unwaged work and to include it in the accounting of each nation's GDP.

11. Dominant development models have been based upon the appropriation of resources from the South by the North and the transfer of ideas, technologies and methodologies from the North to the South. We must build upon alternative models that currently exist in both South and North, which are based on equality, mutual respect, true participation and accountability to all women. These models must be economically and socially equitable and environmentally sound. All development projects must

take into account their effects on women, including the additional workload imposed on women by unsustainable and inappropriate technology.

12. NGO women of the world call upon all peoples and all governments to radically reconsider and transform concepts, assumptions and structures governing social and economic life, and to take action on our recommendations. This process will require the full and equal participation of women of all races, ethnic backgrounds, religions, classes, languages, girls, young women, older women, indigenous women, grassroots women, rural women, urban women, women with disabilities, immigrant women, migrant women, refugee women, internally and other displaced women, women of different sexual orientation, and all other marginalized women.

WE CALL FOR:

1. Access for women to political structures at all levels, and equal political empowerment at all decision-making levels. Accountable, transparent and participatory national and international institutions must be created. Women must have free access to diversified and pluralistic information sources and media which are culturally and linguistically appropriate for receiving and communicating information. Governments must support NGOs and ensure their full participation in planning and implementing all programs and policies.

2. Recognition, protection, compensation, financial and other assistance and full legal status for the millions of women and children, and the victims of nuclear and other environmental catastrophes, many of them widows or orphans, who have been forced to become immigrants, migrants, refugees, internally and other displaced persons or forced into sexual slavery as a result of war, foreign occupation and political and socio-economic injustices. Every effort should be made to protect civilian populations from the adverse effects of economic sanctions, which impair their economic human rights.

3. Universally accessible, high quality, non-discriminatory health care, which use the great diversity of possibilities available in health systems world-wide rather than the present overdependence on Western medicine that overmedicates and pathologizes women's bodies. We require all governments to sponsor and support woman-controlled research for the prevention and cure of HIV/AIDS, to prohibit any form of discrimination of women with HIV/AIDS, and to ensure women's access to information, care, support and treatment of HIV/AIDS.

*Appendix B*

4. Development and sustained use of affirmative action by both the private and public sectors of society to ensure the equality of women.

5. All the media to change the present negative, exploitative and sexualized images of women and children to positive ones respecting us in all our dignity and diversity.

6. A reshaping of education for all children, beginning at the primary levels, to sensitize them about human rights, gender issues, and non-violent conflict resolution, stressing the need for world peace.

7. Full implementation of the UN Decade for Human Rights Education and the prevention of human rights violations against women.

8. New and additional financial, technical and other resources to successfully implement the plans and commitments from the Nairobi, Rio de Janeiro, Vienna, Cairo, Copenhagen and Beijing Conferences, and that member states fulfil their obligations under the Convention on the Elimination of All Forms of Discrimination against Women.

WE DEMAND AN END TO RAPE, AND TO ALL FORMS OF VIOLENCE, SEXUAL EXPLOITATION AND HARASSMENT OF WOMEN AND CHILDREN. WE FURTHER DEMAND AN END TO THE TRAFFICKING OF WOMEN AND CHILDREN AS WELL AS SEX TOURISM.

We seek these transformations in the spirit of service to humanity, partners with youth as agents of change, keeping our children, grandchildren and future generations in our hearts. We are convinced that as women achieve full and equal participation in all the affairs of the planet, peace will be realized, and the well-being of every individual secured.

WE REAFFIRM THAT WOMEN'S RIGHTS ARE HUMAN RIGHTS.

# *Bibliography*

Abel, Elizabeth. "(E)merging Identities: The Dynamics of Female Friendship in Contemporary Fiction by Women." *Signs: Journal of Women in Culture and Society* 6, no. 3 (Spring 1981): 413–435.

Adams, Alice. *Reproducing the Womb.* Ithaca: Cornell University Press, 1994.

Afkhami, Mahnaz, and Erika Friedl. "Introduction." In *Muslim Women and the Politics of Participation: Implementing the Beijing Platform*, edited by Mahnaz Afkhami and Erika Friedl. Syracuse: Syracuse University Press, 1997.

Afzal-Khan, Fawzia. *Cultural Imperialism and the Indo-European Novel: Genre and Ideology in R.K. Narayan, Anita Desai, Kamala Markandaya, and Salman Rushdie.* University Park, PA: The Pennsylvania State University Press, 1993.

Aidoo, Ama Ata. *Our Sister Killjoy: Or Reflections from a Black-eyed Squint.* Harlow, Essex: Longman, 1988.

———. "To Be a Woman." In *Sisterhood Is Global*, edited by Robin Morgan. New York: The Feminist Press, 1996.

Alcoff, Linda. "Cultural Feminism versus Post-structuralism: The Identity Crisis in Feminist Theory." *Signs: Journal of Women in Culture and Society* 13, no. 3 (Spring 1988): 405–436.

———. "Democracy and Rationality: A Dialogue with Hilary Putnam." In *Women, Culture, and Development: A Study of Human Capabilities*, edited by Martha Nussbaum and Jonathan Glover. Oxford: Clarendon Press, 1995.

Alegria, Claribel. *They Won't Take Me Alive: Salvadoran Women in Struggle for Liberation*, translated by Darwin J. Flakoll. London: Women's Press, 1987.

Alegria, Claribel, and Darwin J. Flakoll. *Ashes of Izalco*, translated by Darwin J. Flakoll. Willimantic, CT: Curbstone Press, 1989.
Alexander, Meena. *Manhattan Music*. San Francisco: Mercury House, 1997.
———. *Nampally Road*. San Francisco: Mercury House, 1991.
———. *The Shock of Arrival: Reflections on Postcolonial Experience*. Boston: South End Press, 1996.
———. "Translated Lives: The Poetry of Migration," address given at The Conference on Contemporary Poetry. Rutgers University, April 24 to 27, 1997.
Allende, Isabel. *Eva Luna*, translated by Margaret Sayers Peden. New York: Bantam Books, 1989.
———. *House of the Spirits*, translated by Magda Bogin. New York: Bantam Books, 1982.
———. *Paula*, translated by Margaret Sayers Peden. New York: Harper, 1996.
Alvarez, Julia. *In the Time of the Butterflies*. New York: Plume, 1994.
Angelou, Maya. *I Know Why the Caged Bird Sings*. New York: Random House, 1996.
Anzaldua, Gloria. *Borderlands/La Frontera: The New Mestiza*. San Francisco: Aunt Lute Press, 1987.
———. "Speaking in Tongues: A Letter to 3rd World Women Writers." In *This Bridge Called My Back: Writings by Radical Women of Color*, edited by Cherrie Moraga and Gloria Anzaldua. New York: Kitchen Table—Women of Color Press, 1981.
Appiah, Anthony. "Topologies of Nativism." In *Literary Theory: An Anthology*, edited by Julie Rivkin and Michael Ryan. Oxford: Blackwell Publishers, 1998.
Arteaga, Alfred. "An Other Tongue." In *An Other Tongue: Nation and Ethnicity in the Linguistic Borderlands*, edited by Alfred Arteaga. Durham: Duke University Press, 1994.
Ashcroft, Bill, Gareth Griffiths and Helen Tiffin. *The Empire Writes Back: Theory and Practice in Post-Colonial Literatures*. New York: Routledge, 1989.
Ba, Mariama. *Scarlet Song*, translated by Dorothy S. Blair. Essex: Longman, 1986.
———. *So Long a Letter*, translated by Modupé Bodé-Thomas. Oxford: Heinemann, 1989.
Bakhtin, Mikhail. *The Dialogic Imagination: Four Essays*, edited by Michael Holquist, translated by Caryl Emerson and Michael Holguist. Austin: University of Texas Press, 1981.
———. *Rabelais and His World*, translated by Helene Iswolsky. Cambridge: MIT Press, 1968.
Bedford, Simi. *Yoruba Girl Dancing*. New York: Penguin, 1994.
*Beijing Declaration* and *Platform for Action, Report of the Fourth World Conference on Women* (Beijing, 4-15 September, 1995). New York: The United Nations, 1995. (Printed in their entirety in *Beyond Beijing: Toward the*

*Twenty-first Century of Women*, special edition of *Women's Studies Quarterly* 4, no. 1-2 (Spring/Summer, 1996).

Benhabib, Seyla. "Cultural Complexity, Moral Interdependence, and the Global Dialogical Community." In *Women, Culture, and Development: A Study of Human Capabilities*, edited by Martha Nussbaum and Jonathan Glover. Oxford: Clarendon Press, 1995.

———. *Situating the Self: Gender, Community and Postmodernism in Contemporary Ethics*. Cambridge: Polity Press, 1992.

Bernards, Reena. "Forging Across the Borders of Conflict: Women's Diplomacy." In *Women at the Center: Development Issues and Practices for the 1990s*, edited by Gay Young, Vidyamali Samarasinghe, and Ken Kusterer. West Hartford, CT: Kumarian Press, 1993.

*Beyond Beijing: Women and Economic Justice* (video). Philadelphia: Nightingale Productions and WHYY/TV, 1996.

Bhasin, Kamla. "Challenges for Women's Empowerment and Education in South Asia." In *A Commitment to the World's Women: Perspectives on Development for Beijing and Beyond*, edited by Noeleen Heyzer. New York: UNIFEM, 1995.

Bordo, Susan. *Unbearable Weight: Feminism, Western Culture, and the Body*. Berkeley: University of California Press, 1993.

Bornstein, David. "The Barefoot Bank with Cheek." *Atlantic Monthly* 276 (December 1995): 40–47.

Boserup, Ester. *Women's Role in Economic Development*. New York: St. Martin's Press, 1970.

Bradley, Christine. "Why Male Violence against Women Is a Development Issue: Reflections from Papua New Guinea." In *Women and Violence: Realities and Responses Worldwide*, edited by Miranda Davies. London: Zed Books, 1994.

Bruce, Judith. "The Economics of Motherhood." In *A Commitment to the World's Women: Perspectives on Development for Beijing and Beyond*, edited by Noeleen Heyzer. New York: UNIFEM, 1995.

Buckley, Stephen. "Wedded to Tradition: Marriage at Puberty." *The Washington Post* (December 13, 1997): A1.

Bunch, Charlotte. "Women's Human Rights and Development: A Global Agenda for the 21st Century." In *A Commitment to the World's Women: Perspectives on Development for Beijing and Beyond*, edited by Noeleen Heyzer. New York: UNIFEM, 1995.

———. "Women's Rights as Human Rights: Toward a Re-vision of Human Rights." *Human Rights Quarterly* 12, no. 4 (November 1990): 486–498.

Bunster-Burotto, Ximena. "Surviving Beyond Fear: Women and Torture in Latin America." In *Women and Violence: Realities and Responses Worldwide*, edited by Miranda Davies. London: Zed Books, 1994.

Butler, Judith. *Gender Trouble: Feminism and the Subversion of Identity.* London: Routledge, 1990.
Byerman, Keith E. "Anger in a Small Place: Jamaica Kincaid's Cultural Critique of Antigua." *College Literature* 22, no. 1 (1995): 91–102.
Caputo, John D. *The Prayers and Tears of Jacques Derrida: Religion without Religion.* Bloomington: Indiana University Press, 1997.
Castellanos, Rosario. *The Book of Lamentations*, translated by Esther Allen. New York: Marsilio Publishing, 1996.
———. *City of Kings*, translated by Robert S. Rudder and Gloria Chacon de Anjona. Pittsburgh, PA: Latin American Literary Review Press, 1993.
———. *The Nine Guardians*, translated by Irene Nicholson. London: Readers International, 1992.
Charlton, Sue Ellen. *Women in the Third World.* Boulder: Westview Press, 1984.
Chen, Martha. "The Feminization of Poverty." In *A Commitment to the World's Women: Perspectives on Development for Beijing and Beyond*, edited by Noeleen Heyzer. New York: UNIFEM, 1995.
———. "A Matter of Survival: Women's Right to Employment in India and Bangladesh." In *Women, Culture, and Development: A Study of Human Capabilities*, edited by Martha Nussbaum and Jonathan Glover. Oxford: Clarendon Press, 1995.
Cheriet, Boutheina. "Fundamentalism and Women's Rights: Lessons from the City of Women." In *Muslim Women and the Politics of Participation: Implementing the Beijing Platform*, edited by Manaz Afkhami and Erika Friedl. Syracuse: Syracuse University Press, 1997.
Chetin, Sara. "Reading from a Distance: Ama Ata Aidoo's *Our Sister Killjoy*." In *Black Women's Writing*, edited by Gina Wisker. New York: St. Martin's Press, 1993.
Chinweizu, Onwuchekwa Jemie, and Ihechukwu Madubuike. *Toward the Decolonization of African Literature.* Washington, DC: Howard University Press, 1983.
Chittister, Joan. *Beyond Beijing: The Next Step for Women.* Kansas City: Sheed and Ward, 1996.
Chodorow, Nancy. *The Reproduction of Motherhood: Psychoanalysis and the Sociology of Gender.* Berkeley: University of California Press, 1978.
Chuchryk, Patricia M. "Subversive Mothers: The Women's Opposition to the Military Regime in Chile." In *Women, the State, and Development*, edited by Sue Ellen M. Charlton, Jana Everett, and Kathleen Staudt. Albany: State University of New York Press, 1989.
Cixous, Helene. "Castration or Decapitation?" *Contemporary Literary Criticism: Literary and Cultural Studies*, edited by Robert Con Davis and Ronald Schleifer. New York: Longman, 1989.

———. "Coming to Writing." In *Coming to Writing and Other Essays*, edited by Deborah Jenson. Cambridge: Harvard University Press, 1991.

———. "The Laugh of the Medusa." In *Literary Criticism and Theory: The Greeks to the Present*, edited by Robert Con Davis and Ronald Schleifer. New York: Longman, 1989.

———. *Reading with Clarice Lispector*, translated by Verena Andermatt Conley. Minneapolis: University of Minnesota Press, 1990.

Cliff, Michelle. "Conference Presentation." In *Critical Fictions: The Politics of Imaginative Writing*, edited by Philomena Mariani. Seattle: Bay Press, 1991.

*Community: Changing Roles of Women and Men in Bangladesh* (video). Boston: Oxfam America, 1995.

Counts, Alex. *Give Us Credit*. New York: Random House, 1996.

Crossette, Barbara. "A Manual On Rights of Women Under Islam." *New York Times* (December 29, 1996).

Dangarembga, Tsitsi. *Nervous Conditions*. Seattle: The Seal Press, 1989.

Debold, Elizabeth, Marie Wilson and Idelisse Malave. "A Mother Daughter Revolution." In *A Commitment to the World's Women: Perspectives on Development for Beijing and Beyond*, edited by Noeleen Heyzer. New York: UNIFEM, 1995.

Derrida, Jacques. "The Villanova Roundtable," from *Deconstruction in a Nutshell: A Conversation with Jacques Derrida*, edited with a commentary by John D. Caputo. New York: Fordham University Press, 1997.

Desai, Anita. *Clear Light of Day*. London: Penguin Books, 1980.

———. *Fire on the Mountain*. London: Penguin Books, 1977.

Devi, Mahasweta. "Breast Giver." In *Breast Stories*, translated by Gayatri Chakravorty Spivak. Calcutta: Seagull, 1997.

———. "Draupadi," translated and reproduced by Gayatri Chakravorty Spivak in *Writing and Sexual Difference*, edited by Elizabeth Abel. Chicago: University of Chicago Press, 1982.

———. *Imaginary Maps*, translated by Gayatri Chakravorty Spivak. New York: Routledge, 1995.

Djebar, Assia. *Fantasia: An Algerian Cavalcade*, translated by Dorothy S. Blair. Portsmouth, NH: Heinemann, 1993.

———. *A Sister to Scheherazade*, translated by Dorothy S. Blair. Portsmouth, NH: Heinemann, 1993.

———. *So Vast a Prison*, translated by Betsy Wing. New York: Seven Stories Press, 1999.

Doody, Margaret Anne. *The True Story of the Novel*. New Brunswick, NJ: Rutgers University Press, 1997.

Dostoevsky, Fyodor. *Notes from Underground*. New York: Norton, 1989.

Drakulic, Slavenka. "The Rape of Women in Bosnia." In *Women and Violence: Realities and Responses Worldwide*, edited by Miranda Davies. London: Zed Books, 1994.
Driver, Dorothy. "Reconstructing the Past, Shaping the Future: Bessie Head and the Question of Feminism in a New South Africa." In *Black Women's Writing*, edited by Gina Wisker. New York: St. Martin's Press, 1993.
DuPlessis, Rachel Blau. *Writing Beyond the Ending: Narrative Strategies of Twentieth-Century Women Writers*. Bloomington: Indiana University Press, 1995.
Dutt, Mallika. *With Liberty and Justice for All: Women's Human Rights in the United States*. New Brunswick, NJ: Center for Global Women's Leadership, 1994.
Edin, Kathryn and Laura Lein. *Making Ends Meet: How Single Mothers Survive Welfare and Low-Wage Work*. New York: Russell Sage Foundation, 1997.
Eilersen, Gillian Stead. *Bessie Head: Thunder Behind Her Ears: Her Life and Writings*. Portsmouth, NH: Heinemann, 1996.
Emecheta, Buchi. *The Bride Price*. New York: George Braziller, 1976.
———. *Destination Biafra*. Oxford: Heinemann, 1994.
———. *Double Yoke*. New York: George Braziller, 1983.
———. *The Family*. New York: George Braziller, 1990.
———. *Head Above Water: An Autobiography*. Oxford: Heinemann, 1994.
———. *In the Ditch*. Oxford: Heinemann, 1994.
———. *The Joys of Motherhood*. New York: George Braziller, 1979.
———. *Kehinde*. Oxford: Heinemann, 1994.
———. *Second-Class Citizen*. New York: George Braziller, 1975.
Ezeigbo, Theodora Akachi. "Vision and Revision: Flora Nwapa and the Fiction of War." In *Emerging Perspectives on Flora Nwapa: Critical and Theoretical Essays*, edited by Marie Umeh. Trenton, NJ: Africa World Press, 1998.
Fanon, Frantz. *The Wretched of the Earth*, with a preface by Jean Paul Sartre, and translated by Constance Farrington. New York: Grove Press, 1968.
Ferguson, Moira. *Jamaica Kincaid: Where the Land Meets the Body*. Charlottesville: University Press of Virginia, 1994.
Forche, Carolyn. "Introduction." In *Flowers from the Volcano* by Claribel Alegria, translated by Carolyn Forche. Pittsburgh: University of Pittsburgh Press, 1982.
Foucault, Michel. *Discipline and Punish: The Birth of the Prison*, translated by Alan Sheridan. New York: Vintage Books, 1995.
Gordimer, Nadine. *My Son's Story*. New York: Penguin Books, 1990.
———. *Writing and Being*. Cambridge: Harvard University Press, 1995.

Hale, Sondra. *Gender Politics in Sudan: Islam, Socialism, and the State.* Boulder: Westview Press, 1996.
———. "Gender, Religious Identity, and Political Mobilization in Sudan." In *Identity Politics and Women: Cultural Reassertions and Feminisms in International Perspective,* edited by Valentine M. Moghadam. Boulder: Westview Press, 1994.
———. "Letter: On Nuba Women and Children in Sudan." *Middle East Report* 205 (October–December 1997).
Harjo, Joy. "I Give You Back." In *She Had Some Horses.* New York: Thunder's Mouth Press, 1983.
Head, Bessie. *Maru.* Oxford: Heinemann, 1972.
———. "Social and Political Pressures that Shape Literature in South Africa." In *The Tragic Life: Bessie Head and Literature in South Africa,* edited by Cecil Abrahams. Trenton, NJ: Africa World Press, 1990.
———. *A Question of Power.* Oxford: Heinemann, 1974.
———. *When Rain Clouds Gather.* Oxford: Heinemann, 1972.
Heise, Lori L. with Jacqueline Pitanguy and Adrienne Germain. *Violence Against Women: The Hidden Health Burden.* Washington, DC: The World Bank, 1994.
Herz, B., K. Subbarao, M. Habib, and L. Rainey. *Letting Girls Learn, Promising Approaches in Primary and Secondary Education,* World Bank Discussion Paper 133. Washington, DC: The World Bank, 1991.
Heyzer, Noeleen. "A Women's Development Agenda for the 21st Century." In *A Commitment to the World's Women: Perspectives on Development for Beijing and Beyond,* edited by Noeleen Heyzer. New York: UNIFEM, 1995.
Hill, Kathleen. *Still Waters in Niger.* Evanston, IL: Northwestern University Press, 1999.
hooks, bell. "Conference Presentation." In *Critical Fictions: The Politics of Imaginative Writing,* edited by Philomena Mariani. Seattle: Bay Press, 1991.
———. *Killing Rage: Ending Racism.* New York: Henry Holt and Company, 1995.
———. *Reel to Real: Race, Sex and Class at the Movies.* New York: Routledge, 1996.
Howe, Irving. *Politics and the Novel.* Greenwich, CT: Fawcett Publications, 1957.
Human Rights Watch/Asia. *Rape for Profit: Trafficking of Nepali Girls and Women to India's Brothels.* New York: Human Rights Watch, 1995.
Ibrahim, Huma. *Bessie Head: Subversive Identities in Exile.* Charlottesville: University of Virginia Press, 1996.
James, Adeola. *In Their Own Voices: African Women Writers Talk.* London: James Curry, 1990.

Jell-Bahlsen, Sabine. "Flora Nwapa and Uhammiri/Ogbuide, The Lake Goddess: An Evolving Relationship." In *Emerging Perspectives on Flora Nwapa: Critical and Theoretical Essays*, edited by Marie Umeh. Trenton, NJ: Africa World Press, 1998.

Jhabvala, Ruth Prawer. *Heat and Dust*. New York: Simon and Schuster, 1987.

Kandiyoti, Deniz. "Beyond Beijing: Obstacles and Prospects for the Middle East." In *Muslim Women and The Politics of Participation: Implementing the Beijing Platform*, edited by Manaz Afkhami and Erika Friedl. Syracuse: Syracuse University Press, 1997.

Kincaid, Jamaica. *Annie John*. New York: Penguin Books, 1986.

———. *At the Bottom of the River*. New York: Penguin Books, 1992.

———. *The Autobiography of My Mother*. New York: Farrar, Straus and Giroux, 1996.

———. *Lucy*. New York: Penguin Books, 1990.

———. *A Small Place*. New York: Penguin Books, 1989.

Kristeva, Julia. "Desire in Language." In *The Portable Kristeva*, edited by Kelly Oliver. New York: Columbia University Press, 1997.

———. "From One Identity to Another." *Critical Theory Since Plato*, edited by Hazard Adams. New York: Harcourt Brace Javanovich, 1992.

———. "My Memory's Hyperbole." In *The Portable Kristeva*, edited by Kelly Oliver. New York: Columbia University Press, 1997.

———. "New Maladies of the Soul." In *The Portable Kristeva*, edited by Kelly Oliver. New York: Columbia University Press, 1997.

———. "A Question of Subjectivity." In *Feminist Literary Theory*, edited by Mary Eagleton. Oxford: Blackwell Publishers, 1996.

———. "Revolution in Poetic Language." In *The Portable Kristeva*, edited by Kelly Oliver. New York: Columbia University Press, 1997.

———. "Strangers to Ourselves." In *The Kristeva Reader*, edited by Toril Moi. New York: Columbia University Press, 1986.

———. "The System and the Speaking Subject." In *The Kristeva Reader*, edited by Toril Moi. New York: Columbia University Press, 1986.

———. "Tales of Love." In *The Portable Kristeva*, edited by Kelly Oliver. New York: Columbia University Press, 1997.

———. "Word, Dialogue and Novel." In *The Kristeva Reader*, edited by Toril Moi. New York: Columbia University Press, 1986.

Kristof, Nicholas D. "Stark Data on Women: 100 Million Are Missing." *The New York Times* (November 5, 1991): C1.

Kusterer, Ken. "Women-Oriented NGOs in Latin America: Democratization's Decisive Wave." In *Women at the Center: Development Issues and Practices for the 1990s*, edited by Gay Young, Vidyamali Samarasinghe, and Ken Kusterer. West Hartford, CT: Kumarian Press, 1993.

Lashgari, Deirdre. "To Speak the Unspeakable: Implications of Gender, 'Race,' Class, and Culture." In *Violence, Silence, and Anger: Women's Writing as

*Transgression*, edited by Deirdre Lashgari. Charlottesville: University Press of Virginia, 1995.

Leonard, Ann and Cassie Landers. "Child Care: Meeting the Needs of Working Mothers and Their Children." In *Seeds 2: Supporting Women's Work around the World*, edited by Ann Leonard. New York: The Feminist Press, 1995.

Lerner, Gerda. *The Creation of Patriarchy*. New York: Oxford University Press, 1986.

Lispector, Clarice. *The Hour of the Star*, translated by Giovanni Pontiero. New York: New Directions Books, 1986.

Malti-Douglas, Fedwa. *Men, Women, and God(s)*. Berkeley: University of California Press, 1995.

Maraire, J. Nozipo. *Zenzele: A Letter for My Daughter*. New York: Crown Publishers, 1996.

Marcus, Sharon. "Fighting Bodies, Fighting Words: A Theory and Politic of Rape Prevention." In *Feminists Theorize the Political*, edited by Judith Butler and Joan W. Scott. New York: Routledge, 1992.

Markandaya Kamala. *Nectar in a Sieve*. New York: Penguin, 1998.

Martin, Biddy and Chandra Talpade Mohanty. "Feminist Politics: What's Home Got to Do with It?" In *Feminisms: An Anthology of Literary Theory and Criticisms*, edited by Robyn R. Warhol and Diane Price Herndl. New Brunswick, NJ: Rutgers University Press, 1991.

Martin, Emily. *The Woman in the Body: A Cultural Analysis of Reproduction*. Boston: Beacon Press, 1987.

Martin, John Barlow. *Overtaken by Events: The Dominican Crisis from the Fall of Trujillo to the Civil War*. New York: Doubleday, 1966.

McKinley, James C. "Legacy of Rwanda Violence: The Thousands Born of Rape." *The New York Times* (September 23, 1996): A1.

Miller, Judith. "Taking Two Bosnian Women's Case to the World." *The New York Times* (February 23, 1997): H36.

Mitra, Madhuchhanda. "Angry Eyes and Closed Lips: Forces of Revolution in Nawal el Saadawi's *God Dies by the Nile*." In *Violence, Silence, and Anger: Women's Writing as Transgression*, edited by Deirdre Lashgari. Charlottesville: University Press of Virginia, 1995

Moghadam, Valentine M. "Introduction: Women and Identity Politics in Theoretical and Comparative Perspective." In *Identity Politics and Women: Cultural Reassertions and Feminisms in International Perspective*, edited by Valentine M. Moghadam. Boulder: Westview Press, 1994.

Mohanty, Chandra. "Cartographies of Struggle: Third World Women and the Politics of Feminism." In *Third World Women and the Politics of Feminism*, edited by Chandra Talpada Mohanty, Ann Russo, and Lourdes Torres. Bloomington: Indiana University Press, 1991.

———. "Under Western Eyes: Feminist Scholarship and Colonial Discourses." In *Third World Women and the Politics of Feminism*, edited by Chandra Talpada Mohanty, Ann Russo, and Lourdes Torres. Bloomington: Indiana University Press, 1991.

Morgan, Robin. *The Demon Lover: On the Sexuality of Terrorism*. New York: Norton, 1989.

———. "Our Bodies, Our Souls." *Ms.* (September/October 1997): 58–63.

Morrison, Toni. *Beloved*. New York: Alfred Knopf, 1987.

———. *Paradise*. New York: Alfred A. Knopf, 1998.

Moses, Michael Valdez. *The Novel and the Globalization of Culture*. New York: Oxford University Press, 1995.

Mosse, Julia Cleves. *Half the World, Half a Chance: An Introduction to Gender and Development*. Oxford: Oxfam, 1993.

Mukherjee, Bharati. "A Four-Hundred-Year-Old Woman." In *Critical Fictions: The Politics of Imaginative Writing*, edited by Philomena Mariani. Seattle: Bay Press, 1991.

Nafisi, Azar. "Imagination as Subversion: Narrative as a Tool of Civic Awareness." In *Muslim Women and the Politics of Participation: Implementing the Beijing Platform*, edited by Manaz Afkhami and Erika Friedl. Syracuse: Syracuse University Press, 1997.

Neft, Naomi and Ann Levine. *Where Women Stand: An International Report on the Status of Women in 140 Countries, 1997–1998*. New York: Random House, 1997.

Ngugi wa Thiong'o. *Caitaani Mutharabaini*. Nairobi, Kenya: Heinemann, 1980. Translated as *Devil on the Cross*. London: Heinemann, 1982.

———. *Decolonizing the Mind: The Politics of Language in African Literature*. London: James Currey, 1986.

Nin, Anais. "Birth." In *Under a Glass Bell*. Chicago: Swallow Press, 1948.

*Non-Governmental Organization (NGO) Beijing Declaration*, September 1995 (www.igc.org/beijing/ngo/ngodec.html).

Nussbaum, Martha. "Introduction." In *Women, Culture, and Development: A Study of Human Capabilities*, edited by Martha Nussbaum and Jonathan Glover. Oxford: Clarendon Press, 1995.

———. *Poetic Justice: The Literary Imagination and Public Life*. Boston: Beacon Press, 1995.

Nussbaum, Martha and Jonathan Glover. *Women, Culture, and Development: A Study of Human Capabilities*, edited by Martha Nussbaum and Jonathan Glover. Oxford: Clarendon Press, 1995.

Nwankwo, Chimalum, "The Feminist Impulse and Social Realism in Ama Ata Aidoo's *No Sweetness Here* and *Our Sister Killjoy*." In *Ngambika: Studies of Women in African Literature*, edited by Carole Boyce Davies and Anne Adams Graves. Trenton, NJ: Africa World Press, 1986.

Nwapa, Flora. *Efuru*. Oxford: Heinemann Books, 1966.

———. *Idu*. Oxford: Heinemann Books, 1970.
———. *Never Again*. Trenton, NJ: Africa World Press, 1992.
———. *One Is Enough*. Trenton, NJ: Africa World Press, 1992.
———. *Women Are Different*. Trenton, NJ: Africa World Press, 1992.
O'Connell, Joanna. *Prospero's Daughter: The Prose of Rosario Castellanos*. Austin: University of Texas Press, 1995.
Odamtten, Vincent O. *The Art of Ama Ata Aidoo: Polylectics and Reading Against Neocolonialism*. Gainesville: University Press of Florida, 1994.
Ogundele, Oladipo Joseph. "A Conversation with Dr. Buchi Emecheta." In *Emerging Perspectives on Buchi Emecheta*, edited by Marie Umeh. Trenton, NJ: Africa World Press, 1996.
Ogundipe-Leslie, Molara. *Recreating Ourselves: African Women and Critical Transformation*. Trenton, NJ: African World Press, 1994.
Ogunyemi, Chikwenye Okonjo. *Africa Wo/man Palava: The Nigerian Novel by Women*. Chicago: The University of Chicago Press, 1996.
Okin, Susan. "Inequalities Between the Sexes in Different Cultural Contexts." In *Women, Culture, and Development: A Study of Human Capabilities*, edited by Martha Nussbaum and Jonathan Glover. Oxford: Clarendon Press, 1995.
Ola, Virginia U. "Women's Role in Bessie Head's Ideal World." *Ariel* 17 no. 4 (1986): 39–47.
Ollenburger, Jane C. and Helen A. Moore. *A Sociology of Women: The Intersection of Patriarchy, Capitalism, and Colonization*. Upper Saddle River, NJ: Prentice-Hall, 1998.
Ortiz, Alicia Dujovne. "Buenos Aires." In *Critical Fictions: The Politics of Imaginative Writing*, edited by Philomena Mariani. Seattle: Bay Press, 1991.
Ortner, Sherry. "Is Female to Male as Nature Is to Culture?" In *Women, Culture and Society*, edited by Michelle Zimbalist Rosaldo and Louise Lamphere. Stanford: Stanford University Press, 1974.
———. "Making Gender: Toward a Feminist, Minority, Postcolonial, etc., Theory of Practice." In *Making Gender: The Politics and Erotics of Culture*. Boston: Beacon Press, 1996.
———. "So Is Female to Male as Nature Is to Culture?" In *Making Gender: The Politics and Erotics of Culture*. Boston: Beacon Press, 1996.
Peixote, Marta. *Passionate Fictions: Gender, Narrative, and Violence in Clarice Lispector*. Minneapolis: University of Minnesota Press, 1994.
Perpinan, Mary Soledad. "Militarism and the Sex Industry in the Philippines." In *Women and Violence: Realities and Responses Worldwide*, edited by Miranda Davies. London: Zed Books, 1994.
Phillips, Maggie. "Engaging Dreams: Alternative Perspectives on Flora Nwapa, Buchi Emecheta, Ama Ata Aidoo, Bessie Head, and Tsitsi Dangarembga's Writing." *Research in African Literatures* 25, no. 4 (1994): 89–103.

Pontiero, Giovanni. "Afterword." In *The Hour of the Star*, by Clarice Lispector. New York: New Directions Books, 1986.

———. "Clarice Lispector: Dreams of Language." In *A Dream of Light and Shadow: Portraits of Latin American Women Writers*, edited by Marjorie Agosin. Albuquerque: University of New Mexico Press, 1995.

Reid, Elizabeth. "Development as a Moral Concept: Women's Practices as Development Practices." In *A Commitment to the World's Women: Perspectives on Development for Beijing and Beyond*, edited by Noeleen Heyzer. New York: UNIFEM, 1995.

Reinhold, Amy Jo. *Working with Rural Communities in Nepal: Some Principles of Non-formal Education Intervention*. Paris: UNESCO, 1993.

*Report from Beijing: The 1995 U.N. Fourth World Conference on Women and the Non-Governmental Organization Forum As Seen by U.S. Journalists of Color*, edited by Helen Zia. Kirkland, WA: Unity '99 and the Ford Foundation, 1996.

Reuman, Ann E. "'Wild Tongues Can't Be Tamed': Gloria Anzaldua's (R)evolution of Voice." In *Violence, Silence, and Anger: Women's Writing as Transgression*, edited by Deirdre Lashgari. Charlottesville: University Press of Virginia, 1995.

Robinson, Andrea. "Anita Desai." In *Beyond the Glass Ceiling: Forty Women Whose Ideas Shaped the Modern World*, edited by Sian Griffiths. Manchester: Manchester University Press, 1996.

Rohter, Larry. "Brazil Averts Its Eyes." *The New York Times* (July 4, 1999).

Rosaldo, Michelle Zimbalist. "The Use and Abuse of Anthropology: Reflections on Feminism and Cross-cultural Understanding." *Signs: Journal of Women in Culture and Society* 5, no. 3 (1980): 389–417.

———. "Woman, Culture and Society: A Theoretical Overview," *Woman, Culture and Society*, edited by Michelle Zimbalist Rosaldo and Louise Lamphere. Stanford: Stanford University Press, 1974.

Royte, Elizabeth. "The Outcasts." *The New York Times Magazine* (January 19, 1997): 37–39.

Rushdie, Salman. "Imaginary Homelands." In *Imaginary Homelands*. New York: Granta, 1992.

———. "In Defense of the Novel, Yet Again." *The New Yorker* (June 4 and July 1, 1996): 50.

el Saadawi, Nawal. *The Fall of the Imam*, translated by Sherif Hetata. London: Minerva, 1989.

———. *God Dies by the Nile*, translated by Sherif Hetata. London: Zed Books, 1985.

———. *The Innocence of the Devil*, translated by Sherif Hetata. Berkeley: University of California Press, 1994.

———. *Memoirs from the Women's Prison*, translated by Marilyn Booth. Berkeley: University of California Press, 1994.

———. *Memoirs of a Woman Doctor*, translated by Catherine Cobham. San Francisco: City Light Books, 1989.
———. *My Travels Around the World*, translated by Shirley Eber. London: Minerva, 1992.
———. *Woman at Point Zero*, translated by Sherif Hetata. London: Zed Books, 1993.
Said, Edward. *Culture and Imperialism*. New York: Vintage Books, 1994.
———. *Orientalism*. New York: Random House, 1978.
Scott, James. *Domination and the Arts of Resistance*. New Haven: Yale University Press, 1990.
Sears, Briscella. "What Is Difficult Can Be Done at Once. What Is Impossible Takes a Little Longer: The Beijing Conference." *NWSA Journal*, Special Issue: Global Perspectives, 8, no. 1 (Spring 1996): 179–185.
Sen, Amartya. "Agency and Well-Being: The Development Agenda," *A Commitment to the World's Women: Perspectives on Development for Beijing and Beyond*, edited by Noeleen Heyzer. New York: UNIFEM, 1995.
al-Shaykh, Hanan. *Beirut Blues,* translated by Catherine Cobham. New York: Doubleday, 1995.
———. *The Story of Zahra*, translated by Peter Ford. New York: Doubleday, 1995.
Showalter, Elaine. "Feminism and Literature." In *Literary Theory Today*, edited by Peter Collier and Helga Geyer-Ryan. Ithaca, NY: Cornell University Press, 1990.
———. "Feminist Criticism in the Wilderness." In *Contemporary Literary Criticism: Literary and Cultural Studies*, edited by Robert Con Davis and Ronald Schleifer. New York: Longman, 1989.
Sidhwa, Bapsi. *Cracking India*. Minneapolis, MN: Milkwood Editions, 1991.
Silko, Leslie Marmon. "Lullaby." In *Storyteller*. New York: Seaver Books, 1981.
Smith, Anna. *Julia Kristeva: Readings of Exile and Estrangement*. New York: St. Martin's Press, 1996.
Sohoni, Neera Kuckreja. *The Burden of Girlhood: A Global Inquiry into the Status of Girls*. Oakland, CA: Third Party Publishing Company, 1995.
Specter, Michael. "Trafficker's New Cargo: Naive Slavic Women." *The New York Times* (January 11, 1998).
Spencer-Walters, Tom. "Orality and Patriarchal Dominance in Buchi Emecheta's *The Slave Girl*." In *Emerging Perspectives on Buchi Emecheta*, edited by Marie Umeh. Trenton, NJ: Africa World Press, 1996.
Spivak, Gayatri Chakrovorty. "Strategy, Identity, Writing." *The Post-Colonial Critic: Interviews, Strategies, Dialogues*, edited by Sarah Harasym. New York: Routledge, 1990.
Standing, Guy. "Global Feminization through Flexible Labor." *World Development* 17, no. 7 (1989): 1077–1095.

Stanley Alessandra. "Semantics Stalls Pact Labelling Rape a War Crime." *The New York Times* (July 9, 1998) A3.

Staudt, Kathleen. "Strategic Locations: Gender Issues in Business Management." In *Women at the Center: Development Issues and Practices for the 1990s*, edited by Gay Young, Vidyamali Samarasinghe, and Ken Kusterer. West Hartford, CT: Kumarian Press, 1993.

Stratton, Florence. *Contemporary African Literature and the Politics of Gender*. London: Routledge, 1994.

Sugnet, Charles. "*Nervous Conditions*: Dangarembga's Feminist Re-invention of Fanon." In *The Politics of (M)othering: Identity and Resistance in African Literature*, edited by Obioma Nnaemeka. New York: Routledge, 1997.

Suleiman, Susan Rubin. "Writing and Motherhood." In *The (M)other Tongue: Essays in Feminist Psychoanalytic Interpretation*, edited by Shirley Nelson Garner. Ithaca, NY: Cornell University Press, 1985.

Suleri, Sara. "Woman Skin Deep: Feminism and the Postcolonial Condition." *Critical Inquiry* 13, no. 4 (Summer 1992): 756–769.

Tagliabue, John. "In Europe, Steps Toward a Common Language." *The New York Times* (July 19 1998).

Trinh T. Minh-ha. "Not You/Like You: Post-Colonial Women and the Interlocking Questions of Identity and Difference." In *Making Face, Making Soul: Creative and Critical Perspectives by Feminists of Color*, edited by Gloria Anzaldua. San Francisco: aunt lute books, 1990.

———. *Woman, Native, Other*. Bloomington: Indiana University Press, 1989.

Tucker, Margaret. "A 'Nice-time Girl' Strikes Back: An Essay on Bessie Head's *A Question of Power*." *Research in African Literatures* 19, no. 2 (Summer 1988): 170–181.

Umeh, Marie. Introduction to "Part One: Igbo Women: Culture and Literary Enterprise." In *Emerging Perspectives on Flora Nwapa: Critical and Theoretical Essays*, edited by Marie Umeh. Trenton, NJ: Africa World Press, 1998.

United Nations Development Programme. *Human Development Report 1995*. Oxford: Oxford University Press, 1995.

Uwakheh, Pauline Ada. "Debunking Patriarchy: The Liberational Quality of Voicing in Tsitsi Dangarembga's *Nervous Conditions*." *Research in African Literatures* 26, no. 1 (1995): 75–84.

Velis, Jean-Pierre. *Blazing the Trail: The Village Schools of Save the Children/ USA in Mali*. Paris: UNESCO, 1994.

Walby, Sylvia. "The 'Declining Significance' or the 'Changing Forms' of Patriarchy?" In *Patriarchy and Economic Development: Women's Positions at the End of the Twentieth Century*, edited by Valentine Moghadam. Oxford: Clarendon Press, 1996.

Walker, Alice. *The Color Purple*. New York: Washington Square Press, 1982.

Watt, Ian. *The Rise of the Novel*. Berkeley: University of California Press, 1967.

White, Jonathan. *Recasting the World: Writing after Colonialism*. Baltimore: The Johns Hopkins University Press, 1993.

Wilentz, Gay. "Not Feminist but Afracentrist: Flora Nwapa and the Politics of African Cultural Production." In *Emerging Perspectives on Flora Nwapa: Critical and Theoretical Essays*, edited by Marie Umeh. Trenton, NJ: Africa World Press, 1998.

Wolf, Naomi. *The Beauty Myth: How Images of Beauty Are Used Against Women*. New York: William Morrow, 1991.

*Women Writing in India* (Volume II: The Twentieth Century), edited by Susie Tharu and K. Lalita. New York: The Feminist Press, 1993.

*The World's Women 1995: Trends and Statistics*. New York: United Nations, 1995.

*The World's Women 2000: Trends and Statistics*. New York: United Nations, 2000.

# Index

Achebe, Chinua, 44, 70
Adams, Alice, 64–65
Afkhami, Mahnaz, xvii, 14
Agency: definition, 185; in Dangarembga's *Nervous Conditions*, 129; in Saadawi's *God Dies by the Nile*, 104–5; source of power, 12, 104, 184; women's agency, 12, 22, chapter 8
Aidoo, Ama Ata, 204; association with oral literature, 22–23, 36 n.2; focus on education of women, 137; *Our Sister Killjoy*, 136–46
Alcoff, Linda, 8, 18 n.3
Alegria, Claribel: *Ashes of Izalco*, 194–98; leftist orientation, 194–95
Alexander, Meena, xv; literary discourse, 53–54. Works: *Manhattan Music*, 29–30; *Nampally Road*, 146–47; *The Shock of Arrival*, 53–54.
Alienation: in Aidoo's *Our Sister Killjoy*, 140; in Hill's *Still Waters in Niger*, 211–12; in origins of language, 40–41, 65

Allende, Isabel: storytelling 23. Works: *Eva Luna*, 151, 153; *House of the Spirits*, 23, 68, 113
Alvarez, Julia: historical exploration through fiction, 106, 113; *In the Time of the Butterflies*, 106–13
Anorexia. See Eating disorders.
Anzaldua, Gloria, 41, 47, 54–55. See also *Mestiza* consciousness
Appiah, Anthony, 55 n.1, 56 n.4
Audience, 21, 24, 45, 48, 192, 214; women as, 31, 33

Bakhtin, Mikhail, 26–28, 30, 37 n.6, 54, 56 n.10
"Been toism," in Aidoo's *Our Sister Killjoy*, 141, 143
Beijing, *Declaration*, Fourth World Conference on Women, xvi, 16
Benhabib, Seyla, xv, 8, 18 n.3
Binary oppositions, 11, 131; problematized in Nwapa's fiction, 77
Bosrup, Ester, 3–4
Brain-drain, in Aidoo's *Our Sister Killjoy*, 143–46
Bunch, Charlotte, 5–6, 95

Capabilities approach [to development], 7–8. *See also* Nussbaum, Martha
Carnival/carnivalesque, 49, 50, 56 n.10
Castellanos, Rosario, focus on indigenous people, 113–14. Works: *The Book of Lamentations,* 114–15; *The Nine Guardians,* 114
Chen, Martha 10, 153–55, 156
Cheriet, Boutheina, 14
Chinweizu, 26
Chodorow, Nancy, 64
*Chora,* 49, 64–65, 131
Cixous, Helene, 50–51, 66, 74, 134, 160, 164, 205; on Lispector, 174–75
Clitoridectomy [genital multilation], 16, 63; in Nawpa's *Efuru,* 72; in Saadawi's *God Dies by the Nile,* 102
Colonialism: in Alvarez's *In the Time of the Butterflies,* 107–8; in Dangarembga's *Nervous Conditions,* 129–36; in Emecheta's *In the Ditch,* 162–63; in Kincaid's works, 77–83
Colonial discourse. *See* "Master tongue"
Co-madres, 188–90, 210 n.3
Commodification of women: and origins of patriarchy, 10; reproductive capacity, 62–63
Convention on the Elimination of All Forms of Discrimination Against Women. *See* United Nations
Copyright, irony of, 24
Creativity, xiv, 65–66
Critical mass, 186–87
Crossing borders, xv; in Emecheta's *The Family,* 35; and origins of novel, 50–51. *See also* Exile; *Mestiza* consciousness

Dangarembga, Tsitsi, *Nervous Conditions,* viii, 128, 129–34
Derrida, Jacques 213–14
Desai, Anita, and *mestiza* consciousness, 199. Works: *Clear Light of Day,* 199–203; *Fire on the Mountain,* 33–34
Development, 3; "Gender and Development," 4–5; in Head's *When Rain Clouds Gather,* 165–66, 167–68; "Women and Development," 4; "Women in Development," 4
Devi, Mahasweta, "Draupadi," 89, 91
Dialogue: dialogic community, 8; dialogical imagination, 24, 26–28, 55
Difference, 127, 184; structures of, 9–11
Djebar, Assia, unveiled Algerian woman, 204. Works: *Fantasia: An Algerian Cavalcade* 36–37 n.3; *A Sister to Scheherazade,* 205–9; *So Vast a Prison,* 208
Doody, Margaret Anne, *The True Story of the Novel,* 30–34
Domestic abuse, 91–92
"Double voiced" discourse: in Aidoo's *Our Sister Killjoy,* 138, 141; in Djebar's *A Sister to Scheherazade,* 205, 208; in Kincaid's *The Autobiography of My Mother,* 85
Drakulic, Slavenka, 93
DuPlessis, Rachel, 193

Eating disorders, 123–24, 191; in Dangarembga's *Nervous Conditions,* 130–31, 135
Edin, Kathryn, 158–59
Education of women and girls: as source of agency, 125–26; as waste of resources, 124–25; as way out of poverty, 125
Eilersen, Gillian Stead, 165

Emecheta, Buchi: exile, 159; storytelling, 22–23; welfare mother, 159. Works: *The Bride Price*, 32; *The Family*, 35; *In the Ditch*, 159–64; *The Joys of Motherhood*, 75; *Second-Class Citizen*, 159; *The Slave Girl*, 37 n.5

*The Empire Writes Back* (Ashcroft, Griffiths, and Triffen), xx, 56 n.5

Essentialism, 9, 13, 41, 188

Exile, 38 n.14, 51, 54; in Emecheta's *In the Ditch*, 162–63; in Head's *When Rain Clouds Gather*, 165, 166–67, 168, 172; in Kincaid's works, 77–81

Fanon, Frantz, 123, 191

Female-headed households, 62, 154–55

Feminism: as cultural construct, 47, 50; as defined by Bessie Head, 166; "first-world" [Western] feminism, 4, 36; in *When Rain Clouds Gather*, 169; Marxist feminism, 4

"Feminization of poverty," 151–80; causes, 152–53, 153–54; in Emecheta's *In the Ditch*, 159–64; in Head's *A Question of Power*, 166–72; in Lispector's *The Hour of the Star*, 174–78; redress, 156–59

Foucault, Michel, 104

Fourth World Conference on Women, xv–xvii, 3–19

Fundamentalism: Islamic, xvii; religious, 91, 98

Gaze, 104, 191; in Saadawi's *God Dies by the Nile*, 101–2, 104

Gender: cultural construction of, 11–12; and development, 4; gender analysis, 183; gender asymmetry, 9–11, 61–62; and identity politics, 13; and language choice, 45, 52; as metaphor, 12; in UN documents, 6, 14–15, 16

Girl child, 17, 119–26

"The gift," 213–15

Globalization: and future of novel, 34–35; global conferences (*See* United Nations); global marketplace, 45, 191–92

Gordimer, Nadine: *My Son's Story*, 127–28; *Writing and Being*, 127

Grassroots action: associated with NGO Forum, 15; associated with women's NGOs, 187–89

*Griotte*, Nwapa as, 69

Harem, 36–37 n.3, 204; in Djebar's *A Sister to Scheherazade*, 208, 209

Head, Bessie, storytelling, 24. Works: *Maru*, 173–74; *A Question of Power*,173; *When Rain Clouds Gather*, 166–72

Heteroglossia, 27–28, 54, 56 n.6, 86, 193; in Alvarez's *In the Time of the Butterflies*, 110; in Dangarembga's *Nervous Conditions*, 132; in Emecheta's *In the Ditch*, 163–64

"Hidden transcripts," 19 n.6, 26, 158, 188; in Aidoo's *Our Sister Killjoy*, 138–39, 140, 142–43; in Desai's *Clear Light of Day*, 202, 203. *See* Scott, James

Hill, Kathleen, *Still Water in Niger*, 211–13, 214–15

hooks, bell, 95, 104, 118 n.13, 192

Human rights: relationship to women's rights, 5–7, 95; reproductive rights, xvi, 63; UN Involvement, 5–7, 14; universal human rights, 5–7 (*See also* United Nations)

Ibrahim, Huma, 24, 171

Identity politics, 6, 13–14, 41, 42, 43, 54–55, 55 nn.1, 2, 184
Illiteracy among women, 17–18 n.1, 120

Kandiyoti, Deniz, xv–xvi
Kincaid, Jamaica: anti-colonial stance, 77–79; conflation of colonial/biological mother, 78–82. Works: *Annie John,* 80; *At the Bottom of the River,* 79–80; *The Autobiography of My Mother,* 81–85; *Lucy,* 80–81; *A Small Place,* 79
Kristeva, Julia, xiv; linguistic theory, 40–41, 48–50, 64–65, 78; relation to Bakhtin, 28–29; semiotic-symbolic dichotomy, 49–59, 56 n.9, 84; "subject-in-process," 43. *See also* Chora; Poetic language; Subject-in-process

Lashgari, Deirdre, 40, 46
Lerner, Gerda, 9–10, 18 n.2
Lispector, Clarice: alliance with poor of Brazil, 174; *The Hour of the Star,* 174–78

Magic realism, 26
Malti-Douglas, Fedwa, 99
Market women, 22
Martin, Emily, 65
"Master tongue" [colonial language], 40, 43–44, 51, 54; in Kincaid's *The Autobiography of My Mother,* 82
*Mestiza* consciousness, 29, 37–8 n.9, 53–55, 57 n.11; in Desai's fiction, 199
"Micro-credit," 156–57; Grameen Bank, 156
Mirrors: Lacan's mirror stage, xix; metaphor for anthropology 12; metaphor for language, 28; metaphor for novel, xiv, xix, 127
Moghadam, Valentine, 5–6, 13

Mohanty, Chandra, 11–12, 19 n.9, 29, 78, 198
Morgan, Robin, 91, 94–95, 117 n.7
Motherhood, 61–87; "big mother" as storyteller, 22–23, 24; as cultural construct 64–65; in Emecheta's *The Joys of Motherhood,* 75; in Kincaid's fiction, 77–85; in Nwapa's works, 69–77. *See* "Other" mothering
Mother tongue, 40, 44–45, 46, 48, 53, 54; in Djebar's *A Sister to Scheherazade,* 209; in Kincaid's *The Autobiography of My Mother,* 82
"Multiplex" self, xix, 29
Multivocality, 26–30, 35, 51–52
Muslim: defense of veiling, 13–14 (*See also* Veiling); "Manual for Women's Rights," 96, 117 n.10; objections to West, 13–14; reservations to *Platform for Action* xvi–xvii

Nafisi, Azar, xvii–xviii
Naming, as violence, 40; in Lispector's *The Hour of the Star,* 177
*NGO (Non-Governmental Organisation) Beijing Declaration,* 16
NGO Forum on Women, xv, 15
Novel: African novel, 22–23, 26; Aidoo's *Our Sister Killjoy* as nonlinear novel, 141–46; association with oral literature, 22–24; as "baggy monster," 26–27; classical novel, 27, 31–32, 38 n.11; European novel, 25–27, 31, 32–33; future of, 34–36; history of, 24–34; international literary marketplace, viii, 21–22; Nwapa's *Efuru* as nonlinear novel, 72–75; reading as political act, xviii–xix; women's novels, xx, 36, 192–94

# Index

Ngugi wa Thiong'o, 44–45, 46, 56 n.6
Nussbaum, Martha, xiv–xv; capabilities approach, 7–8; *Poetic Justice*, xviii–xix, 35
Nwapa, Flora: mother of Nigerian women's fiction, 69; focus on barren women, 69, 70–72, 76–77. Works: *Efuru*, 70–75; *Idu*, 76; *One is Enough*, 76–77; *Women are Different*, 77

O'Connell, Joanna, 114
Odamtten, Vincent, 138, 140, 204
Ogunyemi, Chikwenye, 21–22, 27, 47–48, 51–53, 66–68, 190; on Emecheta, 164, 180 n.5; on Nwapa, 69
Orality, 37 nn.4, 5, 44; association with marketplace, 22; association with origins of novel, 26; association with women's novels, 22–24; in Kincaid's *The Autobiography of My Mother*, 83–84; in Nwapa's *Efuru*, 73–74. *See also* Storytelling
Ortner, Sherry, 9, 12
"Other" mothering, 63, 66–69; connected to African female deities, 67; in Hill's *Still Water's in Niger*, 212; in Nwapa's fiction, 71
Otherness, 11, 27, 40–41, 48, 65; of poor in Lispector's *The Hour of the Star*, 177–78
Outlaw culture/outlaw language, 50–51, 55, 193; in Emecheta's *In the Ditch*, 160; in Head's *When Rain Clouds Gather*, 165; in Nwapa's *Efuru*, 74–75

*Palava*: definition, 51–52; *palava sauce*, 52; palaverous discourse in Dangarembga's *Nervous Conditions*, 134–36; palaverous discourse in Head's *When Rain Clouds Gather*, 172; palaverous discourse in Nwapa's *Efuru*, 72–74
Palaver, 22, 23, 51–52; in Emecheta's *In the Ditch*, 164
Palimpsest, 114, 203
Patriarchy: definition, 18 n.2; internalization of, 98; origins, 9–10
*Platform for Action*, xix, 3, 5; on feminization of poverty, 152–53; on mothering, 61–63; reservations to, xvi–xvii, 17; on son preference, 119–20; on stereotypes for women, 183; on violence against women, 90
Poetic language, 49–50, 65, 78, 138; pushed to the edge in Djebar's *A Sister to Scheherazade*, 206
Pontiero, Giovanni, 174
Pornography, 101
Post-colonial: definition, xx; women's novels, 28, 184 (*See also* Novel: women's novels); women writers, 24, 115, 126
Power: in Alvarez's *In the Time of the Butterflies*, 106–9; in Castellanos' *The Book of Lamentations*, 114; in Dangarembga's *Nervous Conditions*, 130; economic power, 151–80; in Nwapa's *Efuru*, 71; redefinition, 190–94; in Saadawi's *God Dies by the Nile*, 100–101; through mothering (including "other" mothering), 63, 67–69, 210 n.3; through writing, 24, 28–29, 42, 97, 99; violence as a result of unequal power relations, 11, 90–91, 98
Public-private/culture-nature dichotomy, 9–11, 12, 22, 117 n.9
Publishing industry, 33, 46

Racism, 16

Rape, 116 n.3, 117 n.11; in Allende's *House of the Spirits*, 113; in Alvarez's *In the Time of the Butterflies*, 109, 110; in Devi's "Darupadi," 89, 91; marital rape in Djebar's *A Sister to Scheherazade*, 206; in *Memoirs from the Women's Prison*, 98; as military strategy/war crime, 17, 93–95, 117 n.6; as prototype of violence in Saadawi's *God Dies by the Nile*, 101–102; resistance to, 96

Reid, Elizabeth, 185–86, 198

Reproductive rights. *See* Human rights

Resistance, 91, 95–97; in Alvarez's *In the Time of the Butterflies*, 109–10; in Dangarembga's *Nervous Conditions*, 131; in Djebar's *A Sister to Scheherazade*, 206–7; education as resistance, 125–26; language "choice" as resistance, 44–48; in Saadawi's *God Dies by the Nile*, 103–6; writing as resistance, 19 n.6, 99, 184, 192–94

Rosaldo, Michelle Zimbalist, 8–9, 12, 61–62

el Saadawi, Nawal: "aeroplane mirrors," xix; choice of Arabic, 46, 97; imprisonment under Sadat, 96–99; orality in, 23; women's advocate, xiv, 96–97. Works: *God Dies by the Nile*, 99–106; *Memoirs from the Women's Prison*, 97–99; *Memoirs of a Woman Doctor*, 119, 120–21; *Woman at Point Zero*, 25, 123

al-Shaykh, Hanan, *The Story of Zahra*, 181–82, 183–84

Said, Edward, 18 n.4, 25, 34, 55 n.1

Scheherazade (also Shahrzad and Shahrazad), 33, 97, 208–9; original legend, xvii–xviii

Scott, James, 19 n.6

Semiotics, 28

Sen, Amartya, 122, 185, 209 n.2

Sexual slavery, 92–93, 116 n.5

Showalter, Elaine, 51, 64, 167

Signifying, 28, 43, 164

Son preference, 119–49; in Aidoo's *Our Sister Killjoy*, 136, 139; in Dangarembga's *Nervous Conditions*, 128; definition, 119–20; effects, 120–25; in Gordimer's *My Son's Story*, 127–28; in Saadawi's *Memoirs of a Woman Doctor*, 119, 120–21

Spivak, Gayatri Chakrovorty, 41–42, 46

Staudt, Kathleen, 186–87

Stereotypes (gender), 181–215, 209 n.1; in Alegria's *Ashes of Izalco*, 197–98; in Desai's *Clear Light of Day*, 201–3; in Djebar's *A Sister to Scheherazade*

Storytelling, 26; market women, 22; place in "harem," 36–37 n.3; place in prison, 23; subversive activity, xviii, 183, 208–9. *See also* Orality

Structural adjustment programs, xvi, xxii n.1, 155–56, 179 n.1

Subject-in-process: in Aidoo's *Our Sister Killjoy*, 138, 140; in Dangarembga's *Nervous Conditions*, 129. *See also* Kristeva, Julia

Subjectivity (construction of the self), 42–43; in Kincaid's *The Autobiography of My Mother*, 85. *See also* Kristeva, Julia, "subject-in-process"; Subject-in-process

Suicide, in Alexander's *Manhattan Music*, 29, 30

"Talking back," 38 n.15, 104, 115, 193; in Alvarez's *In the Time of the Butterflies*, 109

Transgression: as property of language, 28, 43, 52; as property of the novel, 28, 33

Translation, problems of, 45, 46
Tribalism, in Head's *When Rain Clouds Gather*, 168
"Trickster": in Aidoo's *Our Sister Killjoy*, 138; in Emecheta's *In the Ditch*, 164
Trinh Minh-ha, 42, 46–47, 55 n.2

United Nations: charter, 5; *Convention on the Elimination of All Forms of Discrimination Against Women*, 5, 17; *Convention on the Rights of the Child*, 6; Decade for Women, 5; *Declaration on Violence Against Women*, 90; *Forward-Looking Strategies for the Advancement of Women*, 5, 14; gender-ratio, 183; Special Rapporteur on Violence Against Women, 6; UNIFEM, 5; *Universal Declaration of Human Rights*, 5, 14; *Vienna Declaration and Programme of Action* (addressing women's rights as human rights), 6, 94. *See* Fourth World Conference on Women; *Platform for Action*
Universalism: tension with cultural diversity, xiv–xv, 3–19; universal language, 43–45

Valdez, Michael, *The Novel and the Globalization of Culture*, 34–35
Vatican, reservations to *Platform for Action*, xvi, xxii n.3,
Veiling: in Djebar's *A Sister to Scheherazade*, 205, 206–7; motivations for, 13–14, 19 n.7
Violence: against women, 89–118; in Alvarez's *In the Time of the Butterflies*, 106, 108–9; of language, 39–41, 53–54; in Saadawi's *God Dies by the Nile*, 99–106; by state, 93–94, 106–9; *See also* Domestic abuse; Rape

*Violence Against Women: The Hidden Health Burden*, 90–91, 92, 116 n.1

Walker, Alice, viii; *The Color Purple*, 61, 63–64
Watt, Ian, 25
Welfare system, 158–59; as depicted in Emecheta's *In the Ditch*, 160–63
Wolfe, Naomi, 191–92
Woman, as cultural construction, viii, 11, 18 n.3, 42, 198–99
Womanism, 67–68, 69, 167
*Women Writing in India* (Tharu and Lilita), xxi, 36, 149 n.5
Women's discourse, 48–51; in Head's *When Rain Cloud's Gather*, 167; in Alvarez's *In the Time of the Butterflies*, 110; in Nwapa's *Efuru*, 74–75. *See also* Cixous, Helene; Kristeva, Julia; *Palava*
Women's work, 155–56, 185; in Head's *When Rain Clouds Gather*, 167–68, 171; reproductive/domestic tasks, 62, 156

**About the Author**

ELIZABETH MORGAN is a professor of English and Women in Development at Eastern College in St. Davids, Pennsylvania. She has written on the creative process and global poverty, and edited a collection of refugee stories. She has produced films for public television on the revolution in El Salvador and on issues resulting from the 1995 Fourth World Conference on Women in Beijing.